D0323475

– THE CENTURY OF THE CHILD –

– THE CENTURY OF THE CHILD –

The Mental Hygiene Movement and Social Policy in the United States and Canada

THERESA R. RICHARDSON

State University of New York Press

Published by
State University of New York Press, Albany

©1989 State University of New York

All rights reserved

Printed in the United States of America

No part of this book may be used or reproduced in any manner whatsoever without written permission except in the case of brief quotations embodied in critical articles and reviews.

For information, address State University of New York Press, State University Plaza, Albany, N.Y., 12246

Library of Congress Cataloging in Publication Data

Richardson, Theresa R., 1945-
The century of the child : the mental hygiene movement and social policy in the United States and Canada / Theresa R. Richardson.
p. c.m
Includes index.
ISBN 0-7914-0020-4. ISBN 0-7914-0021-2 (pbk.)
1. Child mental health services—United States—History—20th century. 2. Child mental health services—Canada—History—20th century. 3. Child mental health services—Government policy—United States—History—20th century. 4. Child mental health services—Government policy—Canada—History—20th century. I. Title.
RJ501.A2R53 1989
362.2 '088054—dc19 88-24894
CIP

To George S. Tomkins

Contents

Abbreviations

AAPC: American Association of Psychiatric Clinics for children
AFMH: American Foundation for Mental Health Archives, CMC, NYC
AMHF: American Mental Health Association
AM: Adolf Meyer
AFMH: American Foundation of Mental Health Archives in CMC
APA: American Psychiatric Association
Beers Papers: Clifford Whittingham Beers Papers, AFMH
CELDIC: Commission on Emotional and Learning Disorders in Canada
CF: Commonwealth Fund
CJMH: Canadian Journal of Mental Hygiene
CMC: Cornell Medical Center, NYC
CMH: Clarence Meredith Hincks
CMHA: Canadian Mental Health Association
CNCMH: Canadian National Committee For Mental Hygiene
CWB: Clifford Whittingham Beers, papers in AFMH, CMC
DBS: Canada, Dominion Bureau of Statistics
DSM III: Diagnostic and Statistical Manual of the American Psychiatric Association, 3rd. edition
GAP: Group for the Advancement of Psychiatry
GEB: General Education Board, Manuscript Collection in RAC
Greenland Griffin Archives: Queen Street Mental Health Centre, Toronto
Hincks Papers: Clarence Meredith Hincks Papers in Greenland-Griffin Archives
ICD-9: International Classification of Diseases, 9th Edition
IHB: International Health Board/Division, Papers in RAC
LSRM: Laura Spelman Rockefeller Memorial, Manuscript Collection in RAC
NAMH: National Association for Mental Health
NCMH: National Committee for Mental Hygiene
N.Y.: New York State
NYC: New York City

PAC: Public Archives of Canada, Ottawa, Ontario
RAC: Rockefeller Archive Center, Pocantico Hills, N. Tarrytown, N.Y.
RI: Rockefeller Institute, NYC, now Rockefeller University papers in RAC
RFA: Rockefeller Foundation Archives, RAC
RF: Rockefeller Foundation
Salmon Papers: Thomas W. Salmon Papers, Payne Whitney Clinic, CMC, AFMH Archives
TWS: Thomas W. Salmon
WHO: World Health Organization, United Nations, Geneva, Switzerland
WJ: William James
JHU: Johns Hopkins University, and Medical School, Baltimore, Maryland

Preface

Jacques Derrida, when queried in an interview published in *Positions*, posed the rhetorical question, "Dare one maintain that one is the author of books?"

Dare one indeed? Books are fundamentally a collective enterprise from author, to publisher, to printer, to reader. Ideas unfailingly extend beyond the single mind, or written word. They evolve in shared circumstances, in conversation, and in practice. Research is aided by the support and expertise of others.

This research began in experiences and observations as a public school teacher in Oakland, California and found consummation in graduate school in Canada. The questions borrow from the sociology of knowledge, and the method from the classical tenants of historiography, with its sustenance from archival documents. The topic in mental hygiene is one whose primary characteristic is its multiple disciplinary and conceptual dimensions. The subject in childhood is a fleeting period in the ages of life, ephemeral and in transition.

Beyond the artificial boundaries of the beginnings and ending of the contents of written documents, this work also belies closure in another sense. Its intention is rather to open to question the domain assumptions which circumscribe our thoughts and practices as we look to our own future and our children's future.

I would like to thank the individuals who have contributed most directly their time and energy to exchanges which have helped guide my progress. I am especially indebted to Donald Fisher for his sustained encouragement, insights and critical advice; to Neil Sutherland, R. S. Ratner, A. C. L. Smith, R. H. Rodgers, and Charles Strickland for their careful reading of the manuscript and constructive commentary. Marvin Lazerson's support and constructive criticism throughout this project have added not only to this work but to my intellectual growth. A gift without ending. A special remembrance and tribute is due to the late historian of

Canadian curriculum, George S. Tomkins (1920–1985) whose early encouragement and wise counsel proved a timeless guide.

I would also like to thank the faculty and graduate students of the Department of Social and Educational Studies, especially Professor J. D. Wilson, the staff and faculty at the Centre for Policy Studies in Education and its Director Professor Kjell Rubenson, and the members of the Canadian Childhood History Project at the University of British Columbia, who at various points have provided support for both the body and the mind.

This research owes much to the wealth of documentary materials and expert assistance of the staffs of the U.B.C. and University of Toronto libraries, the Rockefeller Archive Center collections of the Rockefeller Foundation, General Education Board, Laura Spelman Rockefeller Foundation, General Education Collections; the Cornell Medical Center Archives and the Payne Whitney Clinic Library, American Foundation for Mental Health Collection; as well as the Griffin-Greenland Archive files on the history of Canadian psychiatry and Canadian Mental Health Association Collection at the Public Archives of Canada. This research was supported by a Rockefeller University Fellowship, University of British Columbia, University Graduate Fellowship and Post-doctoral Fellowship.

Most important, I would like to offer a word of appreciation to my husband, John, as critic, editor, friend and teacher and my daughters, Genevieve, Anne and Nicole. It is for them that I dare to write.

Introduction

> *Now along comes science, which has illuminated so many things in this age of efficiency, and throws light into the dark places of age-long customs. We may expect that many errors will be disclosed and as they are and the faulty practices which grew out of them corrected there will result a better society.* (William A. White, *The Mental Hygiene of Childhood*, Boston: Little Brown and Co., 1919, reprint 1923, p. 190).

Hygiene describes that branch of knowledge which relates to the promotion of health and the prevention of disease. When applied to mental functioning in the early twentieth century, it was described as a science of mental health which covered:

> the health and efficiency of all mentally integrated functions, the behavior and conduct of the organism or personality as dependent on growth and experience. It includes not only what might lead to diseases or disorders of personality but also the fluctuations and deviations of efficiency.[1]

The promotion of health is not a new idea. In the late seventeenth century three branches of "speculative medicine" included "physiologia, hygiene, and pathologia," (anatomy, health, and disease).[2] Between the eighteenth and nineteenth century speculative medicine, still a branch of metaphysics and philosophy, was integrated into the new biologically oriented medical sciences. The concept of "hygiene" was transformed into a search for scientific principles which would conserve health.

A formal movement to create a science of mental health originated in the United States in 1909 and expanded to Canada in 1918. By 1930 over fifty countries were represented at the first International Congress held in Washington D.C. Mental hygiene in the United States and Canada was, broadly speaking, an extension of the twentieth century public health movement, but its policy implications, especially as it concentrated on children, was pervasive. Mental hygiene symbolized and advanced the application of science to social life. It encompassed the medicalization and popularization of psychiatry within the framework of the modern institutional state.

The focus of mental hygienists concentrated on educational and welfare policies directed toward children. Mental hygienists formalized the boundaries between mental health and illness, and in so doing, they refined the protocols which identify contemporary concepts of individual and society, success and failure.

The twentieth century, the primary focus of this work, was ushered in as the "century of the child."[3] The children of this century have grown up in an age of scientific advancement which has incorporated an underlying psychoanalytic emphasis on the importance of early socialization. The mental hygiene movement combined nineteenth century child saving with the idea that the scientific promotion of well-being in childhood could prevent adult dysfunctions. The mental hygiene paradigm originated with the premise that society could be perfected through the socialization of children. Happy, healthy children were argued to be society's best assurance of a rational and productive adult population.[4]

The history of childhood is a relatively new area of study. One of the primary insights, stemming from an historical and sociological concentration on the young since 1960, has been that the social reality of childhood as a life stage has been altered over time, along with changes in the structure of family life.[5] The seminal work by Philippe Ariès, *Centuries of Childhood*, put forth the proposition that childhood is a social category of relatively modern origin.[6] American sociologist, W. I. Thomas, in one of the early sociological studies on "different" children and the emergent institutions for deviant and disruptive youth in the 1920s, pointed out that a prior "definition of the situation," determining what constitutes good health and proper conduct, effectively shapes not only the perspectives but the practices of child rearing.[7] The perception of infancy, childhood and adolescence as socially constructed, rather than incontrovertible and universal, categories is essential to a critical analysis of the mental hygiene movement and its influence on the "definition" of child life in this century.

The Medical Model

This century has witnessed the formalization of the meaning of the stages of the human life cycle described within a categorical framework which identifies adjustment and maladjustment, as well as normality and abnormality. Mental hygienists promoted the institutionalization of childhood as a series of life-events from infancy through adulthood, characterized by psycho-social changes. The institutionalization of social and political reality as a medical "psychobiological" phenomenon contributed to the transformation of interpersonal relations between adults and children. It similarly altered the child's relationship to the state.[8] These changes were accompanied by, and contributed to, the establishment of professional disciplines, whose official role was to intervene into previously private spheres of life. Doctors, psychiatrists, psychologists, social workers and teachers became authorities where family traditions formerly reigned supreme over issues such as personal health, the acquisition of life skills, and child rearing practices.[9]

At the end of the nineteenth and beginning of the twentieth century, medical science provided a major rationale for social as well as public health reform.[10] Medicine served as a successful prototype for the institutionalization of graduate training in universities. Technical experts and professionals filled the ranks of bureaucracies whose mandate was to oversee public interests.[11] Uncovering the mechanisms through which mental hygienists incorporated the methodology and rationale underlying medical reformism is a major aspect of the research presented here. The question is how it was used in the formation of social policy reflecting the mental hygiene paradigm.

The Childhood Gaze

The medical model, as a scientific approach to human problem solving, was derived from an earlier and more fundamental ideological transformation identified here with the concept of "the childhood gaze," borrowed from Michel Foucault's premiere study on the origin of medical knowledge in the clinics and mental asylums of France. The idea of the *childhood gaze* is used throughout this study to refer to the convergence of medical and scientific perspectives as it was lodged within the mental hygiene paradigm. The *childhood gaze* refers to a method of inquiry based on direct observation, a focus of attention on origins and beginnings, and a belief system concerned with reforming public policy.[12]

The mental hygiene movement was complex. Like other Progressive Era social reform movements, mental hygiene exhibited multiple and sometimes contradictory tendencies. Significantly, two facets of the Enlightenment are inseparable in the *childhood gaze*, as an orientation toward science, and mental hygiene, as an orientation toward health. One, a positivistic rationalism directed toward controlling social change from positions of authority according to ideals of order and efficiency; the other a broad based humanism directed toward perfecting the human condition according to equalitarian principles. Similarly, on one hand, mental hygiene was a scientific movement concerned with discovering absolute principles and systematically applying them as solutions to problems in social contexts. The intent was to create a more efficient and ordered society. On the other hand, mental hygiene was a humanitarian movement concerned with human rights and the alleviation of suffering. These dual elements have led to historiographical controversies over the character of Anglo-American psychiatry. It has also led to questions concerning the motivations behind the establishment of children's institutions.[13]

This dualism is clearly problematic as a prescription for social action. Yet, these contradictions are present, though integrated differently, in the views of democracy in Canadian and United States' political and cultural life.[14] Social policy in areas such as child welfare are especially marked by the internal dynamics of these contradictions.[15] The characteristic of dependency, as self-imposed or as a product of external conditions, and the resolution to the problem in government responsibility or volunteerism, remain topics of great significance for on-going and future debates on the proper role of the modern state in areas of policy which concern health, education and welfare.[16]

This dualism is a focus of this study. The problem is examined in the relationship between knowledge and power in the institutionalization of ideas. The adaptation of mental hygiene ideas into a paradigm which served as an instrument of social transformation reflects the relationship between the internal dynamic of ideas and the external forces which shape them. Ideas, in this sense, are understood as field or context dependent. This dependency between ideas and context, biography and history, contributes to the apparent contradictions and unintended outcomes which characterize progressive social policies concerning children, including mental hygiene. The degree to which knowledge, which is promoted as a universal by elites remains shaped by external events, is a question which is examined through the historical record.

Social Movements in Mental Hygiene

The role of power in the formalization of knowledge and the institutionalization of ideas produced by the mental hygienists is clearly a primary concern in this research. It is examined by way of the individuals and institutions which fostered the movement. This includes the National Committee for Mental Hygiene in the United States, founded in 1909 by Clifford Beers, and the Canadian National Committee for Mental Hygiene, founded by Clarence Hincks in 1918. The mental hygiene paradigms on normality and abnormality in childhood evolved out of two related movements in the 1920s and 1930s. The first is child guidance, which legitimated the classification of mentally disordered children and substantially contributed to the formalization of child psychiatry. The second, mental hygiene paradigm, was an equally important element in scientific child study which established a psychology of normal development.[17]

Mental hygiene became an international movement of great consequence with special significance for the United States and Canada.[18] In spite of the recent concentration by social historians on twentieth century social movements, mental hygiene has received relatively little scholarly attention in the United States. It has received even less attention in Canada.[19] Mental hygiene as an interdisciplinary and international phenomena is examined in this research from a perspective which attempts to integrate the interdependency of its disciplinary perspectives as well as its geographical diffusion.

Twentieth Century Philanthropy

The progress of the mental hygiene movement and its offshoots in child guidance and child study also inescapably includes the role of twentieth century philanthropy. The brokers of knowledge mediating mental hygiene were the general purpose philanthropies, represented by the Rockefeller family chain of charitable organizations, and the Harkeness family Commonwealth fund. While there is a substantial body of literature on the origins and work of twentieth century foundations, we have only just begun to critically evaluate their relationship to social organization.[20] Philanthropies have had a significant impact on social policies in health, education and social welfare.[21] The influence on children's policy related to mental hygiene was dominated in the 1920s and 1930s by Rockefeller related philanthropy in child study research and the Commonwealth Fund in child guidance.[22] The philanthropies have also played an international role in the legitimation and development of the medical and social sciences. In this process, the boundaries between child related academic disciplines, especially in health, education and welfare, were forged.

The structure of power in legitimating knowledge is an important aspect of the institutionalization of any idea over related ideas. Mental hygiene, in its relationship to philanthropies, suggests a strong correspondence between successful ideas and the power of mentors. Ideas promoted by the powerful, however, are not produced in isolation, but are related to larger systems of social and cultural changes. Further, selected ideas are not exchanged intact. They are, in fact, transformed in the process of their institutionalization. As pointed out by a celebrated historian of the French Revolution, Alfred Cobban, the determination of causality in good history and good social science must include an assessment of the relative contribution of external social forces and the dynamics of individual biography.[23] This study is an attempt to achieve a balance between the broader scale of historical time and the more particular sequences of experiential change in a description of the "mechanics of the process" which legitimated mental hygiene in two national contexts.

Inquiry into the Body, Mind, and Estate of Mental Hygiene

This study is divided into three parts which represent not separate elements but parts of a puzzle which function together even as they evolve chronologically: Part I, The Body (the medical model): Part II, the Mind (the legitimation of psychiatry); and Part III, the Estate (the medicalization of public policy).[24]

Chapter one is concerned with the transition from eighteenth and nineteenth century institutions to the "century of the child." The field of inquiry examined in chapter two is the professionalization of medical knowledge described in the establishment of Johns Hopkins Medical School. Chapter three focuses on the establishment of large scale American philanthropy, represented by the Rockefeller family as organizers and promoters of scientific ideas. The last two chapters in the section relay the interplay between individual personal biographies of the founders of mental hygiene and the larger social forces which led to the establishment of the first two national committees in the United States and Canada.

Part II is concerned with the application of medical knowledge to child life and the separation of maladjusted and adjusted children into two paradigms, which legitimate the social recognition of non-normal and normal progress in childhood. Chapters six and seven follow the institutionalization of child psychiatry from the mental hygienist's concern over juvenile delinquency to concern for mentally disordered children in the child guidance movement in the 1920s and 1930s. Chapters eight and nine look at the parallel movements at research institutions in Canada and the United States, where scientific child studies funded by Rockefeller founded a psychololgy of normality.

The final section, chapters ten through twelve, covers the formalization of child psychiatry in U.S. and Canadian institutions. Differences between Canadian and U.S. approaches to mental hygiene are also explored in relationship to the underlying dynamics of the private and public dimensions of social life, as shaped by configurations of knowledge and power.

– Part I –

The Body

The Childhood Gaze and the Medical Model

The child is more precious than the problem. The only field in which experiment on the human being is recognized, or rather practices without recognition, is medicine, where the material is already threatened with destruction through sickness, and the physician introduces an experimental change . . . which gives a chance of preserving life and restoring health. (W. I. Thomas, *The Unadjusted Girl*, Boston: Little and Brown, 1923, pp. 244–5).

Biographies of Mental Hygiene

This book is dedicated to Humanity in its own behalf, by one whose rare privilege it has been, and is, to speak for those afflicted thousands of human beings least able to speak for themselves. (Clifford Whittingham Beers, original preface to *A Mind That Found Itself*, draft manuscript, January 1907, Beers Notebooks, AFMH Archives, CMC, NYC).

Part I

The Body

Chapter One

The Childhood Gaze

As a science of preserving normality, mental hygiene applies a systematic prescription for problem solving. The orientation is clinical, individualistic, and utopian. Mental hygienists sought to perfect both the body and mind of man as well as his society. The mental hygiene paradigm is part of the rationale which developed in support of, and in response to, the sense of the public order which evolved out of the heritage of the childhood gaze expressed in nineteenth century institutions.

While public perceptions of what is normal and abnormal shape psychiatry more than other medical disciplines, mental hygienists tried to contribute to the establishment of an empirical body of knowledge in the scientific study of disorders of the mind. In spite of attempts to medicalize mental illness, other than in cases of verifiable disease or injury, "madness" remains, as it has throughout history, a kind of social deviance where aberrant behavior, or thought, is ultimately a matter of breaching established concepts of normative behavior. Mental illness, from this standpoint, is more of a social construct than physical illness, in that its symptoms are circumstantial and its reality is a matter of opinion which has been formalized in social practices. The application of the concept of mental illness to children is surprisingly recent.

The mental hygiene movement developed a way of looking at childhood that was grounded in the natural sciences as a template for the social sciences. Scientific research directed toward children was especially influenced by medicine, which served as a clinical example of systematic problem solving. The medical model, as incorporated into the public health campaigns of the turn of the century, was seen by advocates to constitute the ultimate applied version of science which served both the biological and social sciences.

Science and Medical Reform

The rising international concern over normal and abnormal children was part of the nineteenth century scientific movement to classify and rationalize what was observable in nature as well as human life. The physical and mental well-being of children and youth became a focus of attention reflecting a new vision which emphasized the principles of prevention.

The dynamic behind the direction of reform was borrowed from the rapid expansion of technical and scientific knowledge made in the first half of the nineteenth century, which contributed to the advancement of medicine as a science. The expansion of this knowledge base was greatly facilitated by an international exchange of both leadership and technology.

Reformist preventive medicine gained momentum from the excitement derived from the technological and conceptual breakthroughs of nineteenth century men of science. For example, the invention of the microscope in 1830 led to the discovery of the biological origin of diseases. In the 1860s and 1870s, pathologists in bacteriology uncovered the microbial causes of typhoid, malaria, tuberculosis, diphtheria, dysentery, tetanus, and cholera. These findings were applied to the cure of diseases in the 1880s and 1890s.[1] In March 1882, Robert Koch announced his discovery of the tubercule bacillus. The same year, Louis Pasteur discovered the principles of vaccination in the effective immunization against anthrax in sheep. The possibility arose of protecting human populations from early and unnecessary death. Potentially the scourges of deadly diseases could be eliminated altogether through preventive vaccinations. Pathology became the central focus of advanced medical research, with the most potent practical application of the knowledge gained termed "hygiene." Hygiene assumed the designation as "state medicine, public health or preventive medicine."[2]

Prior Conditions for a Mental Hygiene of Childhood

The technical advance of scientific research applied to human life and progress and a growing concern over youth served as two interrelated steps in the addition of mental phenomena to the concept of hygiene and its concentration on childhood. A combination of forces came to play in focussing the mental hygiene movement on childhood as the key to adult mental health. Nineteenth century social changes which shaped the family and habits of the work place were critical to the development of the twentieth century mental health paradigm, with its focus on reforming public policy in the direction of prevention in childhood. Children were gradually conceptually segregated by age. Only later was their cognitive and emotional life elaborated as different from adults and as having significant consequences in later life.[3] The segregation of children encouraged separate popular categories for normal, dependent, neglected, and delinquent groups of the young by age. The success of the mental hygiene movement hinged upon the subsequent transition to the idea that social progress was tied to the quality and progress of early life.

Throughout the nineteenth century, children were increasingly identified with age-specific institutions separated from similar adult institutions. The general institutional expansion of the nineteenth century was, to a very great extent, directed toward this pattern of segregating child from adult society. The transformation in social institutions also fostered the medicalization of the concept of childhood as the emergent medical model was built into the expanding institutional structures.

Institutions which took in children in the nineteenth century were increasingly seen as necessarily unique from similar institutions for dependent or criminal adults.[4] The institutional differentiation of children occurred first with those individuals who have been subsequently classified as dependent or deviant, and who currently tend to be labeled disadvantaged, handicapped, or suffering from some form of "disorder" either mental, physical, or behavioral.[5] These children were identified by nineteenth century child savers as morally disordered, witnessed in the circumstances that they were "wayward," and "lacked parental guidance." The trend to control the circumstances and upbringing of the young was not isolated, but occurred in Canada, England, and other parts of the western world as well as the United States.[6]

Nineteenth century institutions at first tended to randomly combine categories of age in the same way that such institutions lacked formal distinctions between categories of deviance such as aberrant lifestyles or behavior, as opposed to indigent or dependent individuals who could not help themselves, or the criminal whose antisocial acts broke laws. Early prototypes for age-specific institutions did exist, however. The Boston Female Asylum (1800), the New York Orphan Asylum (1806), The Boston Asylum and Farm School for Indigent Boys (1814), and the Baltimore Manual Labor School (1847) were among the earliest of United States child-specific organizations. Even these examples lacked the division between delinquent and dependent children.[7] Both delinquency and dependency were identified with pauperism. One consequence of this line of thought was that where "pauperism" was considered "the enemy," crimes committed by the young became a symptom reflecting the moral disease of poverty.

In 1824, the Society for the Prevention of Pauperism assumed the title, the Society for the Prevention of Delinquency.[8] The first call for the separation of youthful criminals from adults, and the creation of the first segregated institutional setting for children who broke the law occurred as part of the House of Refuge.[9] It was children who were deviant in this way who later became the first object of psychiatric interest.

The nineteenth century developed a variety of other public institutions which also evolved toward the separation of child and adult groups. Asylums, workhouses, almshouses, prisons, and special schools were restructured in order to differentiate among various classes of "normal," "defective," "dependent," and "delinquent" by age. In the advance of the *childhood gaze* with the scientization of medicine, and the medicalization of social problems, deviance was gradually transformed in the minds of reformists from a moral into a medical disease.

Childhood and Social Deviance

While asylums, and later hospitals, for the insane were part of the advance of scientific methodology in classifying distinctions among populations, the emphasis was not on youth. Mental hospitals and asylums were largely filled with adult populations. In 1880, the average age was 43.5 years. Seventeen percent were over the age of sixty years.[10] A great number of those incarcerated as insane were alcoholics or were suffering from the debilitating effects of advanced syphilis. This remained the major factor in commitment until the late 1920s. The expansion of public institutions for the insane took place in the mid to late 1800s. The early years were marked by an optimism which has been termed a "cult of curability."[11] Prior to 1820, only one state in the United States took responsibility for the insane. By 1875, there were more than sixty institutions in thirty-two states. The "cult of curability" waned in the face of what appeared to be a gigantic increase in the number of insane in the general population. Insanity was increasingly thought to be due to hereditary factors of biological origin independent of psychological characteristics.[12]

In Canada, the first provincially operated lunatic asylum was established in New Brunswick in 1835. Dorothea Dix, the early American advocate for the reform of the treatment of the insane, campaigned in the Maritime provinces of Canada as well as in the New England states.[13] Alarming statistics concerning the census of insane from the United States and Britain also encouraged the growth of Canadian asylums. By 1913, there were twenty-eight institutions representing all ten provinces.[14] In the early years in both the United States and Canada, the insane were often put in nonspecific instituions such as jails and almshouses. Similarly, there were no legal restrictions to placing juveniles in the asylums.

The weak division between youth and adult is witnessed in the "Record of Lunatics in the Temporary Lunatic Asylum in the City and Parish of Saint John from the first of January to the thirty-first of December 1837."[15] There are fifty-four cases cited, of these there are six minors, four nineteen year olds, one fourteen and one eleven year old. These cases also illustrate the degree to which insanity as a moral affliction was considered curable. The eleven year old, Michael Mullen, is identified as being afflicted with "ordinary insanity." Admitted the twenty-fourth of August, he was discharged as "cured" less than a month later on the eighteenth of September. The fourteen year old is cited as an "idiot" who was "remaining unimproved." Two "furiously mad" nineteen year old females are also cited as discharged as "cured." Another nineteen year old was discharged "improved" while the fourth afflicted with "ordinary insanity" remained "unimproved."[16]

The Orphans' Home and Female Aid Society was incorporated in Toronto in 1851 by members of the city's elite.[17] The concern with neglected children on the streets of Toronto led to a variety of institutions from reformatories to industrial schools to an array of charities.[18] One change in the disposition of dependent and neglected children which altered their placement in non-age segregated settings was the enactment of legislation which regulated children's aid societies and controlled the placement of children in private and institutional care.[19] In Canada, a Royal Commission on the Prison and Reformatory System of Ontario was set up in the year 1890 with J. W. Langmuir as chair. An outcome of the Commission was "The Children's Charter," or "Gibson Act," passed in 1893, which led to the appointment of J. J. Kelso as Superintendent of Neglected and Dependent Children.[20]

Child immigration became an issue in Canada which nearly superseded the problem of unsupervised and delinquent children.[21] Between the years 1869 and 1919, seventy-three thousand children were sent from various parts of the United Kingdom to Canada under the auspices of charitable organizations. The earliest group came from the Kirkdale Workhouse in Liverpool under the supervision of Maria S. Rye, followed shortly by children from the Revival Refuge and Home of Industry of Spitalsfield, London, with Annie MacPherson.[22]

In the period between 1891 and 1921, the Canadian population increased from almost five million to almost nine million.[23] In the Western provinces up to forty-two percent of the children under ten years old had parents who were foreign born.[24] The rapid increase in the foreign born population was argued to contribute to social problems from criminality to labor agitation.[25] The objective was not to stop immigration, which was imperative for nation building, but to ensure "quality" immigrants who would become good citizens and good workers.

A child immigrant, who was without family protection, a child who committed a crime, or who was orphaned, or vagrant, could be considered dangerous, or a criminal, in the nineteenth century. He or she was not likely to be declared mad. Gradually, however, as judging from the evolution of posts such as J. J. Kelso's, childhood was separated as more flexible and curable than similar circumstances might indicate with adults. Children were considered to be morally vulnerable and in need of training and protection rather than punishment. Insanity was looked upon as an adult problem. Any mention of the possibility of insanity in young children was rare, and when it occurred it was viewed from a theoretical or speculative basis.

From a Pathology of Childhood to Psychiatry In the Century of the Child

The first attempted systematic view of a psychiatry which could encompass a broad range of ages, was a theoretical work by Hermann Emminghaus published in the year 1887. The conceptual basis for a psychiatry of childhood was not established until the year 1905 in Freud's *Three Essays on the Theory of Sexuality*. Freud's primary interest, nonetheless, was in the psychology of the adult, not the child. Yet, his idea that the treatment of adult psychosis required an introspective search into childhood events gave impetus to the psychiatric examination of children.

Adolf Meyer, a Swiss immigrant psychiatrist who was central to mental hygiene and the professionalization of American psychiatry, contributed the notion of "psychobiology." He stressed the importance of the body-mind as a continuum, which also introduced a dynamic attitude toward the origins of mental illness as a developmental issue. Technical advances in psychometry in the early twentieth century created the capacity to measure individual differences. This added a predictive element to child study based on differential expectations according to intellectual capacity. Mental testing, which remains a relatively inaccurate tool, is still used to legitimate the presence of inequalities in ability which are not remediable.

The school-age population, made accessible by the successful nineteenth century establishment of common schools and the legislation of compulsory school laws, offered an unprecedented opportunity for large scale public intervention into child life, first in moral training, then in physical health and finally in mental well-being. European and British moral and medical reform predated efforts in the United States and Canada.[26] "School hygiene" was an early battleground in the campaign for public health reform.

Medical inspection of schools was legislated in Brussels in the year 1874. In England, advocates first attempted to uplift the physical health of children in the schools in the 1880s. Efforts in the United States and Canada followed. The early popular works such as Kerr's, *School Hygiene*, sold thousands of copies on an international market and were frequently reissued and updated. The connection between physical health and environmental conditions led to campaigns for sanitary school facilities. Open air classrooms, nursing, and dental services were included as a part of the public institution of the school. By the early twentieth century, coinciding with the testing, eugenics, and mental hygiene movements, arguments were made for the preservation of physical health in order to preserve mental health. In 1913, four years after the establishment of the first national committee for mental hygiene, revised works on school hygiene included chapters on mental testing, descriptions of the brain, and discussions of emotional development in childhood.[27]

The formal child psychiatry movement in the United States evolved in conjunction with the U.S. mental hygiene inspired child guidance movement of the 1920s and 1930s which first took up directly the problem of delinquency as a mental problem.[28] The first English language text in child psychiatry, written by Leo Kanner, was not published until the year 1935.[29] Psychotherapy with children remained underdeveloped and formally unrecognized in the United States or Canada until after the second World War.

While children in the nineteenth century were seen as a resource for family welfare, the twentieth century has increasingly individualized childhood and placed children under observation as objects of investigation.[30] Only in this century have systematic studies been conducted and widely disseminated in order to determine how children behave and what they learn at various ages. And, only in this century have we made this a paramount consideration in our social institutions. The biological and clinical sciences have become a rationale binding social and behavioral practices.[31] The professionalization of medical science was central to the advance of mental hygiene and child psychiatry in the particular form that it has taken in the United States. The relative differences in the evolution of the medical model and the status of its medical practitioners in Canada shaped mental hygiene and psychiatry differently in that context. The elevation of scientific curriculum in higher education, the growth of graduate university instruction and advanced training in medicine took an early lead in the United States at Johns Hopkins University in the late nineteenth century.

Chapter Two

The Spirit of Johns Hopkins and the Medical Model

The *childhood gaze* was implicated in the development of scientific curriculum in the modern university and especially in medical education. Without this occurrence scientific child study would not have had a foundation upon which to build in the years after the first World War. The legitimation of science in professional education is best illustrated in the establishment of Johns Hopkins University and its graduate medical school.

The men who were instrumental in making Johns Hopkins the model for American higher education, and especially graduate education in medicine and psychiatry, were also instrumental in formalizing the mental hygiene movement with the establishment of the National Committee for Mental Hygiene. William Welch, William Osler, and Adolf Meyer, in particular, played central roles in directing philanthropic funds toward the support of research in mental hygiene and related medical sciences. Simon and Abraham Flexner were influential promoters of scientific research and its accompanying ideology within the Rockefeller philanthropies.

Johns Hopkins served as a catalyst for the building of institutions from which the childhood gaze could be disseminated. It provided an early setting which nurtured the scientific study of children in the formative years of individuals who became major influences on twentieth century thought about child life. This included G. Stanley Hall, John Dewey, and John B. Watson. Meyer encouraged the discipline of psychology to move away from philosophy toward clinical research, just as he helped legitimate the scientific orientation of American psychoanalysis and psychiatric medicine. American behaviorism and clinical psychology was also initiated at Johns Hopkins in the work of Hall and Watson.

Johns Hopkins Medical School helped to elevate to social leadership status a cadre of scientific medical men imbued with an ideology perfectly tailored to advance the ideological orientation of mental hygiene. William

Welch, as the first dean of medicine, felt that science was on a "threshold" of eliminating diseases of the mind which had been "more devastating [to mankind] than any upheavals of nature or any wars."[1] William Osler, first head of the department of medicine, initiated a campaign against tuberculosis and called for other massive public preventive health campaigns to "fight for the day when a man's life shall be more precious than gold."[2]

Medical Men as Social Leaders

The revolution in public health in the latter part of the nineteenth and early twentieth century necessarily began in the restructuring of medical education and the building of a new social leadership. Medicine was used as a guide for the reconstruction of university based graduate professional schools, which also served to form a base for the education of a new scientifically oriented cadre of politically influential social leaders. Standards were established for medical education which ultimately became the model for the American university system, with consequences for post professional education in particular.[3] These innovations depended on the legitimation of medical knowledge as scientifically valid. Johns Hopkins University served as a template for the application of science to the study of the human life cycle. The model of university and graduate training as it evolved at Johns Hopkins was especially relevant to the historical convergence of the theme of the childhood gaze, medical reformism, mental hygiene, and scientific philanthropy in the twentieth century.

Establishing Johns Hopkins University

The University was originally endowed by the Baltimore Quaker merchant of the same name. Hopkins was influenced by his fellow townsman, George Peabody, who had been instrumental in the southern states in pioneering educational philanthropy. Hopkins had come to believe that the most enduring needs were "a university, for there will always be youth to train; and a hospital, for there will always be suffering to relieve."[4] On his death in 1873, two overlapping boards of trustees (one for the university and one for the medical school) were set up to establish two interrelated institutions with seven million dollars divided between them.

The result was unique: the first true university, in a modern sense, in America and the first organically connected medical facility with post graduate medical education. Johns Hopkins combined the most advanced scientific medical research with clinical hospital experience in a university setting. Clinics were established for both physical and psychiatric disorders. The role of the university was defined according to European and especially Germanic tradition, as providing the insights of 'true enlightenment' and 'scientific discovery.' Johns Hopkins helped redefine the position of doctors from marginal figures with ill defined status to positions of prestigious social leadership based on their possession of the necessary knowledge and qualifications to solve fundamental and pressing social problems.

An impending alliance between university based researchers and large scale donors in the newly formed general purpose American philanthropies constructed a mechanism which fostered a systematic approach to social policy based on the supposedly objective grounds of methodical investigation. The institutionalization of social policy on the basis of medical research often directly intervened into traditional social practices associated with family life and child rearing. The success of this endeavor rested heavily on legitimizing leadership training in institutions of higher education. Before the founding of Johns Hopkins this had yet to be accomplished, even though the movement toward scientific curriculum and university reform had been initiated as early as the year 1869 by Charles Eliot in his inaugural address as President of Harvard University.[5] The university idea and the role of higher education in fostering scientific progress took focus at Johns Hopkins in the 1880s.

The Vision of Johns Hopkins

The vision of Johns Hopkins University was largely shaped by its first president, Daniel Coit Gilman. Gilman was a contemporary of other great university presidents including Charles Eliot, Andrew White of Cornell, and James B. Angell of Michigan. These men strongly supported the introduction of scientific curriculum in addition to the traditional classic curriculum. Gilman, like his contemporaries, was concerned with upgrading science, including the medical sciences, as an integral part of a university. Medicine was to be connected with research and clinical facilities in a hospital setting. Gilman was unusual in that he also gave strong support for the introduction of post graduate university work. This was in contrast to most other college presidents who were concerned with upgrading and differentiating undergraduate university traditions from secondary curricula.

Gilman's views were influenced by his experience as a graduate student in Germany. German universities had reached their peak of productivity by the year 1870 and they had become a mecca for Americans and Canadians seeking advanced work.[6] Instruction in theology, law and philosophy excelled, as did the medical sciences. Basic research was pursued with diligence, and the scholar, and researcher, was looked upon with high prestige. The goal of university education was to further the horizons of human knowledge rather than to simply train applicants for practical certificates. The pursuit of pure understanding in clinical and laboratory studies revolutionized the basic sciences upon which modern technologies with practical application were founded. Part of the impact of the *childhood gaze* was a millennial belief in a future shaped by scientific knowledge. The premonition of a better world was not grounded in the abstractions of metaphysics but in the readily apparent advances being made through scientific research. Gilman and his contemporaries were profoundly impressed by the intense and exciting intellectual atmosphere which prevailed in the laboratories of Europe.[7]

Upon his return from Germany, Gilman helped organize the Sheffield Scientific School of Yale in the German tradition.[8] In the year 1874, Gilman's reputation at Yale, and as president of the University of California since 1872, led to an offer by the trustees of Johns Hopkins University which "involved nothing less than creating a new institution without restriction of precedent or the interference of political manipulation."[9] This offer, was well suited to Gilman's temperament and breadth of view. The organizational model created by Gilman at Johns Hopkins University reflected the tenor and direction of the European precedent which had so impressed him. He succeeded in bringing this revolution in the production of scientific knowledge back to the United States at a strategic point in the nation's growth. Johns Hopkins came to serve as a model for promoting innovations in the structure and utility of esoteric knowledge which fit well within an expanding entrepreneurial and technically oriented society.

The University Idea

The years 1876 to 1890 were the adolescent years of American universities. Before 1876, the opening of Johns Hopkins, there had been only immature beginnings of higher education in the United States. In the fifteen years after its establishment, Johns Hopkins along with Harvard University approached maturity in that they were able to provide training and opportunities previously available only in Europe. After 1890, other universities in the United States and Canada began to experiment with the "university idea." Notable schools which made this effort included: Cornell, Columbia, Stanford, Michigan, California, Yale, Toronto, and McGill. Fifteen major graduate schools or departments, inspired by the model provided at Johns Hopkins, were established by the end of the nineteenth century.[10] The university was distinguished from a college, in the JHU ideal, by offering a diversified undergraduate curriculum which was nonetheless differentiated from graduate level instruction in professional fields. Harvard officials had previously taken the position that there should be no arbitrary differentiation between graduate and undergraduate studies. Charles Eliot commented that "the single most brilliant experiment in the development of graduate education and research was the one made at Johns Hopkins. It influenced all the others."[11] Eliot wrote to Gilman on his retirement: "There is not a university in the country that has not benefited by what you have done . . . Your Medical School has been a real inspiration."[12]

The experience of attending Johns Hopkins has been described by the early fellows as thrilling and exhilarating:

> Here at last, so we felt, the American university had been founded. The beginning . . . was a dawn wherein 'twas blessed to be alive. Freedom and wise counsel one enjoyed together . . . One longed to be a doer of the word, and not a hearer only, a creator of his own infinitesimal fraction of a product.[13]

The Doctors

The American portrait artist, John Singer Sargent captured the sense of awe associated with men of science by immortalizing the founders of the medical school at Johns Hopkins in the classic work, "The Four Doctors."[14] The painting reveals the elevation to sovereign status that the medical profession was to take to heart in the United States in the following decades.[15] The legitimacy of medical leadership was argued to be more fundamental than the simple acquisition of material power, since it was based in the doctor's esoteric access to scientific knowledge about life and death, health and disease. This belief was cultivated by the creators of the medical tradition at Johns Hopkins.

The dynamic of the medical school at Johns Hopkins was that of active social and medical reformists. The doctors of the Sargent paintings at Johns Hopkins and their students formed an intimate network which tied together medical and social reform, mental hygiene and philanthropy in the Progressive Era. Two of the major individuals who took part in coalescing this network, William Henry Welch and William Osler, are portrayed by Sargent.

William Henry Welch, The Dean of Medicine

William Welch, often hailed as the dean of American medicine, was perhaps the most important figure both at Johns Hopkins and as a liaison between science, medical reformism and funding agencies. Welch became one of the most active founders of the mental hygiene movement. He served as vice president (1909–1923), president (1923) and honorary president (1924–1934) of the National Committee for Mental Hygiene as well as president of the American Foundation for Mental Hygiene (1928–1934) and the International Committee for Mental Hygiene (1923–1934).[16] He helped secure ideological support for the mental hygiene movement as well as funds to sustain it by way of his professional contacts, which were numerous. He served in executive positions in Rockefeller related philanthropies in the Sanitary Commission, International Health Board, and Rockefeller Institute among others. He coincidentally served on the Board of Trustees of the Carnegie Institution of Washington and the Milbank Memorial Fund. His biographers give a partial list of over eighty scientific and civic organizations, largely dealing with public health, medicine, and the social sciences, to which he belonged.[17]

Mental hygiene was a coordinated part of Welch's more general activism. All of these areas were linked in Welch's mind with social reform. To Welch, medical science and the elimination of disease was as practical a means of social intervention as was urban renewal and public welfare. Welch saw poor housing, sewage problems, and industrial conditions as part of the etiology of physical, mental, and moral disease. Weak character, alcoholism, and pauperism were essentially problems of sanitation, curable by way of medical intervention.[18]

William Osler, The Family Doctor

The other figure of international fame depicted in Sargent's portrait was Canadian born William Osler. Osler was one of the most widely celebrated clinical teachers of medicine of his day, and he remains a classic role model for the moral leadership of the family doctor. Osler was an eloquent spokesman for the application of the medical model in solving a wide variety of social problems. He was known for his keen wit and charismatic discourses on the nobility of the cause of preventive medicine. He viewed scientific medicine and pathology as a practical extension of a democratic social conscience properly directed toward uplifting the common man. He rose to become a world leader in public health which helped to legitimate mental hygiene in Canada, the United States, and England.

In the year 1905, he resigned from Johns Hopkins to become Regius Professor of Medicine at Oxford, England. His prestige was accorded an ultimate sanction when he was knighted in the year 1910.[19] His published works and addresses greatly influenced the orientation toward science of major figures in the history of general purpose philanthropy. The most notable case of this was his influence on Frederick T. Gates, personal advisor to John D. Rockefeller, Sr., who felt that he had been drawn to the support of medical research after reading a treatise by Osler on the need for the advancement of medical knowledge and the potential of scientific research.[20]

The students of Welch and Osler were equally illustrious, for among them were included Simon Flexner of the Rockefeller Institute of Medicine (Rockefeller University), and his brother, Abraham Flexner who, in the year 1910, wrote the influential Carnegie study of *Medical Education in the United States and Canada.*[21] Harvey Cushing, became a renowned medical educator and researcher at Harvard University and biographer of Osler.[22] One of the first of a succession of Canadian students to come to Johns Hopkins, Lewellys F. Barker, became the first president of the National Committee for Mental Hygiene.[23]

In addition to pioneering scientific medicine, laboratory research in pathology, and medical education, Johns Hopkins also served as a model for the advancement of psychiatry and psychology. Johns Hopkins legitimated clinical research in a university setting and placed the support of medical science behind psychiatry, neurology, and their related fields in preventive public health. Johns Hopkins was also at the forefront of the advancement of psychology, which, at other universities at the turn of the century, was undistinguished from philosophy. One of the pioneers in psychiatry, Adolf Meyer, elaborated the early rationales for developing a science of mental hygiene based in his idea of "psychobiology" which set the stage for the clinical traditions of child psychology and child psychiatry.

Adolf Meyer and Psychobiology

Adolf Meyer was a Swiss born neuropathologist whose arrival in the United States signaled a movement on the part of asylum psychiatrists to improve the scientific aspects of institutional psychiatry. Meyer was a respected and established laboratory researcher in Europe. He introduced methods of laboratory science to the care and study of psychiatric patients as well as methods for the collection of clinical records at Worchester. His efforts were recognized widely in the burgeoning medical fields of the era. The influence of his experiences in the asylum and Hall's influential emphasis on biology and behavior directed Meyer toward a holistic approach to mental illness, based on a theory which emphasized the interplay between mental and physical states.[24] By 1898 Meyer's European neuroanatomical orientation evolved into the "psychobiological" approach which became the center piece in his philosophy as well as a central premise in mental hygiene.

Meyer was hired at Johns Hopkins by William Welch, where he became director of the Phipps Psychiatric Clinic. The clinic operated a social service department which served both adults and children. During the formative period for the Phipps Clinic, which opened in 1913, Meyer served as a pivotal figure in the mental hygiene movement.[25] Meyer greatly contributed to the legitimation of psychiatric interest in childhood, which became fundamental to mental hygiene's contention that preventive mental health care necessitated intervention into child and family life. Meyer's interests were reinforced by the theories of Freudian psychoanalysis, as well as by his medical colleagues at Johns Hopkins with their public health orientation. His psychobiology also had affiliations with the developing environmental or behavioral approach to psychiatric illness. This is evidenced by his support for John B. Watson who conducted laboratory work in the Phipps Psychiatric Clinic at Johns Hopkins in the years just prior to and just after the first World War.[26]

G. Stanley Hall and Early Child Study

G. Stanley Hall was one of the dominant figures in psychology and education in the Progressive era whose personal history sometimes intersects and sometimes runs parallel to the story of the *childhood gaze* and mental hygiene. A student of William James at Harvard, Hall was recommended to Gilman for a professorship in psychology and pedagogics at Johns Hopkins in 1882. In the year 1883, Hall published *The Contents of Children's Minds*, one of the earliest serious attempts to examine the psychology of the child.[27] As chair of a new department at Johns Hopkins, Hall initiated a model psychological laboratory grounded in his experiences in experimental psychology in Europe. While William James had previously established a "psycho-physics" laboratory at Harvard, Hall's laboratory at Johns Hopkins is considered the first true clinical laboratory in the United States.[28]

Hall, similar to Gilman, received a graduate education in Europe where he was profoundly influenced by the power of scientific clinical research. Hall, as did Gilman, felt a responsibility to advance scientific curriculum upon his return to the United States. At Johns Hopkins, Hall gathered around him men who later went on to make significant independent contributions to the development of science. Among his students at Johns Hopkins can be counted: James McKeen Cattel, John Dewey, and Joseph Jastrow.[29]

By 1888, Hall had become the foremost critic of secondary and higher education in the United States. In 1889, he was asked to become president of the newly founded Clark University, which he subsequently organized according to the principles embodied by Johns Hopkins under Gilman. Hall's vision was, however, modified even more sharply toward the German model of post graduate scientific research. Hall also influenced Adolf Meyer during this period in his early work in the United States as a pathologist at Kankakee State Hospital for the Insane in Worchester, Massachusetts. Meyer had in part been attracted to Worchester because of the presence of Hall and his students in psychology at nearby Clark University. Meyer and Hall developed reciprocal exchanges where Clark students received clinical training at Kankakee.[30]

Hall's early interest in and advocacy of child study had long term consequences. Hall sought the attention of educators and incipient psychologists through his journals, *The Pedagogical Seminary* (1891) and the *American Journal of Psychology* (1887), as well as lectures at Clark and through his professional leadership in other organizations.[31]

Hall's perception of children was in part a refinement of the conceptualization of Rousseau's noble savage. Hall added to this idea, however, Charles Darwin's notion of the survival of the fittest. He saw the stages of childhood and adolescence in human development as a reflection of natural processes in a recapitulation of the history of the race. "The adolescent," according to Hall, "is neo-atavistic, [where the] later acquisitions of the race slowly become prepotent." Hall described adolescent "development [as] less gradual and more salutatory," than a child's. To Hall it was "suggestive of some ancient period of storm and stress when old moorings were broken and a higher level attained."[32]

The child study movement, encouraged by Hall, expanded in the 1880s and 1890s. However, child study as an independently organized movement was relatively short-lived even though it boasted study groups in a number of states and was counted among the two or three most vital topics in educational circles up to World War I. Hall hoped to permanently establish child study in the National Education Association. His first attempt was in the year 1891 at the Annual Convention of the NEA held in Toronto. He was, however, more successful at the 1894 NEA meetings, partly due to having popularized his ideas at the World Columbian Congress held in conjunction with the 1893 Exposition in Chicago. In spite of this the formal aspects of the movement were in decline by 1904 when Hall's treatise on child study, *Adolescence*, was published.

Nevertheless, the impact of child study was more pervasive than its official organization or temporal existence might imply. Hall's ideas on child study filtered into other organizations such as the Mother's Congress, precursor to the contemporary Parent Teacher Associations. It became a part of the developing academic disciplines which were to become the official guides for child life in the twentieth century.[33] One of the long term contributions of the child study movement, as conceived by Hall, was the great forward thrust that it gave to the theme of the *childhood gaze* in the legitimation of a scientific perspective which bolstered the medical model.

Hall's concentration on the mental life and development of children, combined with his publicly visible position, did much to further research on children on an international level. One author speculates that Alfred Binet's early experimental work on individual differences in children was spurred by Hall's early publications on the study of children.[34] Hall was also instrumental in introducing Freudian theory to the United States. Hall was host to Freud's only visit to the U.S. at the twentieth anniversary of the opening of Clark University in the year 1909.[35]

Hall's influence was extended by the fact that his students at Clark became highly influential leaders. For example, Lewis Terman, professor of educational psychology at Stanford University, dominated the presidency of the American Psychological Association in the inter-War period. Terman worked to professionalize public school psychologists as experts on standardized testing and student placement. He was co-author of the Stanford Binet intelligence scale.[36]

Another of Hall's students, Henry H. Goddard, introduced Binet's tests to the United States.[37] Goddard was scientific director at Vineland Training School for the Feebleminded in New Jersey, where the Army intelligence scales were developed during the first World War. Goddard was a strong advocate of the eugenics and testing movements.[38]

A third student, Arnold Gesell, was the founder of the Child Development Clinic at Yale in 1911. His clinical work in child development helped to establish this field. These figures, among other students of Hall at Clark, did much to shape educational psychology, special education, and early childhood research in a formative period in the early twentieth century.[39] Hall and his students were, in a sense, a product of the diffusion of the spirit of Johns Hopkins which they used to structure their own research.

The Heroic Age of Medicine

It is clear that the men who first came to Johns Hopkins University were already convinced of the social value of the application of scientific knowledge. They did not get the idea of using science to protect human welfare from Johns Hopkins but from the ethos and ethic of the advance of science in the *childhood gaze* which gave Johns Hopkins its "spirit." The men and women in higher education who came after the clinical pioneers at Johns Hopkins had the benefits of the their early theories, techniques and organizational models. The National Committee for Mental Hygiene and the Rockefeller Foundation also inherited the intellectual climate which John Hopkins had carried with vigor into the twentieth century.

Practitioners in the new science of medicine sought to establish public policies that would improve the quality of human life. The medical image of progress captured the imagination of the formulators of scientific philanthropy. The combination of philanthropy and science created one of the great alliances of modern times in that it brought substantial resources to bear on the production and dissemination of a particular set of ideas. It made it financially feasible to establish institutions which supported and made powerful a medical paradigm in the name of human progress. In this period, the field of scientific medicine, supported broadly by philanthropy, was established as a dominant profession in the United States.[40]

The years between 1880 and the first World War have been called the "heroic age of medicine."[41] There was a reciprocal relationship between public health reform and the philanthropies which took shape in the first decades of the new century. The beneficiaries of early entrepreneurial capitalism applied their resources and organizational talents to philanthropy in this period. The attempt was to apply science to human welfare in the same sense as industrialization and technology had rationalized the economic sphere in the nineteenth century.

By the beginning of the twentieth century, the *childhood gaze* had taken on an institutional character in the form of graduate professional education. Scholars pursued through clinical studies the advance of the medical and social sciences. The new knowledge base in preventive and public health medicine was conceived as the ultimate tool for social reform. Systematic investigation assumed a universal status whose legitimacy was based in its supposed objectivity.[42] The language of reform was a part of the symbolic order of the *childhood gaze*. Through the *childhood gaze* the mental hygiene of childhood came to be viewed as a path to social salvation.

Chapter Three

The Midas Touch and the Power of Science

The elaboration of the *childhood gaze* in scientific medicine and public health intersected with the history of large scale twentieth century general purpose philanthropy.[1] The diffusion of medical reform as pioneered at Johns Hopkins and its formal establishment in institutional practices on a broad scale was greatly advanced by the advocacy and resources made available by major U.S. philanthropies.

Benevolent donations to education and welfare are an established tradition in western societies. Throughout the nineteenth century, charitable enterprises fostered the ideological underpinnings of mental hygiene in the advance of the social sciences. The charitable tradition was pursued on a relatively large but unsystematic scale in the United States in the nineteenth century by men such as George Peabody and Henry Phipps. The character of economic expansion in the nineteenth century created a situation, however, which was unprecedented.

Modern American philanthropic foundations directed resources in the twentieth century which were larger than any private pool of wealth the world had previously experienced in charitable organization. The rationale for large, private donations for public purposes was perfected in the modern era by men such as Andrew Carnegie. The concentration of philanthropic interventions in public health and the expansion of the scale of this work on an international basis was advanced by John D. Rockefeller, Sr. and the Rockefeller family of philanthropies.

The Science of Philanthropy in the Twentieth Century

Charity in western, and especially British, culture was traditionally directed toward public issues. The tradition of charity imported from Britain in the American Social Science Association (A.S.S.A.), which was established in the year 1865, directly contributed to the professionalization of the social and behavioral sciences.[2] The Conference of Boards and

Charities separated from the A.S.S.A. in 1879 to become the National Conference of Charities and Correction, forerunner to the contemporary Conference of Social Work. These increasingly professional groups in the "helping services," and other voluntary reform societies helped establish children as priorities for public intervention between the years 1825 and 1900.

The Society for the Prevention of Pauperism helped establish the first House of Refuge for delinquent juveniles in New York in 1825. A progression can be seen from the 1820s to the Chicago Women's Club which contributed to the formalization of juvenile law in the first juvenile court in Chicago in 1899.[3] The establishment of large scale scientific philanthropy in the early twentieth century also took on public concerns, but on a magnitude which distinguishes it from earlier efforts in terms of the vastness of the resources brought to bear on a problem. Scientific philanthropists promoted formal professional training in the helping services as part of their unwavering belief in the systematic methods of science.

The benevolent society and charitable organization tradition became formalized and diversified in the course of the nineteenth century. The modern general purpose foundation with its unique scientific orientation, however, was a twentieth century phenomenon with specific historical roots in the United States.[4] Scientific philanthropy was enormously influential in shaping twentieth century U.S. institutions. It has been noted that "very few important cultural projects of any size are consummated . . . without having experienced either the direct or indirect impact of foundation philosophy or influence."[5]

F. Emerson Andrews, first director of the Foundation Library Center, defines foundations as non-governmental, nonprofit organizations, which are established to maintain and further social, educational, charitable or religious activities for the common welfare. They are supported by a principal fund and governed by trustees or directors.[6]

General philanthropic foundations evolved in the past one hundred years, although their major development has been in the shorter time period since 1917.[7] In the year 1910, the Encyclopedia Britannica did not deem them important enough for an entry. Fifty years later, forty-five thousand tax-exempt organizations were listed at the Foundation Library Center. Of these, eleven percent were endowed with one million dollars, less than two percent had access to one to ten million dollars, and less than one half of one percent had over ten million dollars at their disposal.[8] While the absolute numbers of philanthropies have increased, and the funds disbursed and held as assets by these agencies have soared with inflation, the number of large powerful foundations has remained small.[9]

The large twentieth century foundations were a product of the unique circumstances of nineteenth century economic growth and social changes.

The U.S. in the nineteenth century was witness to the establishment of a cadre of elites who acquired great wealth and power independent of their family of origin. The characterization of the self-made man fits steel magnate, Andrew Carnegie; oil baron, John D. Rockefeller, Sr.; and, automobile empire builder, Henry Ford.[10]

Andrew Carnegie's 1889 essay, "The Gospel of Wealth," stated the case of the philanthropist in terms which postulated that the wealthy, and therefore the competent, had a responsibility to the less competent to provide leadership for the benefit of the common good of society. To Andrew Carnegie, the problem of the twentieth century was the "proper administration of wealth," and this endeavor "bound the rich and the poor."[11]

The responsibility of the wealthy to advance society justified economic inequality on the basis of competence. The way to social progress, it was argued, should be led by an elite vanguard represented by men of proven ability. Carnegie argued for the development of a science of philanthropy in order to guide this elite in the distribution of funds in the public interest.

Carnegie incorporated the Carnegie Institution of Washington on the fourth of January, 1902. Shortly thereafter, he gave the newly formed Board of Trustees ten million dollars to:

> encourage, in its broadest and most liberal manner, investigation, research, and discovery and the application of knowledge to the improvement of mankind.[12]

Carnegie's act, in its scope and breadth, directly stimulated the development of other major philanthropies along these same lines. This included the philanthropies of John D. Rockefeller, Sr.

The Rockefeller Family of Philanthropies

Rockefeller philanthropy was the major patron of medical science and philosophy in the first half of the twentieth century. A general model for the organization of scientific philanthropy slowly emerged out of early charitable organizations to encompass basic principles and practices.[13] Just like the "university idea" had to be stabilized, the idea of "scientific philanthropy" had to be formalized. Whereas Carnegie provided the originating point, Rockefeller provided the business-like theorems which have come to characterize large scale twentieth century philanthropy. These theorems continue to influence corporate philanthropy and contemporary governmental spending in health, education, and welfare areas once dominated by philanthropy.

Rockefeller philanthropy came to exert pressure not only on the form of scientific charitable giving but on the focus of philanthropic work.

Medicine and mental hygiene were an early concentration. The principles for the operation of responsible philanthropy, which have given the Rockefeller Foundation its position of high regard in philanthropic circles, evolved not through one but several Rockefeller family philanthropies. John D. Rockefeller, Sr. and his advisors experimented with six different organizational forms between the years 1903 and 1928, the period which encompasses the establishment of the mental hygiene movement.

In the year 1901, John D. Rockefeller, Sr. established the Rockefeller Institute for Medical Research with a total gift of 60.6 million dollars figured on the market price of securities of the day. Two years later, in 1903, the General Education Board (GEB) was established for the promotion of education in the United States with a gift of 129 million dollars. The Rockefeller Foundation (RF) itself was established in 1913 with a gift of 182.8 million dollars. In the year 1918, the Laura Spelman Rockefeller Memorial (LSRM) was created with a gift of 73.9 million dollars to further the projects of John D. Rockefeller, Sr.'s first wife. In the year 1923, the General Education Board's work was carried to other countries with the creation of the International Education Board (IEB) with a gift of twenty million dollars from John D. Rockefeller, Jr.

When the IEB spent its funds in five years it was liquidated. That same year, the LSRM was consolidated with the Rockefeller Foundation, but certain special programs were continued under the Spelman Fund of New York with a gift of ten million dollars, until it too was consolidated with the Rockefeller Foundation. The expenditures of these Boards to 1950 were 451.5 million dollars for the Rockefeller Foundation, 296.7 million dollars for the General Education Board, 55.3 milion dollars for the Laura Spelman Rockefeller Memorial, and 18.3 million dollars for the International Education Board. Between the years 1917 and 1928 alone, ten million dollars were spent on schools of hygiene and public health, and 3.7 million dollars were spent on research fellowships in math, science, and medicine in the United States, Canada and Europe.[14]

Origins: "Value in the Sphere of Bestowal"

In placing wealth in the "service of mankind," both John D. Rockefeller, Sr. and his advisor Frederick T. Gates were concerned with the value of the "sphere of investment as well as the sphere of bestowal." Gates, in particular, was interested in applying the principles of science to philanthropic endeavors.[15] John D. Rockefeller, Sr. did not accumulate his fortune by acting hastily or without forethought. As he turned to seriously consider the organizational imperatives his philanthropic enterprises should follow, he was similarly of cautious and prudent disposition. Rockefeller's forte was building empires which were capable of adapting themselves to various social and economic pressures over time. Rockefeller looked to precedents and suggestive openings in areas which had a ready-made clientele that begged for the vision of large scale development. The area of public health loomed forward as one of critical need.

Gates, a Baptist minister and former head of the American Baptist Education Society, had become principal aide to John D. Rockefeller, Sr. in 1892. His role was to direct Rockefeller's increasing forays into philanthropy. In the year 1896, the senior Rockefeller retired from the management of Standard Oil to devote his time to his philanthropic activities. A year later his son, John D. Rockefeller, Jr., graduated from Brown University and essentially began a life career in philanthropy. The Rockefellers and their collaborator, Gates, agreed that charitable work was an enterprise as serious as business, and one which ought to be based on rational principles.[16].

Gates' personality was forthright and independent, even in his relationship with John D. Rockefeller, Jr. and Sr. It is said that he preferred to strengthen his argument when opposed rather than back down. Raymond B. Fosdick, a close associate and president of the Rockefeller Foundation during the years 1936–1948, describes Gates as:

> fearless, often fiery in his words, powerful in exhortation, with a mind that was too precipitous to be always tolerant, and with a voice that thundered from Sinai.[17]

Gates viewed the Foundation as more than a common responsibility. In his retirement speech before the Rockefeller Foundation Board, he reminded the trusteees:

> When you die and come to approach the judgement of Almighty God, what do you think He will demand of you? Do you for an instant presume to believe that He will enquire into your petty failures or your trivial virtues? No! He will ask just one question, 'What did you do as a Trustee of the Rockefeller Foundation?'[18]

Gates was an important link in directing the Rockefeller fortune toward scientific medicine. In 1897, Gates read Osler's *Principles and Practice of Medicine*. In this book, Osler argues strongly for the reform of medicine through the promotion of scientific research. He describes with eloquence the potential long range benefits of large scale public health intervention which would be made possible through science. Gates was profoundly moved:

> When I laid down this book, I had begun to realize how woefully neglected in all civilized countries and perhaps most of all in this country, had been the scientific study of medicine . . . It became clear that medicine could hardly hope to become a science until medicine could be endowed and qualified men could give themselves to uninterrupted study and investigation, on ample salary, entirely independent of practice. To his end, it seemed to me an Institute of medical research ought to be established in the United States. Here was an opportunity, to me the greatest, which the world could afford, for Mr. Rockefeller to become a pioneer.[19]

Filled with these thoughts Gates brought his case before Mr. Rockefeller.

> I remember insisting . . . that the mere fact that he, Mr. Rockefeller, had established such an institute of research . . . would result in other institutes of research in a similar kind, or at least other funds for research being established, until research in this country would be conducted on a great scale and that out of the multitudes of workers, we might be sure in the end of abundant rewards even though those rewards did not come directly from the institute which he might found.[20]

The Rockefeller Institute, 1901

The establishment of the Rockefeller Institute in the year 1901 was the end product of Gates' insight gained from Osler. Gates envisioned the Institute's medical work as "a kind of theological research." Addressing a group of scientists, Gates is quoted as having described the Institute as a "theological seminary." This comment was greeted with laughter. "Why do you laugh?" Gates countered:

> I am now talking of the religion, not of the past but of the future, and I tell you that as this medical research goes on you will . . . promulgate . . . new moral laws and new social laws, new definitions of what is right and wrong in our social relations.[21]

One history of the Institute notes that if the medical doctors and researchers at Johns Hopkins and the Rockefeller Institute were "therapeutic nihilists," Gates' "accommodation of religion to science [was] on the terms of science." The intensity of the idea of medical research as a mission and the ability to focus this mission in organizational outlets added a dimension and a destiny to the theme of the *childhood gaze* which was furthered by Rockefeller philanthropy in the years to come.[22]

The first Board of Directors of the Institute included Simon Flexner of Johns Hopkins, who became director, and William Welch also of Johns Hopkins.[23] The researchers and directors of the Institute were an amazingly homogeneous group in age, background, experience and interests. Only one individual had not studied in Germany, and many shared graduate study experiences at Johns Hopkins.[24]

Two things stand out about the Institute. First, the Institute was important in furthering and establishing the philanthropic use of the theme of the *childhood gaze* in scientific medicine and public health research. Secondly, it furthered the scientific orientation of Johns Hopkins University as a demonstration for other philanthropic projects designed to advance scientific knowledge for the public good.

The Institute also pioneered the international focus of Rockefeller philanthropy. The Institute's clientele was conceived to be international from the outset.[25] Canadians, for example, were included in the original conceptualizaton of the Institute.[26] Life and death, and the intervention of science, were understood within the German tradition as transgressing political boundaries for the "good of mankind."

The laboratories organized in 1910 worked on the prevention of epidemics, contagious diseases and on the advancement of a basic understanding of human biology critical to normal growth and development. Much of the routine work and signficant discoveries at the Institute contributed both to general health and to infant and child health in its work on hygiene, nutrition and disease control.[27]

The General Education Board and the Sanitary Commission

Other early Rockefeller philanthropic endeavors evolved models for the large scale application of elite knowledge for the general good. The General Education Board and the Sanitary Commission for the Eradication of Hookworm Disease in the Southern States were notable projects of this nature. The General Education Board officially began its work in 1903. It essentially became a steering committee for the earlier non-Rockefeller philanthropies in the South. Its success was in adapting and coordinating on a much grander scale than would have otherwise been possible, the work which had been initiated by others. The GEB also served as a precursor for what was to become important international projects on the part of Rockefeller related philanthropy in both education and public health.[28]

The first full scale model for public health work was established in 1909 in the Sanitary Commission for the Eradication of Hookworm Disease in the Southern States. Hookworm disease was indeed a widespread health hazard in the rural South which contributed to the physical and mental disabilities of those afflicted. The Sanitary Commission became the world's largest full scale campaign for the eradication of a single public health problem. None of the predecessors of the Sanitary Commission in public health campaigns undertook the eradication of a pervasive health problem within a defined geographical unit of such large scale, nor did any of the others have the financial support represented in the Commission.[29] The Sanitary Commission pioneered multi-level services which ranged from public education, to laboratory studies and clinical treatment.

The eradication of this disease served as an influential demonstration project for other international Rockefeller related work in public health. The director of the project, Wickliffe Rose, who was trained as a philosopher, shared with Frederick Gates what one author has noted as "an amateur's fervor in his belief that science held primacy over all other forms of human activity."[30] Rose's belief in the power of science to solve public problems reflected the enthusiasm of other Rockefeller affiliates of the day:

> Science is the method of knowledge. It is the key to such dominion as man may ever acquire over his physical environment. Appreciation of its spirit and technique, moreover, determines the mental attitude of a people, affects the entire system of education and carries with it the shaping of a civilization.[31]

This perspective outlived the Sanitary Commission. The International Health Board was created in 1913 to absorb the Commission and to elaborate its mission to solve other broadly defined public health problems on an international scale. The IHB's programs eventually operated in sixty-two countries on six continents.[32]

The Rockefeller Foundation: Innovator in the World of Philanthropy

All of these efforts provided models for the 1910 establishment of the major Rockefeller effort in philanthropy, the Rockefeller Foundation. The earlier Rockefeller supported public health enterprises also provided a testing ground for the funding of innovative public health efforts later adapted by the Rockefeller foundation officials in their efforts to make the mental hygiene movement live up to the ideals of science and the elevated goals of preventive medicine. It is with a touch of irony that mental hygiene was probably more likely to receive a sympathetic hearing from Foundation Trustees due to the early public health campaigns. Conversely, mental hygienists also acquired a yardstick for success, which measured performance at a level which psychiatry as "mental medicine" found difficult to match.

Resistance to the Charter of the Rockefeller Foundation

It was the possibility of shaping civilization which caught the imagination of Frederick Gates as he argued for the establishment of the Rockefeller Foundation. In light of Gates' frequent admonition that the accumulation of assets continued to outpace Rockefeller's charitable outlays, on the 29th of July 1909, John D. Rockefeller, Sr. set aside fifty million dollars worth of shares in the Standard Oil Company of New Jersey to be used for the endowment of a philanthropic organization to be known simply as the Rockefeller Foundation.[33] This sum is in contrast to the ten million dollars with which Carnegie had initiated the Carnegie Institute of Washington D.C. in 1902. In March 1910, a bill was put before the United States Senate requesting incorporation of the Rockefeller Foundation. Rockefeller could have initiated his organization with a simple deed of trust but he wanted to set an example for the establishment of a corporate structure in scientific philanthropy which was based on a business model.

It is paradoxical that, if the early attempts to charter the Rockefeller Foundation at the federal level had been successful, a precedent would have been set for a considerable degree of public intervention into the organizational functioning of modern philanthropy. This was not to be.

The attempt to incorporate the Foundation was met with determined opposition for fear that the Foundation would use the government for its own purposes. The William H. Taft administration and the Congress were not alone in feeling that Rockefeller's request for a charter amounted to an "indefinite scheme for perpetuating vast wealth."[34] This feeling was exacerbated by negative publicity and imposing court cases such as the one concerning Standard Oil. Judge Kenesaw Mountain Landis had fined the Standard Oil Company of Indiana 29.2 million dollars in 1908 for monopolistic practices and the corruption of public officials. Appeals were still pending.

Serious questions were raised concerning the public's right to oversee and have a measure of control over private charitable expenditures which were directed at the public interest. Congress added numerous amendments to the proposed bill which were accepted by Rockefeller. These included: the limitation of the total assets to one hundred million dollars; that there be no accumulation of foundation income; that Congress could dissolve the foundation in one hundred years; and, that the election of trustees be subject to veto within sixty days by the President of the United States, the President of the Senate, the Speaker of the House of Representatives of the presidents of Harvard, Yale, Columbia, Johns Hopkins, or Chicago universities.

After three years, Congress still could not confirm the charter and it was withdrawn by Rockefeller and placed in the state legislature of New

York, where it was passed without further arguments and without the limits of the amendments. Two of the amendments have nominally been used in the organization of Rockefeller philanthropy, namely, the nonaccumulation of assets and the dissolvability of any one foundation.

The search for organizational guidelines did not end with the charter. Gates argued that maximum benefits would be derived if Rockefeller funds provided prototypical programs for other charities to follow. This rationale became a policy protocol which served to structure Rockefeller philanthropy. A new vision of the role of charity evolved where philanthropy was conceived as responsible for creating, marketing, and testing ideas, institutional models, and social programs. Demonstration projects and model institutions were funded for a specific time period in order to serve experimental objectives. Secretary of the Rockefeller Foundation, Jerome Greene, later explained in a speech before the Commercial Club of Cincinnati:

> So far as the Rockefeller Foundation is concerned, it strenuously avoids the creation of a relationship of continuing dependence upon the favor of the Foundation for the perpetration of any of the charitable or educational currents to which it contributes, and its greatest satisfaction is derived from those lines where after a preliminary period of experiment or demonstration entire responsibility is assumed by governmental or other permanent agencies.[35]

Scientific philanthropy in this sense differed from traditional charity whose individual contributions served to bolster the short term needs of specific populations. Rather than set up funds for one purpose in perpetuity Rockefeller preferred a dynamic model which was not locked into any one time period.

In the same way that the funds were not indefinitely tied to specific projects, they were also freed from the personal control of the donor. In the year 1917, John D. Rockefeller, Sr. relinquished the right to make personal designations of the Foundation's funds. Up to that time he had made contributions of one hundred to one hundred thousand dollars to various charity organization societies and Baptist missionary organizations largely based in New York, city or state. Many of the donations went to child related causes including the Children's Aid Society of New York, Girls' Branch of the Public Schools Athletic League in New York City, New York Milk Committee, New York Child Labor Committee, Parks and Playgrounds Association of the City of New York, Public Education Association of the City of New York, Public Schools Athletic League of the City of New York, superintendent of New York schools, and the state and four local Y.M.C.A.'s. Additionally, Rockefeller supported the Eugenics Record Office at Cold Springs Harbor, Long Island, and the United Hospital Fund of New York.[36]

After 1917, the Board of Trustees was responsible for policy and the distribution of Foundation funds. However, the Rockefeller family remained active in the Foundation's work. In 1917, John D. Rockefeller, Jr. stepped down from the presidency of the Foundation, taking instead, the position of chairman of the Board of Trustees, which he held until 1939. He retired April 3, 1940, having spent a lifetime devoted to philanthropic work. Rockefeller philanthropy during this period was characteristically broadened from John D. Rockefeller Senior's local and specific charitable interests. The subsequent scientific approach to philanthropy differed from the earlier charity primarily on the basis of its universalistic orientation.

This new imperative as stated in the Foundation's first annual *Report* in 1913, was "to promote the well-being of mankind throughout the world." In the pursuit of "policies and lines of work which were likely to present the largest possibility of permanent and far-reaching usefulness, there was general agreement that the advancement of public health through medical research and education . . . afforded the surest prospect of such usefulness." The zeal with which this was spoken reflected the heritage of Johns Hopkins University Medical School, the Rockefeller Institute, Sanitary Commission and International Health Board/Commission, in the believe that the:

> diagnosis of disease can be made with certainty and that it can be cured and easily prevented . . . People, physicians, state boards of health, county and municipal officers [are] all eager to cooperate . . . [when] an intelligent public interest is awakened in hygiene and in modern scientific medicine and in practical measures for permanent public sanitation.[37]

Mental hygiene was considered a part of the public health problem to be solved through scientific investigation. It was specifically named as "one of the important subjects" to be undertaken.

A Philanthropic Mandate for Mental Hygiene: Eradicating the Evils of Society

The subsequent problems and tensions in the mental hygiene movements as it contributed to child health stem in part from its relationship to the organizational structure of philanthropy, and to scientific philanthropy's particular vision of the *childhood gaze.* The majority of the work of the Rockefeller Foundation in its early years focussed on issues in public health and medicine which were peripherally, of not directly, related to mental hygiene. The Foundation's mandate in the field of mental health was broad both in rhetoric and practice. It was conceived as the fundamental link between the "natural and social sciences."[38] Psychiatry and the medical model served as an underlying theme determining the general value of projects as contributing to human welfare as much as it contributed to the methodological approach to problem solving favored by the Foundation.

The method and theme of medicalization and mental hygiene are evident in the development of Foundation policy from an early date. At a meeting of the Trustees on October 27, 1915, Secretary Jerome Greene addressed the "close interrelation of many of the familiar evils of society" which were of central importance to the work of the philanthropy. Included among the evils of which Greene spoke were: "insanity, feeblemindedness, alcoholism, drug habits, prostitution, crime, venereal disease, infant mortality, child labor, illegitimacy, pauperism, divorce, bad milk and other food, bad housing, tuberculosis, and typhoid fever." The interrelationship between insanity and the other evils were considered to be strongly linked.[39]

A committee was formed to investigate and report on the "actual and desirable activity in these fields with a view to their proper correlation."[40] This correlation remained an underlying focus of Rockefeller related philanthropy which was to preserve the resources inherent in the minds of the nation's and the world's young. Greene wrote to Harvard President Charles W. Eliot underscoring the importance of the coordination of

> social health and welfare [activities. He emphasized] that contributions to health . . . are the surest means of doing an unqualified good to the human race, but it seems to me that there can be no better application of philanthropy than in efforts to promote the intellectual and spiritual life of the human animal made healthy by medical research and preventive medicine.[41]

In the year of its creation, the Rockefeller Foundation entered into a cooperative relationship with the National Committee for Mental Hygiene. The interest of the Foundation's advisors in mental hygiene predated the formal establishment of the organization. In a sense, the creation of scientific philanthropy, the rise of modern medical science, and the formalization of the mental hygiene movement were mutually supportive events which lent each other its character. As Raymond Fosdick points out, "The Foundation was a child of the era in which it was born, and it has been shaped by its environment."[42] Mental hygiene was a part of the original era, and a mutual contributor to the ongoing environment.

Rockefeller Foundation interest in mental health was expressed in independent projects and in support for the National Committees for Mental Hygiene. Inter-War mental hygiene projects were largely funded through the Rockefeller Foundation, General Education Board and the Laura Spelman Rockefeller Memorial. Rockefeller support was supplemented by other philanthropies such as the Harkness family Commonwealth Fund. The Commonwealth Fund was established in 1918 by the wife of Stephen Harkness, a partner of John D. Rockefeller, Sr. in Standard Oil. While the Fund was unequivocally independent, its activities often complemented or paralleled the work of the Rockefeller Foundation especially in the area of mental hygiene. Additionally, as was the case with other contemporary charitable organizations, the Commonwealth Fund's leadership was profoundly influenced by the example set by Rockefeller philanthropy.

Early mental hygiene studies and surveys were elaborated in the 1920s into research and training programs designed to establish psychiatry, psychiatric social work, and psychology in public policy and in institutions of higher learning. In the year 1933, under Alan Gregg, director of the Division of Medical Sciences, psychiatry "broadly interpreted" was formalized as the major thrust of the Foundation's work.[43]

Dilemmas of the Midas Touch

Although monopoly capitalism and its offspring in scientific philanthropy have periodically come under serious political and legislative attack in the United States, no other country has so favored the development of large scale philanthropies. Canada has no match for these organizations. The legality and ideology behind incorporated private tax-exempt institutions, organized for the purpose of providing for the "public good," survived the early vicious controversies such as the three year deadlock of the U.S. Congress over the charter of the Rockefeller Foundation. While the foundations have periodically come under review, their existence has never been seriously in danger.[44]

The identification of the private interests of entrepreneurs with the public good was a common and pervasive belief of the originators of scientific philanthropy. This strategy seems to have worked reciprocally between philanthropists, reformers, and the public, at least in influencing popular rhethorical descriptions of industrialists and their practices.

Social problems were often reinterpreted, and only partly seen even by more radical contingencies of reformers, in terms of the unequal distribution of material rewards and income. There was an ambivalence which extended into the populist camp as well. Both rhetorically and practically public thought and action was torn between suspicion and respect for the successful self-made man no matter how he earned his new status. Patriotic ideas in individual freedom, fair play, and democracy could be interpreted to either support or condemn the mandarins of industrial power.

This found popular expression in odd juxtapositions. For example, the 1880s witnessed the popularity of Edward Bellamy's utopian socialist novel *Looking Backward*. Bellamy's world was based on a vision of well being for all in a planned social order which maintained high standards in an atmosphere of rationalized inequalities.[45] The syndicalist movement, on the other hand, spawned labor organizations such as the International Workers of the World (the I.W.W.), which attempted to organize a better and more communal world based on the ideal of a brotherhood of equals.[46]

Neither utopian socialism, with its scientific and technocratic reordering of politics and economics "from above," nor the more populist and communal orientation toward political and economic organization "from below," was to dominate middle class reform. Reform efforts in education, public health, and welfare often waged a war of rhetoric but showed little practical concern with the *underlying* political and economic causes of the discrepancies between individual lives. The emphasis was on the reduction of disease and ignorance through efficient leadership, and a better understanding of individual pathology through scientific intervention. This ideological emphasis was articulated and encouraged by industrial leaders turned philanthropists.

An early student of the reputation of American financiers, Sigmond Diamond, followed up on the public's perception of the individuals who appeared to succeed where many other failed or only partly succeeded. Diamond studied John D. Rockefeller, Sr., Pierpont Morgan, Andrew Carnegie, George Peabody, Henry Ford, and John Astor. He found that public media in magazines and journals during the life time of these men of wealth advanced the reputation of the entrepreneur based less on:

> the business activities or of the methods by which is fortune was made than on consideration of the destination of his wealth.[47]

Industrial philanthropists, encouraged this view. They were outspoken in their justification of the accumulation of vast resources on the grounds that they returned more to society than they took. They argued, and apparently the arguments were publicly accepted, that men of wealth provided essential social leadership, and successfully, as well as efficiently, redistributed their gains in benefits to noble causes which in turn provided for the common good.[48]

Diamond identifies the verbal mechanisms philanthropists used for legitimating the logic of their activities as a "double language."[49] The first, internal to their mutal class and status interests, and the second language directed toward public consumption:

> this last truth to tell, was a brand of special pleading with public opinion to whom success of the financier is presented as the typical triumph of the self-made man, the condition necessary for the nation's prosperity.[50]

This double language of rationalization, Diamond notes, is on one hand a personal and human reaction. On the other hand, it is the:

> customary reaction of any dominant class which feels its prestige waning and its privileges threatened. In order to camouflage itself it is necessary for it to confuse its own fate with that of the city, of the nation, its own private interests with the public interest.[51]

The rationalization of philanthropy in the twentieth century helped transform the issues of social justice away from economic or political confrontations toward the *childhood gaze* couched in scientific and pseudoscientific explanations of personal and interpersonal failures.

Philanthropy was not alone in its double language. Mary O. Furner illustrates this point in her description of the progression of the American Social Science Association, as it evolved from a conglomerate charity organization toward the modern professional associations of the contemporary social sciences. The A.S.S.A., according to Furner, tended to look at:

> illness, crime, and social pathology as curable by measures that promoted physical and moral health; voluntary, collective efforts to reduce the economic insecurities of the industrial system were vastly preferred by reformers in almost every case to basic changes in the system.[52]

The tone, however, was optimistic in that the failures of society could be reversed (cured), or prevented by professionally guided systematic effort.

Interestingly, those individuals in academic circles in the new sciences of social organization, i.e., economics, political science, sociology, social work, public health and psychology, were required to conform to the rhetoric of the institutionalization of philanthropy. Those who were outspoken in their critique of the accumulation and distribution of the inequalities of capitalism were likely to find themselves censured or ostracized by colleagues, administrators, and the philanthropist/industrialist patrons who provided resources for the scientization of academia and the professionalization of higher education.[53]

The major early philanthropies of the twentieth century were formalized in the midst of a controversy over the validity of emphasizing elite (whether social or technical/professional) versus egalitarian (popular) mechanisms for public decision making in democratic states. The controversies and dynamics of the two approaches to distributing material benefits of social progress, as well as political power over deciding social policy, reflected similar discrepancies in the budding social sciences and the voluntary organizations which were their precursors. Many of the Progressive Era reform groups expressed internal contradictions in their attitudes toward public and private interests, individual rights and the nature of democratic institutions. The settlement movement, public health reform, school expansion, child saving, and child study are a witness to efforts to mediate between reforms "from above" or "from below." The mental hygiene movement was inescapably established in the tradition of these contradictions in middle and upper class twentieth century social reform efforts.

Adolf Meyer's early presence on the Committee was as critical to its character and organization as Beers. Meyer suggested the name "mental hygiene" which denoted the promotion of a science of mental health. Meyer established the preventive format for the movement as directed toward social psychiatry rather than institutional reform. One of Meyer's main interests was in the advancement of professional psychiatry through scientific research.[19]

Beers' and Meyer's interests were consistently in direct conflict. Meyer's reading of Beers' draft of the autobiography was highly critical. He opposed Beers' notion of a publicly oriented national organization. He saw Beers' version of public critiques of psychiatry as unprofessional propagandizing.[20]

After some thought, Meyer agreed to collaborate with Beers in editing the manuscript into a platform which they could mutually support. Meyer's revisions, however, altered the work both in form and content. Meyer favored a professional organization oriented toward scientific and clinical research controlled by physicians and psychiatrists, a view diametrically opposed to Beers' objectives. Meyer increasingly considered Beers' to be "hypercritical" and unbalanced.[21]

Beers was annoyed by Meyer's proposals but still felt that he could direct the changes for his own purposes. He wrote James: "I am securing the support of the medical profession . . . before long, I shall have the medical jury fixed."[22] Beers even conceded to Meyer's insistence on medical rather than lay leadership for the movement. Beers described his version of medical leadership as exhibiting the "desired medical color." Medical color, in Beers' words, would be "secured by selecting as officers of the association members of the medical profession itself *as to seem at least in the eyes of the members of that profession, to be a medical movement*."[23]

Beers still hoped to offset the power of psychiatrists by way of including a counterbalancing group of nonmedical members. A "well balanced medical-layman control of the National Association for Mental Hygiene will render what might be called megaphonic service for the medical profession by giving voice to authoritative opinion and advice which heretofore has not even succeeded in reaching all members of the medical profession itself, let alone the public at large."[24] Meyer's responded pointedly to Beers on his apparent need for and resentment of the professional approbation of medical circles: "If you don't want medical staff directing the organization, then I might also become an obstacle to your own aims and those of your society."[25] Beers paid little attention to Meyer's admonitions. The autobiography was designed, in Beer's mind, to wrest control out of the hands of the medical elite such as Meyer.

The autobiography, whatever else its literary or clinical value, is also a deliberately written piece of inspirational literature and propaganda. Written as a persuasive argument, the first editions contain introductory letters such as "medical color" from Adolf Meyer, William James and Stewart Paton.[26] The large appendix includes supplementary material designed to attract financial backing for the National Committee for Mental Hygiene. Beers wrote in the margin of one copy: "perhaps this . . . will strike you as being flippant, nevertheless, it brought forth what I needed."[27]

Beers' carefully edited final draft retained the classic quality noted in the early drafts read by James. It was published in 1908 amid the high praise and favorable publicity which Beers had so painstakingly constructed for the purpose of launching his movement.

After the publication of *A Mind That Found Itself*, the conflicting views of Meyer and Beers over the objectives and organization of the movement came to a head. Beers' interest was in expansion, publicity and the pursuit of funds. He wanted to immediately establish a national association. The immediate lack of funds for expansion tended to favor Meyer's efforts to avoid a national movement. Meyer also paternalistically felt that he was helping Beers. "I wanted him to learn something of what he wanted to get the money for . . . I felt the work should be on a foundation of knowledge and not merely of dreaming."[28] However, the attention and support Beers attracted with his book set up a momentum which was difficult to offset.

A compromise was reached where Beers was persuaded to begin with a state society in Connecticut rather than a national association as he had originally planned. Meyer argued that a state level society should provide a practical demonstration of the functioning of an organization to promote mental hygiene before expansion could be seriously considered. Meyer insisted that "not depending on a large association [was] . . . the only correct policy."[29]

Meyer worried that the still primitive state of psychiatry needed rather to attend to research and "essentials outside of legislative propaganda."[30] He noted that the high expectations and enthusiasm of nonprofessionals could do more harm than good. He stressed the point that "I feel very keenly that people who give money without knowing very clearly what it is for are rather dangerous helpers."[31] Meyer increasingly felt that Beers with his ideological stance and grandiose schemes was a decidedly dangerous helper.

Over the few months preceding the founding of the Connecticut Society, Beers was more successful in expanding mental hygiene than Meyer was in limiting its expansion. Two months after the acclaimed publication of *A Mind That Found Itself*, thirteen founding members of the Connecticut Society for Mental Hygiene gathered in New Haven at the home of Anson Phelps Stokes to launch the movement.[32] The second meeting listed over one hundred members.[33] Plans were made, over Meyer's objection, to establish a national association. In a last minute compromise, the title of the national organization was changed from an association to the less formal connotation of a committee.[34] Membership was to include both medical professionals and influential political, social and economic leaders in the style of a voluntary organization.

The first meeting of the National Committee was held on February 19th 1909. Among those present were Russell H. Chittenden, head of Yale University Sheffield Scientific School; President Jacob G. Schurman of Cornell University; Anson Phelps Stokes, secretary of Yale University; neurologist, August Hoch; Julia Lathrop, Illinois Board of State Commissioners of Public Charities; Chicago physician, Henry B. Favill; Charles P. Bancroft, head of New Hampshire State Hospital; William James; Adolf Meyer, William Welch and Lewellys Barker from Johns Hopkins University. Meyer became chairman of the executive committee with Bancroft, Chittenden, James, and Lathrop. Favill became president with Bancroft and Welch, vice presidents.[35] Beers was appointed temporary secretary.

Upon achieving the position of secretary, Beers proceeded with an ambitious publicity plan for the Committee. This action prompted Meyer to respond with barely contained anger.[36] James attempted to intervene and mediate the two positions but they were not reconcilable. James greatly respected Meyer's professionalism, yet he valued Beers' potential contribution to the cause of mental hygiene. He reluctantly concluded, "I can see both sides — it is a case of the ox and the wild ass, not working well in double harness."[37]

The continuing and most persistent problem which superseded the bickering over policy was the imperative need for funding. This too created policy problems. After James and others had made unsuccessful personal appeals to John D. Rockefeller, Sr., it was deemed that a formal request be drafted.[38] Not surprisingly, Meyer and Beers disagreed on the content and orientation of the document. Meyer condemned Beers' tendency toward an "unprofessional" use of statistics, "exaggerated length," and "emotionalism." "The appeal," Meyer commented, "leaves [me with] an impression as if I had gone through a troublesome dream — that is not the most favorable attitude on which to plan action of a somewhat optimistic character."[39]

A revised version containing letters from William James and Anson Phelps Stokes requesting thirteen million dollars, was finally delivered in June 1909. John D. Rockefeller, Sr. and his advisors were deeply involved during this period in finalizing the Rockefeller Foundation. The request, which seemed out of place at the time, was declined. Even though funds were not granted, the proposal was influential in that it contributed to the Rockefeller Foundation's eventual orientation toward mental hygiene. Mental hygiene was legitimated as a vital yet underdeveloped division of medicine greatly in need of research and support.[40]

The inability of the Committee to secure solid research funding increased Meyer's frustration. He decided to resign his official role and to independently contribute to the advance of extramural psychiatry.[41] Meyer's resignation took effect in 1911; he shortly thereafter joined Johns Hopkins University as director of the Henry Phipps Psychiatric Clinic, which opened a year later. Meyer remained a dominating influence in mental hygiene, helping indirectly to determine policy and provide a rationale for the movement while sidestepping the burdensome and time consuming arguments with Beers.[42]

Meyer substantially influenced the formal structure and orientation of the mental hygiene movement. His orientation toward a professional leadership on the committee was never seriously questioned, even though his resignation appeared to make Beers the victor in their disagreements. In addition, Meyer had, along with the active work of Welch and James, greatly facilitated the legitimation of the National Committee in the eyes of professional organizations such as the American Medico-Psychological Association, the forerunner to the American Psychiatric Association.

Thomas W. Salmon: The First True Mental Hygienist

Thomas W. Salmon was largely responsible for moving mental hygiene toward a working hypothesis, namely, that mental illness arises out of harmful experiences in childhood. Born in 1876, he died in a boating accident at the age of fifty-one, his work in professionalizing psychiatry as yet incomplete. Thomas Salmon, according to Meyer,

> really was the mental hygienist in psychiatry. I don't know if he had a very keen interest in the theory of psychiatry or in research-pathological anatomy and matters of that sort. He was in it for the mental hygiene that was contained in psychiatry.[43]

Salmon followed Meyer in efforts to professionalize psychiatry through the NCMH and to advance a scientific emphasis in mental hygiene. He became a leader in establishing psychiatry in medical education necessary for the professionalization of the specialty. Salmon's activities in other organizations in addition to the National Committee, included the American Psychopathic Association, the National Institute of Social Science, and the American Psychiatric Association.[44]

Salmon reshaped Beers' vague notion of an advocacy association, and Meyer's professional orientation, into a large scale public health effort coordinated by medical personnel. The new vision for the National Committee was as a partner with top level government officials, backed by the resources of large scale philanthropy and endorsed by its leadership. Salmon and Meyer agreed on many key issues. Both men sought to circumscribe Beers' orientation as potentially of negative impact or unworkable, and to channel the movement into what they considered to be a more fruitful and scientifically accurate direction. Salmon, however, unlike Meyer was also a practical organizer interested in applied research and the expansion of clinical practices in public mental health advocacy. It was this latter orientation which interested the Rockefeller Foundation officials.

The Salmon Years

By arguing for the development of a scientific approach to extramural psychiatry, Salmon secured Rockefeller support for mental hygiene. Both the National Committee for Mental Hygiene and the Rockefeller Foundation can be said to have been influenced by "the Salmon years." George Vincent, president of the Rockefeller Foundation (1917–1929), is reputed to have attributed the Foundation's commitment to mental hygiene and psychiatry to the influence of Thomas Salmon.[45]

Salmon rose from a minor public health service functionary to the position of a highly respected, politically effective advocate for the use of applied psychiatry to social problems. As first medical director of the NCMH, Salmon formulated and shaped the public health orientation of the policies and practices of the Committee. He set up protocols which were influential in mental hygiene circles over the next two decades. Salmon also influenced the activities of the Rockefeller Foundation as a paid consultant to the Board of Trustees from 1915 to 1922.[46] He was appointed chief of psychiatry in the U.S. Army during World War I. On his resignation from the NCMH in 1922, he became the first professor of psychiatry at Columbia University Medical School where he helped establish a state funded Psychiatric Institute. Salmon worked diligently to secure the support of government and philanthropy for medical training in psychiatry, which he foresaw as the single most critical long term issue in the success of the mental hygiene movement.[47]

Salmon's transfer from the Public Health Service, to the NCMH was precipitated by a gift from Henry Phipps to the National Committee. In 1911, Phipps sent fifty thousand dollars to William Welch, president of the National Committee. Half of this sum was to be spent for the purpose of creating a "Special Committee on Survey and Improvement of Conditions" among the insane. It was generally agreed that Salmon "seemed to be the man best fitted to serve as Special Investigator."[48]

Salmon drew up a master plan of action for the Committee which included a series of surveys. Salmon emphasized two prerogatives: the elimination of defective populations and the preservation of health in normal children. He insisted that the Committee provide leadership for preventive action concerning social problems related to increases in insanity due to syphilis, alcohol, immigration, heredity, and the marriage of the feeble-minded. On the other hand, he favored earlier recognition of psychiatric problems by way of establishing "dispensaries, [the] mental examination of school children, [and the] teaching [of] medical psychology to [public school] teachers."[49] Salmon borrowed from ideas pioneered by William Welch and William Osler, the psychobiology of Adolf Meyer, and the clinical emphasis on dynamic psychology favored by G. Stanley Hall and his students. Salmon's views were also encouraged by the popular rise of social Darwinism. Darwinism underscored the authority of scientific investigation which strongly supported a medical approach to social problem solving. Biology and evolutionary theory drew attention to family heredity as a factor in the etiology of abnormality.[50]

When Salmon joined the NCMH in the year 1912, he undertook mental hygiene surveys of institutions which housed large numbers of delinquent and dependent children. In an early survey of Baltimore, ten percent of the children were identified as abnormal. As a public health officer, Salmon's early solution to the problem of the insane and defective stressed prevention through deportation. This new line of inquiry in the NCMH took him into an arena where deportation was not an option. Salmon turned to earlier prevention.

Unlike Meyer, Salmon was not opposed to making mental hygiene a public issue. He favored the legislative propagandizing Meyer had opposed. Salmon initiated the preparation of a summary of legislation related to mental hygiene in order to determine the changes which needed to be made. He then set about educating the public on the changes in laws which he deemed important. In keeping with the forms of popular education of the day, a mental hygiene exhibit was presented at the International Congress on Hygiene and Demography held in Washington D.C. in November of 1912. This exhibit, which Salmon and Steward Paton prepared, became an important tool of mental hygiene propaganda for many years to come. It emphasized mental hygiene work with children in parent education, child rearing, and the prevention of delinquency. Additionally, the danger to the general public of the uncontrollable proliferation of defective gene pools by way of uncontrolled immigration or uncontrolled marriages of defective or diseased persons was compared to an epidemic.[51]

Salmon also sought to legitimize mental hygiene in professional circles. During this first year, Salmon instigated the formal recognition of the National Committee by the American Medico-Psychological Association in a resolution adopted in Atlantic City, May 30, 1912; and by the

American Medical Association, also in Atlantic City, June 6, 1912. The Committee sent delegates to the Fourth International Congress on School Hygiene held in Buffalo, New York. The Congress, chaired by Charles Eliot, attracted prominent figures from the United States and Canada.[52] Topics included child study, sex hygiene, the need for special facilities for defective and delinquent children, school inspection and psychiatric clinics.[53]

As Salmon became increasingly instrumental in determining the policies of the National Committee it was essential to consolidate the power structure of the committee.

At the Annual meeting of the National Committee for Mental Hygiene in 1913 the problem of the leadership was resolved. The position of medical director was created as chief officer. This placed Beers' position as executive secretary as subordinate to Salmon as medical director. The issue of scientific leadership was essential to Rockefeller support, a condition which Beers did not fully understand. He was infuriated at what he felt was the usurpation of his movement by medical professionals. In order to redress his grievance, Beers contacted Charles Eliot, vice president of the NCMH, one of the most influential NCMH figures in a non-medical field. Eliot had intimate knowledge of the Rockefeller Foundation having served as a member of the General Education Board since 1908.[54] Beers asked Eliot to intervene in preventing "a small group of men, more or less withdrawn from the public eye [from becoming] the principal agent for promoting improvements in the care of the insane." However, Beers had underestimated Eliot's support for the scientific side of the mental hygiene movement which Salmon had come to represent. Eliot reminded Beers that "the Rockefeller Foundation will always be glad to hear any proposals of the National Committee which may have the endorsement of Dr. Thomas Salmon for I know that the gentlemen who manage most of the Rockefeller trusts have a high regard for [his] judgement and efficiency."[55] This was Beers' last attempt to eliminate or undermine the scientific aspect of the professional orientation of the NCMH.

Salmon took on an increasingly vital role in negotiating with John D. Rockefeller, Sr. and his advisors. In December, August Hoch and Salmon approached Jerome Greene, secretary of the Rockefeller Foundation, with a proposal for financing the NCMH's mental hygiene surveys.[56] The Rockefeller Foundation agreed to fund the surveys as a means of supporting the NCMH in a way which would also contribute to its own mental hygiene program. The Board of Trustees, in a unique action on its part, appointed Thomas Salmon to a salaried position on the Board as "its advisor in matters relating to mental hygiene," and "lent" him to the National Committee.[57] The Board essentially adopted the NCMH through the dual services of Salmon. Salmon served this function for the next seven years.

Mental Hygiene and War Work

Largely due to Thomas Salmon, the first World War played a significant role in the mental hygiene movement even though the initial response appeared to deter the advance of the idea. No state societies were added during the War years. Canada entered the War in 1914 and the United States in the spring of 1917. The Rockefeller Foundation placed increased priority in War relief work in Europe during this period. This accounts in part for the Foundation's reluctance to engage in large scale funding of the NCMH. In 1917 most of the medical leadership of the National Committee, including Thomas Salmon, entered military service. The long term effect of the War was to legitimize and publicize the need for preventive mental health in the post War period.

In February of 1917, Stewart Paton, Pierce Bailey, and Salmon approached Surgeon General William C. Gorgas concerning the need for psychiatric screening and clinical work in the military service. Salmon was sent to survey the mental status of the Canadian army. He was to report back to Gorgas on the need for psychiatric screening among soldiers during wartime. The idea of clinical screening of recruits was not original; Lewis Terman, Edward Thorndike, Robert Yerkes and Henry Goddard, devised intelligence screening tests for the Army in Goddard's laboratory at Vineland Training School. The two versions became known as the Army Alpha and Beta tests. These tests pioneered massive testing programs which were to become common place research and diagnostic tools with children. Yerkes' supervision of testing in the Army did not include psychiatric screening or clinical services. In the United States Army, clinical psychology and psychiatry concerned with the mental status of soldiers occurred independently. The proposal presented to Gorgas for a psychiatric division in the U.S. Army in Europe was accepted. Salmon was subsequently asked to direct the program as chief of psychiatry for the U.S. Expeditionary Forces in France.[58]

In this official capacity, Salmon devised programs for psychiatric care in the army and initiated a professional training course for social workers as psychiatric aids at Smith College. These programs served as models for post War programs, in psychiatric social work.

After the War, Salmon reported his conclusions on psychiatry and war experiences to both Canadian and U.S. audiences. Salmon, through the official position as director of the National Committee, brought the organization into active war work as well. The National Committee contributed to the war effort by recruiting psychiatrists and neurologists, organizing records, printing medical examinations, and arranging after care facilities.[59]

Salmon, as head psychiatrist of the Expeditionary Force in France during World War I, drew up extensive plans for psychiatric services during wartime. He also developed civilian versions of these plans elaborating what he saw as the battlefield of "everyday life." The first line of this battle was to be in out-patient care for school children and in-patient children's units in general hospitals. Psychiatric Institutes would have out-patient services for disturbed children in child guidance clinics. State psychiatric hospitals and treatment centers would have out-patient and in-patient services for all age groups. Ideally the child guidance clinic would not be set up under the criminal justice system, or in affiliation with the courts or reformatories. Instead, they would be connected with university based research hospitals which would also provide advanced psychiatric training in child psychiatry.[60]

After returning to civilian life, Salmon began to badger the Rockefeller Foundation to proceed with what he was beginning to see as the most urgent area of psychiatry. Salmon wrote Edwin Embree of the Foundation, "We are used to saying that the children's courts constitute the first line of attack on the problem of juvenile delinquency but truancy from school is an even earlier phase of anti-social tendencies."[61]

Clifford Beers' vision culminated in the creation of the national movement, yet he lost his objective almost at the moment of his success. The movement had a dynamic of its own. Once mental hygiene had taken root it continued to expand, taking on many of the characteristics of propaganda most feared by Adolf Meyer, in spite of its medical leadership and rationale based in the propagation of a science of mental health. The convergence of the idea of the *childhood gaze* with research had achieved an institutional legitimacy at Johns Hopkins University. A further step was achieved with the acquisition of support from medical reformers and the financial advocacy of large scale philanthropy. Adolf Meyer carved a medical model out of Beers' personal vision and Thomas Salmon gave the movement substance and direction.

Chapter Five

The Canadian National Committee: The Politics of Privilege

The Canadian late nineteenth and early twentieth century experience, in spite of similarities with the United States, also differed significantly. These differences contributed to major divergences between the United States and the Canadian National Committees for Mental Hygiene, in spite of their mutual ideology and the shared leadership which characterized the early phases of the mental hygiene movement.

The Canadian Sense of Order and Nation-Building

The Canadian National Committee for Mental Hygiene was established nine years after the U.S. Committee, stalled in part by the first World War. Another reason for the different trajectory of Canadian mental hygienists was a reflection of the character of Canadian society at the turn of the century. The timing and character of Canadian nation-building in the nineteenth century differed from the rapid growth of the United States in spite of the fact that Canadian institutions such as schools, asylums and hospitals equalled their U.S. counterparts. Canada, whose French origins predated the settlement of New England, nonetheless, took on a slower pace in its expansion across the continent.

A transcontinental economy was barely achieved in Canada at the turn of the century and a nationally integrated urban system was not achieved until the early 1920s.[1] By the second decade of the century, most of the productive agricultural land was occupied and a strong manufacturing industry had emerged. Foreign capital remained important to the economy. Prior to the first World War, Great Britain was the major source of foreign capital. After World War I, the United States increasingly assumed this role, and by 1926, the United States was the dominant foreign investor in Canada.[2]

The bulk of Canadian development occurred at a later date than in the United States for numerous reasons. No national industrial economy existed at the time of the Confederation of modern Canada in 1867. The British North American colonies tended not to rely on each other but instead shared a common external orientation to Great Britain or the United States. The rate of population growth actually declined in the 1880s and 1890s, which was attributable to out-migration exceeding natural growth.[3] In 1891, the Canadian total population stood at five million in comparison with sixty-three million United States citizens. A vigorous prairie settlement policy established in 1896 brought three million immigrants to Canada between 1896 and 1914 with four hundred thousand arriving in 1913 alone. The wheat boom on the prairies stimulated the inter-regional movement of goods and people, helping to forge a transcontinental economy on a national scale.[4] The population had increased to seven million in the 1911 Census and to nearly nine million in 1921. These figures are still appreciably less than the United States census figures for the same period which had risen to over the one hundred million mark.[5]

Not only did Canadian nation-building occur after the United States, the nation-building process in Canada also differed significantly in political and economic character, especially in its elaboration of the relationship between the individual and the state. Part of the ideology of the nation-building process in the United States was based on a Republican version of the "agrarian myth." Republican and democratic beliefs were intertwined with the image of the yeoman farmer as the embodiment of political and social values. The right of the individual to ownership and exploitation of land and resources was a central aspect of the American version of this ideology. With land ownership went the privileges of citizenship, political independence, economic status, social and self-respect. The advance of the individual in a Darwinian struggle for survival assured the advance of the nation. The land policy which incorporated these beliefs encouraged the dispersion of the public domain to private hands in one hundred sixty acre plots for either cash or equivalent labor. The principles of the reservation of land from private ownership, the practice of crown ownership and lease-hold tenure, which characterizes Canadian land policies and distribution of natural resources, are in stark contrast to nineteenth century U.S. counterparts.[6]

The Canadian conception of the state and the retention of state ownership expressed in "crown lands" was a product of Canada's colonial heritage and unique social and economic history. In the early nineteenth century two-sevenths of all public land was tied up in Crown and Clergy Reserves. Of the 4.5 million acres which were transferred to individuals or groups, the distribution was characterized by extreme favoritism. Loyalists received two hundred acres, ex-officers could claim up to five thousand acres, Legislative Councillors got six thousand acres apiece, and entire townships were granted to "entrepreneurs" for speculative purposes.[7]

The oligarchy of upper Canada acquired the name of "The Family Compact." Versions of the "Family Compacts" or "Chateau Cliques" of Halifax, Fredricton, Quebec and Toronto, did not go without criticism and opposition.[8] Nevertheless, as John Porter has pointed out, modern Canadian society retained families of ascribed wealth and prominence over the generations. These families have taken on the traditional philanthropic role of overseeing the common good which is the accepted "duty" of those of high status. It is not surprising that the families of traditional rank, largely of British Protestant origin, have contributed more than their disproportionate share to an emergent corporate elite in the twentieth century. These precedents have extended into the post World War II era, indicated by the fact that at mid-century, the upper one percent of the income recipients in Canada received forty percent of their income from stocks.[9]

While there is little reason to believe that the United States and Canada have different levels of material inequalities, it has been postulated that "Canada is more elitist, ascriptively oriented and particularistic than the United States."[10] The possessive individualism of an agrarian frontier made inroads upon monarchical traditions in Canada but did not eliminate them. As A. R. M. Lower comments, "The perpetration of monarchical forms, even though the life has long since gone out of them, doubtless serves to act as a curb upon the fullest expression of democracy."[11] The monarchical tradition encompasses an ideological perspective as well as a set of institutions. It presents an organic view of society where the crown and leading classes, in conjunction with government institutions, are responsible for molding the character of individual members of society. The role of established leadership is to measure "wealth against commonwealth" in the preservation of a just society and to assure orderly social change.

American conservative intellectuals at the turn of the century relied on individualistic values justified by Darwinian and Spencerian models as the basis for progressive reformism. Canadian counterparts owing more to Burke than to Darwin looked to the state for moral direction as a legitimate basis for collective reformism. Canadian organic conservatism has shaped Canadian individualism, materialism, and democratic values. Similarly, Canadian liberal traditions emphasize the role of the state in exercising authority in the collective interest. The tendency has been to champion unencumbered provincial rights and jurisdiction over individual property and civil rights. This has been a significant constitutional and ideological difference between the United States and Canada.[12]

There is ample literature to explain the differences in Canadian and U.S. by the comparative strength of conservative values in each of the societies.[13] However, as H. V. Nelles points out in his study of Ontario, conservative values are also retained because to some extent they are functional. We need to offer explanations for the maintenance of traditions on this basis. Nelles submits that the origin of provincial land policy in Ontario may result from an underlying aspect of a monarchial tradition and unique environmental factors which support not only the elitist aspects of privilege but also a collectivist outlook. He postulates that the:

> maintenance of the old, imperial habit of authority into the industrial age stemmed primarily from the interaction of interest groups and moderately conservative ideology, within an agriculturally barren environment. The lumbermen, the [Canadian] Shield, and the threat of direct taxation sanctioned a set of resource laws that preserved the germ of an earlier collectivist, conservative conception of the state. The interaction of these ideological and material forces blunted the individualistic, appropriative, liberal qualities—in short the "American-ness" of the northern Ontario frontier.[14]

Further, the interaction between diverse political values stemming from Canada's dual French-English heritage, and its diverse geographic environment did not allow a single conception of land use during the period of its agrarian transformation. "Like democracy itself, Canadian agrarianism was more a condition and less of a theory than in the United States."[15]

Children, Poverty, and Canadian Public Health

It is instructive for the timing of mental hygiene, after World War I, that Canadian nation-building took place precisely during the period when the medical model and the primacy of the scientific method in the *childhood gaze* was established. If the transcontinental development of Canada differed in its timing, value orientations and policies from the United States, it differed less in the physical conditions which faced the urban dwellers of the late nineteenth century.

Urbanization followed a pattern similar to that of the U.S. which rose from 13.1 percent in 1851 to 34.9 percent in 1901.[16] However, discrepancies between provinces varied widely with Ontario (40.3 percent), Quebec (36.1 percent), and British Columbia (56.4 percent) leading. Saskatchewan, by comparison, was as yet undeveloped with 6.1 percent urban. The British Columbia statistics are also misleading in that they reflect the rapid growth of the city of Vancouver after the arrival of the transcontinental railway in 1885. Vast territories in the province remained uninhabited or isolated until the 1930s. Canadian urbanization increased to 47.4 percent in 1921 and to over fifty percent in 1931.[17]

The language describing urban conditions paralleled that used in the United States. C. Dade in, *Notes on the Cholera Seasons of 1832–1894*, described the city of York as filled with "crowded and loathsome hovels, cellars putrid and stagnant water, dunghills with animal and vegetable garbage reeking in the scorching rays of the summer's sum."[18] These conditions brought active reform movements in Canada as they did in the United States. The fight against health hazards, civic corruption and vested interests can be seen in the social programs of English and French-Canadian nationalists, in the struggles of organized labour, as well as in the concerted efforts of social organizations to improve the lives and welfare of children.[19]

Of the social conditions which reformers sought to cure, public health, and especially child health, became a major issue in both the United States and Canada. In Massachusetts of one thousand live births in 1855–1859, 123 badies died. This figure rose to 170 per thousand live births in 1870–1874. It was not until the turn of the century that this trend was seriously reversed, dropping to 116.7 in 1910 and 78.7 in 1920.[20] In Winnipeg there were 207 deaths per thousand live births in 1912, 106 deaths in 1915, and 78 per thousand births in 1921.[21] Life expectancy in the year 1900 was 48.2 years. By the year 1970, this figure was 71.7 years with the increase mainly between birth and fifteen years of age.[22] Foreign-born mothers and those in rural communities were likely to give birth without medical attention. Their infants were unlikely to ever see a doctor.[23] The major killers of children were diarrhoea and dysentery and communicable diseases like diphtheria, scarlet fever, small pox, typhoid fever, malaria, whooping cough, and measles.[24] Children in institutions had the least expectation of survival.[25] John Spargo, in *The Bitter City of the Children*, brought to popular attention the high rates not only of rickets and malnutrition, but of tuberculosis as well. Hunger, disease, and poverty were recognized as social problems of widespread notoriety.[26]

Canadian Mental Hygiene Advocates

A movement for the reform of medicine and asylum psychiatry in the nineteenth century had been present in Canada as well as in the United States. From the early years of the twentieth century, reformists were concerned with public policies on mental deficiency, immigration, public health and schooling. However, the movement did not come together as mental hygiene prior to World War I as it had in the United States under Clifford Beers' tutelage.

In 1914, four years before the actual founding of the CNCMH, the Canadian Medical Association appointed a committee on mental hygiene with public health activist and physician Helen MacMurchy as chairperson. MacMurchy asked for a year so that the committee "might present a comprehensive resumé of the progress made in mental hygiene in this and in other countries and we hope also to be prepared to make suggestions for further progress in the conservation of mental health in Canada."[27] The report of the Committee on Mental Hygiene to the Canadian Medical Association was not presented, since the 1915 meetings were canceled due to the war in Europe and Canada's early participation.

The Lady Doctor and Public Health

Helen MacMurchy laid much of the public health ground work for the Canadian mental hygiene movement. Her interests, however, were not in psychiatry or professional standards but in public health and children's policy. She was a major force in developing mental hygiene concerns in health policy in Canada especially as these issues touched Canadian children.

MacMurchy brought together the Canadian eugenics and mental hygiene movements. She purposefully aroused official and public concern over the presence of feebleminded and delinquent populations as a long term public health hazard. The formation of the Canadian National Committee for Mental Hygiene came together around the issue of mental retardation rather than mental illness. Eugenic overtones were significant aspects of the early mental hygiene movement in both the U.S. and Canada.

The first committee of the American Medico-Psychological Association (forerunner to the American Psychiatric Association) on applied eugenics included leaders in the U.S. National Committee on Mental Hygiene on its executive committee. This included Lewellys F. Barker, Walter E. Fernald, Irving Fisher, and Elmer E. Southard.[28] Applied eugenics in the United States was exemplified by the Eugenics Research Association with its conferences at Cold Spring Harbor. Rockefeller funds were important in the establishment of Cold Spring Harbor and the expansion of eugenic ideas on social hygiene which crossed into mental hygiene.[29]

Canadian eugenics was similarly concerned with illegitimacy, venereal disease, criminality and prostitution. A public protest had been initiated in the year 1896 at a National Council of Women in Canada by A. M. Roseburg of Hamilton. By 1899, local councils were petitioning their respective legislatures urging the provision of custodial facilities for "feebleminded women." MacMurchy was involved in an official investigation to determine the actual number of mentally defective women in Ontario. In

1906, she was appointed the Inspector of the Feebleminded in the Department of the Provincial Secretary.[30] In 1908, a society was organized in Nova Scotia which concentrated on children.[31] The membership of the Toronto Society became the nucleus around which the Canadian national committee was organized.[32] By 1913, fifty societies existed for the "protection" of the feebleminded.[33]

MacMurchy's professional experiences contributed to her private and official views on public health policies in eugenics and mental hygiene. MacMurchy advocated the identification and segregation of defective populations. She also favored widespread public educational campaigns and strong civic action to contain and identify defective individuals. She gained positions of personal authority and respect which furthered her ability to bring about public action. As a witness to her independence and personal perseverance: she succeeded, after graduating in medicine from the University of Toronto, in becoming the first woman intern at the Toronto General Hospital. She also studied in the United States where she was influenced by the Johns Hopkins tradition and especially William Osler's brand of public health advocacy. From 1913 to 1920, she was assistant inspector and then inspector of hospitals, prisons, and public charities for the Department of the Provincial Secretary of Ontario. She was appointed chief of the Division of Child Welfare when it was established under the Dominion Department of Pensions and National Health in 1920.[34]

As Inspector of the Feeble-Minded in Ontario, MacMurchy studied and wrote reports on the widespread danger of racial decline if action was not taken to curb mental deficiency.[35] In 1910, she was placed in charge of medical care of the Andrew Mercer Ontario Reformatory for Women where, two years later, she conducted a special survey into the care of children at the Industrial Schools located in Toronto and in Mimico. This work brought her into the position of serving as an expert witness in the juvenile courts.

Through this experience she became adamantly concerned with the connection between mental problems, immorality, and juvenile crime. She sought allies in her campaign to identify and segregate mentally defective delinquent children brought before the court. MacMurchy's tenure on the medical faculty at the university and Toronto General Hospital from the years 1905 to 1920, coincided with the tenure of influential alienist-psychiatrist C. K. Clarke, the first professor of psychiatry at the University of Toronto and dean of the medical school, as well as chief of psychiatric services at Toronto General Hospital. MacMurchy asked Clarke to help set up a juvenile psychopathic clinic in the Hospital which would serve as a testing service for the juvenile court.

Clarke, who became the first medical director of the Canadian National Committee for Mental Hygiene, was also a critical figure in the eugenical phase of the Canadian movement. His beliefs closely coincided with MacMurchy's. However, due to his personal experiences as an asylum psychiatrist, Clarke strongly opposed mixing normal and defective populations even for the purposes of testing. In order to maintain the separation of the medical hospital and incipient psychiatric testing service, Clarke asked the voluntary social service department of the hospital to sponsor the juvenile psychopathic clinic. The head of the service, Mrs. D. A. Dunlap, agreed. The clinic was subsequently opened under the auspices of the social rather than medical services of the hospital on April 8, 1914.

A young physician, Clarence Hincks, who also became a central figure in establishing the Canadian mental hygiene movement, was hired to direct the clinic with a colleague, O. C. J. Withnow. By 1919, this clinic had handled over five thousand children as cases referred through the juvenile court.[36] The juvenile psychopathic clinic brought together four of the major figures in the formation of the Canadian National Committee, MacMurchy as advocate, Clarke as first medical director, Hincks as assistant and eventual director of both the Canadian and U.S. National Committees, and Dunlap as a mentor.

Clarence M. Hincks: Prospector for Mental Hygiene

Hincks' apprenticeship in psychiatry in Clarke's psychopathic clinic at Toronto General, his work with the children referred from the juvenile court, and his affiliated work as medical inspector of schools occurred at a formative period of his own thinking. The experiences forged a direct link to Hincks' enthusiastic role in the establishment of the Canadian National Committee for Mental Hygiene. In Hincks' words:

> After working with Dr. Clarke in the out-patient clinic for two or three years I became restless and impatient. I felt that the knowledge about mental illness and mental deficiency which we had acquired ought to be put to use somehow across Canada. I knew that many of our asylums were inadequate and our immigration screening was poor. I was aware that we were not doing what should be done to help rehabilitate the psychiatric casualties among our soldiers. No one was doing anything about prevention.[37]

In late 1917, Hincks approached Clarke with the possibility of developing some plan to expand psychiatric care in Canada. Clarke suggested a visit to New York to discuss the issue with U.S. authorities in "medical, psychiatric and neurological science." Hincks left immediately on this quest for suggestions and ideas. In the process of his inquiries he was introduced to Clifford Beers.[38] Beers offered Hincks a copy of his book and explained his vision of an international association for mental hygiene.[39]

Hincks was fascinated by the idea of a Canadian National Committee. Upon his return to Toronto, Hincks wrote Beers of his decision to start an organization. "It is my aim to widen the scope of the Ontario Association [for the Care of the Feebleminded]." The issue of feeblemindedness was to be subsumed within the more comprehensive concerns addressed by the National Committee. Hincks felt that his transition would "be easy" in that "Dr. C. K. Clarke will [probably] be elected to the presidency [of the Association for the Protection of the Feebleminded]."[40]

Hincks began to plan the first meeting. It was not long before he wrote Beers, "I have interviewed practically all the Toronto people I would like to see connected with committee, [such as] Sir Robert Falconer, Lady Eaton . . . the nucleus of a strong Canadian National Committee."[41]

One consequence of the War was the freedom it afforded Clifford Beers to reaffirm his position of influence in the Committee's work. Beers was disgruntled by the fact that the building of an international organization, as well as the growth of local and state societies, had ceased during the War. Unencumbered by opponents to the expansion of the Committee, Beers was more than happy to help Hincks establish an affiliated Canadian National Committee. This was the first step toward his dream of an international organization.

Beers was summoned to Toronto to meet the first select group of potential members and donors. The organizing meetings of the Canadian National Committee for Mental Hygiene took place in the Spring of 1918. The official organization of the mental hygiene movement was extended beyond the national boundary of the United States. While mental hygiene societies extended around the world by 1930, the majority of the actual work continued to be conducted in the United States and Canada.[42]

The first meeting of the Canadian National Committee for Mental Hygiene was held at the home of Mrs. D. A. Dunlap, head of the social service unit which hosted the psychopathic clinic.[43] Thirty national leaders in social, political, and business, as well as medical circles were invited to meet Beers. After introductory comments by Clarke and MacMurchy, Beers made an impassioned speech for the establishment of a Canadian mental hygiene committee.

The audience proved particularly receptive and the Canadian mental hygiene movement was launched with acclaim. Twenty thousand dollars in pledges financed the incipient organization.[44] Charles F. Martin, a physician from Montreal, was made president. It was hoped that by splitting the leadership between the Montreal and the Toronto group, the national character of the organization would be strengthened. An impressive group of vice presidents were commandeered, including: Lord Shaughnessey, Sir Lormer Gouin, Sir Vincent Meredith and Sir Robert Falconer. C. K.

Clarke became the top executive officer as medical director and Clarence Hincks was made his assistant and secretary. The executive board consisted of Colin K. Russel, Peter H. Bryce, J. A. Dale, C. J. O. Hastings, W. H. Hattie, Vincent Massey, J. D. Page, C. A. Porteous, and Peter Sandiford.

The roster of members reveal a broad section of the Canadian established elite. The deans of medical facilities, university presidents, premiers, top governmental chiefs of staff, and major business executives figured prominently in the CNCMH membership. While the Committee was national in scope, two-thirds of the members were from Canada's most heavily populated provinces of Ontario and Quebec. Unlike the American Committee which was dominated by medical leadership, the membership of the Canadian Committee was from a cross section of influential citizens. Thirty-five percent of the members were related to the medical profession, twenty-two percent were in official governmental positions and seventeen percent were business leaders. Social and philanthropical leadership comprised twelve percent of the Committee's membership.

The actual organizing work was largely done by Beers and Hincks. Both were enthusiastic about the effectiveness of what they called "drawing room meetings" or "teas" similar to the one at the Dunlap's. Hincks encouraged the expansion of the concept into other parts of the country. Beers agreed to go anywhere there was an audience.[45]

Hincks took full advantage of his social contacts. Lady Eaton, as an old friend of Hincks, was a case in point. She recalled that "[Hincks] called me and asked me to help him with one of these meetings" and that "ten-thousand dollars was pledged" that afternoon for the cause of mental hygiene.[46] The Committee continued to expand but in a controlled manner. The Committee decided from an early stage not to encourage local groups but to emphasize a strong and unified national organization which would work through other voluntary and governmental agencies.[47]

Within three months of the first drawing room meeting, an organizing meeting of the executive committee was held at Chateau Laurier in Ottawa. A constitution very similar to that of the National Committee in the United States was adopted. An official thank you note was sent to Beers to acknowledge his help in setting the CNCMH in motion.[48]

Clifford Beers found a world view compatible with his own in the organization of the Canadian Committee.[49] Significantly, he did not resent the professional leadership of the Canadian mental hygiene movement, especially as it was balanced with an elite non-medical group of promoters. Clarence Hincks' methods of organization and fund raising were similar to the methods Beers' favored. Clarks' and Hincks' institutional reform orientation clashed less with Beers' advocacy for the insane than Salmon's scientific public health reform.[50] The Canadian National Committee, its influential membership cajoled by Hincks' and Beers' inspirational speeches, forged ahead.

Beers tried to retain his authority over the progress of the Canadian movement in the years after the War. This included attempts to shape both the funding and the direction of research. The Rockefeller Foundation with its ample resources loomed as a major source of support, yet these potential funds also undermined Beers' influence as a successful fund raiser. When Hincks approached Beers with the idea of sending in a proposal to the Foundation on the study of delinquency, Beers tried to suppress Hincks' enthusiasm.[51] The proposal may in fact have been granted. It was very close to the work which the Rockefeller Foundation and the Commonwealth Fund were in the process of reviewing on the advice of Thomas Salmon. Beers successfully discouraged Hincks with the argument that studies on delinquency were unfit for Canada as local not national in scope.[52] In spite of Beers' success in this case, he was not able to retain his position of influence in Canada any more than he could in the United States. Mental hygiene, it seemed, had a momentum of its own.

Eugenics, The Survey and Clinic in Canada

The period between 1918 and Clarke's death in 1924 was the first phase of organized Canadian mental hygiene.[53] Surveys conducted by C. K. Clarke and Clarence Hincks were an important part of the early work. The provincial surveys gathered statistics in juvenile courts, jails, schools, homes for dependent children, industrial schools, and hospitals for the insane and retarded. The search for "mental abnormals" included "insane, feebleminded and epileptic" classifications in populations ranging from dependent children and delinquents to prostitutes, immigrants and criminals. The surveys were also used as "educational" devices to influence provincial politics and institutions as well as urban legislation, where possible, concerning any organization which served children.[54] The survey work most clearly approaches a search for a definition and formalization of categories of abnormality.[55] The work in Ontario and Quebec was especially interesting since the National Committee was the most active in these provinces.

The first official action of Charles Martin, the Montreal based president of the Mental Hygiene Committee, was to formalize a clinical psychiatric service. Twelve days after the opening of the Quebec office of the CNCMH a part-time outpatient clinic was set up at the Royal Victoria Hospital. The clinic was held every Wednesday afternoon and served both adults and children. It was supervised by three psychiatrically oriented physicians, Colin Russel, Gordon Mundie and A. G. Morphy. They were assisted by one full-time and two part-time social workers. In the first seven months 188 patients were examined.[56]

Psychiatric services had been nominally provided by Colin Russel prior to the Royal Victoria Hospital Clinic. The clinic opened with four physicians who had received training by William Tait, a professor of psychology at McGill University. The early referrals were dominated by mentally deficient patients. This reflected the eugenic emphasis of the early work by the Montreal Local Council of Women. Gradually, however, a larger variety of patients was seen as referred by the Family Welfare Association, the Women's Directory, the Children's Bureau, the Catholic Social Service Guild and the Federation of Jewish Philanthropies.[57] Among the 701 patients tabulated by 1922, there were 10 infants and 278 adolescents. Male adolescents slightly outnumbered the females. This was said to be due to the fact that the juvenile court predominantly referred males. However, of the adult group three-fourths of the patients were female. Court and social agencies referred approximately the same number of patients. In comparison with the 156 court referrals there were 65 medical referrals from doctors and only 15 patients referred from family sources.[58] A little over one-third of the patients were determined to be feebleminded, one-quarter delinquent and one-fifth insane. A very small group of three percent were determined to be "psychoneurotic."[59]

The problem of juvenile delinquency was considered an important issue in Montreal but it was only the non-Catholic Juvenile Court Committee which granted permission to have children examined by a psychiatrist at the clinic. Addresses before the Kiwanis Club and Rotary Club were made and a petition sent to Premier Taschereau to try to persuade him to use his influence to allow all children in the court to be screened. Cooperation was solicited from the Health Department under Dr. Boucher but the majority of the mental hygiene work continued to be directed toward the English-speaking population. While the Quebec government allowed A. H. Deslodge of the Montreal Branch of the CNCMH to examine the children in the Boys' Farm and Training School at Shawbridge and to look into improving the classification of inmates of insane asylums, it avoided comprehensive public policies in mental hygiene in agencies which resisted interference.[60]

In October of 1919, permission was granted for a survey of all of the pupils in Protestant Public Schools in Montreal. The original suggestion for the survey was in the year 1913.[61] Eight schools were surveyed and 355 children recommended by teachers were given the Stanford Binet individual intelligence test and 440 were given the Otis Group Intelligence Tests. All students were also "examined for neurotic conditions, psychosis and physical defects."[62] The primary purpose of the testing was to encourage the provision of special classes. The published version refers to Adolf Meyer's description of training "emotional needs." American psychiatrist, William White, is also cited as an authority who encourages training geared toward individual difference with the goal of the child's "greatest efficiency and happiness." While mental testing was instrumental to the survey, the results of such tests were minimized as only one of many tools for assessing children.[63]

A similar study was done in non-Catholic schools in Toronto at about the same time by E. J. Pratt.[64] The differences between the two studies is interesting. The Toronto study was an exhaustive study on one school rather than a broader survey. While the Toronto study was considered to use a "psychiatric" approach in understanding "moody isolation," "explosive and irresponsible conduct," and "apathy or responsiveness," the emphasis was not on happiness or internal mental processes. Instead, the focus was on identifying how children could be "efficiently" directed toward "industrial life." The intelligence scores were correlated with social factors such as gender, father's occupation and the overall health of the child.[65] It was this type of non-psychiatric social and occupational adjustment which was to dominate Canadian mental hygiene in the years to come.

In Toronto, the connection between the staff members of the National Committee for Mental Hygiene and Toronto General Hospital which had been critical to the organization of the movement, continued to dominate activities in the early phases of the committee's existence. C. K. Clarke and Hincks conducted a comprehensive review of the work of the psychiatric clinic from April 1914 to April 1922. The survey included fifty-six hundred cases which had been classified by the clinic out of over six thousand referrals.[66] The clinic served both child and adult populations but the number of minors under twenty years of age constituted sixty-two percent of the case load. This included 212 infants between the ages of one and five years, and 816 school age children between six and ten years. Preadolescents and adolescents constituted the largest age group with 1788 cases of individuals between eleven and fifteen years of age.[67] There were slightly more males than females. Clarke listed 280 cases of "juvenile psychosis." He typed 168 juveniles as having dementia praecox, 25 of which were cited as having a combination of dementia praecox and mental deficiency. Another 44 children were classified as psychopathic, 28 as epileptic, 13 with general paresis and 2 as manic depressives. Of the 130 children referred from the immigration service and subsequently identified as retarded, all but 3 came from the Barnardo Home, which assisted child migration.[68]

Sources of referral to the Toronto clinic included the public health department, public schools and social agencies as well as the juvenile court. Clarke noted that "before the establishment of a psychiatric department in connection with the juvenile court the great majority," of these defective children would have simply been labeled "delinquents."[69] Clarke and

Hincks were aware that their insistence on the genetic abnormality of delinquents conflicted with other studies in the United States, notably William Healy and August Bronner's work in the Chicago Juvenile Court. Clarke's argument was that child immigration in Canada had encouraged the entrance of defective children, which added to other problems such as delinquency and prostitution. Clarke was a need for early identification and he recommended permanent institutionalization to prevent immoral behavior and the spread of defective genes. One nineteen year old girl listed with a mental age of twelve was used as an example. She left school to work when she was fifteen years old. She began to frequent "dance halls" and was once caught stealing. Due to the fact that there was nothing unusual in her appearance, Clarke found her prognosis poor, especially in that her "good looks make it difficult to save her from herself and society from her evil influence."[70]

Clarke used three general categorical types under the term mental abnormality: mental deficiency, mental diseases and deviant conduct. Sometimes intelligence tests were used to determine mental incompetence but Clarke often made observational determinations of pathology which had little objective grounding in scientific fact. Clarke's use of labels included Goddard's unfortunate categories of mentally deficient individuals as morons, imbeciles and idiots. He also used such descriptions as: feebleminded, moral imbeciles, dull normals, slightly mentally retarded and apparently normal." to add to the confusion, Clarke added high and low grades in her determination of defectiveness. One fourteen year old girl was cited as having a "sluggish brain" because "she does not know the name of Lake Ontario and says Toronto has a population of one million."[71]

Clarke also included behavior as a category of mental abnormality. Individuals typed as odd, disruptive or immoral could be recommended for special classes, permanently institutionalized or deported in spite of an "apparently normal intellect."

This latter group mimics most closely the early mental hygiene studies in the United States, which in spite of their scientific facade relied heavily on moral considerations. Case descriptions from Clarke's institutional surveys of the Children's Aid Society, Women's Gaol Farm, and Victor Mission Rescue Home in 1922 and 1923, describe children and youth from one to nineteen with a series of disparaging labels.[72] Most objectionable were individuals Clarke considered overtly engaged in immoral acts or bad habits such as "selling booze." This also included thieves, truants, weak characters, and "dope fiends." Children with undesirable associations were variously interpreted as: "frivolous, carefree, vagrant, incorrigible or easily led." Other children are cited for faults such as running away, not dressing themselves properly, not being able to read, having speech problems, "acting childish," or being ignorant of information which Clarke considered obvious. Clarke was critical of children who he felt were untruthful or lazy, faults which he identified with a "lack of ballast," a euphemism for emotional instability or maladjustment.

Clarke did not distinguish developmental differences between adults and children. He used quasi-psychiatric terms when he felt the child indicated a potentially chronic mental dysfunction. This included designations such as "psychopathic, general paresis, manic depressives or dementia praecox," as well as the less formal "nervous types, the emotionally unstable and shallow natured." Physical stigmata were considered indications of mental dysfunction. Such descriptions ranged from poor teeth, eyes or hearing, to the shape of the cranium, ears, hand or palate. One child simply "looked odd."

It is significant that Clarke saw all of these types of abnormal designations under the more general heading of mental diseases and that he saw them as biologically based, morally offensive and potentially dangerous. Labels were indiscriminately applied to all age groups, although the younger children were more likely to be deferred for future follow ups. The records of one eight year old where diagnosis was supposedly deferred described him, nevertheless, as "not to be trusted." Clarke observed that he had "behavior faults" and that he was at minimum "bad tempered."

A few children received positive reports. One child of eight, with a mental age of over nine, was credited as being "no trouble" and "good natured" even though she was illegitimate and her mother was listed as a "moron." Another child of seven, also illegitimate, who had a "speech defect" and was "deaf," nevertheless received the favorable note of "seeming bright [and] plays."

"Getting Everybody Upset Over the Child"

The Canadian mental hygiene movement was similar to the United States movement in that it popularized a medical perspective in eliminating social problems prior to any substantial advances in scientific research concerning the causes or cure of mental abnormality. The movement tended to propagandize public policies more than it advanced scientific knowledge. Canadian mental hygienists, as did their U.S. counterparts, tended to do what Adolf Meyer found most irritating in getting "everybody upset over the child."[73] Canadian mental hygienists emphasized volunteerism and a combination of eugenics and public health reform. This was reinforced by the sources of funding support for the CNCMH.

Early resources for mental hygiene came from Canadian contributions to the Lady Byng of Vimy Fund, established by the wife of the Governor

General in March of 1922. Lady Byng contributed ten thousand dollars and Sir William Price offered fifty thousand. Other pledges ranged from twenty-five thousand to one thousand dollars. Recruited by Hincks and Beers, the CNCMH's patrons were counted among the most powerful and affluent members of Canadian society.

The interests of elite patrons encouraged work which cooperated with business, government and established voluntary benevolent agencies. This orientation drew the Canadian National Committee away from the professionalization of mental hygiene as a medical discipline and encouraged an identification and affiliation with voluntary and quasi-governmental agencies.

The slowness of professional growth in Canada was due to the differences in the timing of the expansion of higher education and graduate education on a broad scale. Rather than attempt independent organization, Canadian professionals consistently sent delegations to U.S. meetings and conferences. The lack of professional strength in Canada substantiated the strong charitable tradition.

The Canadian Council on Child Welfare, for example, had a great deal of impact on the Canadian mental hygiene movement. The Council was composed of a number of affiliated autonomous agencies including the Canadian Association of Child Protective Officers, the Canadian National Committee for Mental Hygiene, the Canadian Social Hygiene Council, the Canadian Tuberculosis Association, the Religious Education Council of Canada, the Canadian Girl Guides Association, the Boy Scouts' Association, the Federation des Femmes Canadiennes-Françaises, and the Mothers' Allowance Commissioners of the Provinces.[74] While the Montreal group was generally more oriented toward psychiatric medical perspectives than the Toronto group, there was nothing to match the United States' combination of professionalization, medicalization, and philanthropy.

— Part II —

The Mind

Paradigms of Childhood

They who say all men are equal speak an undoubted truth, if they mean that all have an equal right to liberty, to their property and to the protection of the laws. But they are mistaken if they think men are equal in their station and employment, since they are not so by their talents. (Voltaire, quoted in *Farmers Almanac*, 1987.)

A great truth is a truth whose opposite is also a great truth. (Thomas Mann, *Essay on Freud*, quoted in Jerome Kagen, *The Nature of the Child*, New York: Basic Books, 1984.)

Chapter Six

The Child of the State and Mental Hygiene

The direct link between the mental hygiene movement and children's policy embraced the extension of *parens patriae* powers, the authority of the state as a surrogate parent, in juvenile courts and compulsory schooling in the ongoing expansion of nineteenth century children's institutions. Thomas Salmon's argument that preventive mental hygiene necessarily concerned children evolved over several years before childhood became a central feature of mental hygiene work.

Children, nonetheless, had figured prominently in the 1912 NCMH mental hygiene exhibit. Henry Goddard's approach to the feebleminded and the popular emphasis on eugenics was evident as an influence.[1] Salmon extended the mental hygiene surveys to cover mixed adult-child institutions. He came to stress the importance of studying a variety of institutions rather than just concentrating on hospitals for the insane. Salmon's list of institutions to be examined included: almshouses, jails, schools, and institutions for the feebleminded, orphaned, dependent or neglected child.

Salmon first turned his attention toward early intervention through the juvenile court, parental or truant school; secondarily toward the public school, and finally toward the family home. He argued the incontrovertible fact that the insane population was dispersed throughout these settings and that many of these social settings were either specifically organized for children or had mixed age populations.

Related developments paralleling the mental hygiene movement also directed attention toward child life. Salmon was aware of the establishment of Meyer's psychiatric clinic and laboratory at Johns Hopkins University, which was designed to serve both adults and children. The establishment of the Children's Bureau under the Department of Labor legitimated the emphasis on solving social problems by focussing on children's issues. President Theodore Roosevelt's warning at the 1909 White House Conference on Dependent Children that the "ranks of criminals and other enemies of the state are recruited in an altogether undue proportion from children bereft of their natural homes and left without sufficient care," was an added impetus to action. White House Conference spokesmen claimed that in 1904 there were ninety-three thousand institutionalized dependent children, fifty thousand additional neglected and dependent children in private homes, and twenty-five thousand juvenile delinquents.[2]

From Moral to Mental Order: Medicalizing the Deviant Child

The most important single change in children's legal policy which has shaped the twentieth century was the application of the principle of *parens patriae* in the institutionalization of the juvenile courts. The separate courts generally served juveniles between six and sixteen years of age. Previously a child under common law over the age of seven was considered to be criminally responsible in most states. The establishment of the juvenile court not only separated the child from adult proceedings and placement but redefined the child offender not as a criminal but as a delinquent.[3] In this way the child gained the protection of the court but lost certain rights to the protection of due process. These courts attracted all varieties of child and family problems and placed them before the prerogative of the magistrates. The use of probation was a significant addition to child placement since it necessitated the expansion of services and personnel to oversee these provisions. Children's services increasingly concentrated on professional guidance through the school and home rather than through residential institutions.

The Illinois Juvenile Court Law of 1899, as the first statutory example, became a model for similar legislation in twenty-two other states.[4] The Juvenile Delinquency Act of Canada, a statute of 1908, also reflected the Illinois legislation.[5] Child dependency problems were increasingly seen as "the story of the complications of poverty, immorality and other delinquencies, disease and mental defect."[6] The courts of Illinois by law dealt with three classes of children, namely, the dependent or neglected child (homeless or destitute), the child who was in the street instead of school (truant), and the delinquent child (violators of the law, incorrigible children, and those growing up in "idleness and crime").[7] A consolidation of earlier laws, the juvenile court legislation combined the industrial and training school acts, along with all laws relating to dependent children, distinguishing the child from adult by age in terms of the process of state intervention and the possibilities for placement.[8]

The first child guidance clinic originated in affiliation with this court. The idea of a neurological clinic evolved in large measure out of the Juvenile Protective Association in conjunction with the encouragement of Julia Lathrop, then of Hull House settlement, later chief of the Children's

Bureau. Lathrop was appointed chair of a committee to set up an investigatory team to study the causes of truancy and delinquency.[9] Adolf Meyer suggested physician and neurologist, William Healy, as principal investigator. Lathrop invited Allen Burns, of the juvenile court, and Healy to Hull House to discuss the establishment of a special court-affiliated clinic for children. Member of the Board of Trustees of the Juvenile Protective Association and local philanthropist, Ethel S. Dummer, agreed to fund the experiment for five years.[10] In 1908, Healy, a secretary, and Grace Fernald, his first assistant psychologist, began a consultant service in the juvenile court of Judge Pinckney. After six months the "team" began to do pre-trial examinations of the defendants to advise the court of the "true cause" of the child's delinquency.[11] It was decided to officially open a juvenile psychopathic institute in affiliation with the court to more thoroughly study the young offender.

There were few earlier precedents for such a clinic. The very first clinic for children was created in 1896 by Lightner Witmer, professor of psychology at the University of Pennsylvania. A principal in one of the public schools asked Witmer to examine a boy who wouldn't learn. Witmer determined that the child was visually impaired. Witmer established a clinic for the remediation of practical disabilities of learning which he termed clinical psychology.[12] Witmer worked exclusively with mentally retarded children and did not interpret aberrant behavior as reflecting psychiatric problems other than mental retardation.[13]

One further example of the early clinical examination of children occurred at the Vineland Training School for the Feebleminded under the direction of Henry H. Goddard, one of G. Stanley Hall's students. Goddard introduced mental testing into an institutional environment. In the year 1910, he published an American version of the French 1908 Binet-Simon intelligence scale. He also described connections between low test scores and various forms of social deviancy, elaborating in the process three different classes of feeblemindedness: imbeciles, idiots, and morons. Goddard closely associated feeblemindedness with immorality and criminality. Italian anthropologist Cesare Lombroso had developed a similar theory on criminality and the biology of degeneracy based on physiognomy. Lombroso's view was subsequently discredited. Nevertheless, the ability to test clinical features of mental processes in intelligence tests furthered a renewal of a Darwinian approach to deviant behavior.

In 1909, Healy opened the precedent-setting Juvenile Psychopathic Institute. Healy experimented with Binet-Simon intelligence scales as revised by Goddard. One of Healy's goals was to examine the relationship between delinquency and "bad heredity" in feeblemindedness. However, Healy moved away from degeneracy theories and eugenic arguments of "born bad." He concluded that the inheritance of mental peculiarities and physical characteristics had a bearing on delinquency but there was no direct inheritance of discrete criminalistic traits. He found most of the delinquents' intelligence normal. This left the way open to the interpretation of problems of delinquency as due to other learned factors, such as family influence and emotional disturbance. Did "extroverted symptomatic behavior . . . in morbid fantasy life . . . precede pathological lying and accusation?" Healy never completely resolved this question.[14]

Augusta F. Bronner joined the clinic in the year 1913. She was a psychologist trained at Columbia under learning theorist Edward Thorndike. She had been attracted to the clinic during a summer class she took from Healy at Harvard. As a prelude to his growing recognition, Healy gave two lecture sessions at Harvard in the summers of 1912 and 1913. Healy began to publish a series of articles on systems for recording data on criminals (1909, 1913), tests for mental classification (1911), case studies, epilepsy, causes of crime (1912), inheritance, female delinquency (1913), and retardation (1914). In 1915, he published his major work *The Individual Delinquent*. Bronner published *The Psychology of Special Abilities and Disabilities* in 1917.[15] Healy's clinic was the first to add the component of mental unbalance to children in a clinical setting which became the trademark of child guidance. Healy's clinic was a beginning which had a profound effect on Thomas Salmon of the National Committee for Mental Hygiene.

Parens patriae was increasingly influenced by the medical model of preventive mental hygiene work with the young. These complementary perspectives claimed legitimacy based on the child's best interest and the general good. The twentieth century professionalization of juvenile court workers, social workers, educators, public health and child development experts was a corollary of expanded concepts of *parens patriae* responsibility.[16] The National Committees for Mental Hygiene and their philanthropic mentors took up in the twentieth century the banner of the earlier child savers as advocates for the extension of public responsibility for child life. The successful medicalization of childhood came to rely on the testimony of a new class of experts in the medical and social sciences rather than on the moral prescriptions of the advocates of generations past.

Salmon was influenced by the evolution of the Chicago juvenile court and psychopathic clinic. He kept in close touch with the psychopathic clinic by way of the overlapping membership between child savers and mental hygienists such as Jane Addams and Julia Lathrop. Adolf Meyer also served as an early consultant to the juvenile court and encouraged the establishment of the psychopathic clinic.

The Early Projects on the Mental Hygiene of Deviancy

By 1915, Salmon was ready to put forth a comprehensive proposal which began to pull these ideas together into a preventive framework characteristic of mental hygiene. This was also his first year as a paid employee of the Rockefeller Foundation. Salmon proposed to the Foundation a comprehensive study of the psychopathology of crime as "a chronological arrangement of the material . . . from childhood."[17] Salmon suggested a clinical study of the inmate population of Sing Sing prison to cooperate with a "mental clinic" in the children's court of New York city. Salmon first sugested that William Healy be made the director of the project, however, Healy declined the offer. Bernard Glueck, a psychiatrist Salmon had met while in the Public Health Service, accepted the position.[18]

The study at Sing Sing was begun in 1916 with an appropriation from the Rockefeller Foundation of $47,500 over three years. The mental clinic for children was opened in Franklin C. Hoyt's court in New York. Successive appeals to the Rockefeller Foundation to continue support for the study of the psychopathology of crime emphasized the "essential" connection between the Sing Sing study and the children's court. The clinic was to create guidelines for other clinics, and to "standardize research studies" on psychopathology and delinquency.[19] The purpose of the clinical studies was to "discover unstable, mentally deficient and mentally disordered individuals who, later, would in many instances, go to prison for offenses committed not because of criminal instincts but because of mental inefficiency or mental abnormality of one kind or another."[20]

Glueck later described Salmon's part in structuring the Sing Sing research in its relationship to child guidance:

> Indeed from the very first, Doctor Salmon was particularly interested in having us bring to light the intimate relationship between childhood maladjustment and later criminal careers . . . Moreover . . . he had always emphasized a preference for preventive measures as against the purely corrective enterprises and the Sing Sing studies he looked upon as a prelude to child guidance.[21]

Salmon was not as shy as Healy in drawing direct connections between children filtered through the juvenile court and mental illness. He saw the courts as institutions which were age specific but which still failed to make the distinctions between various age related populations in terms of normal and abnormal development and predilections. Salmon pushed the NCMH to take the position that in the children's court "the greater proportion of the difficulties do not deal with criminalism at all, but with many other disorders of conduct which, for administrative convenience, are dealt with by that tribunal." Further, "in many instances police intervention has not been the initial step in bringing them to public notice. Sick children, neglected children, psychopathic children, feebleminded children, all come to this court whenever their conduct seriously interferes with standards established by social conventions."[22] Salmon, in this way, moved the idea of a children's psychopathic clinic away from the study of delinquency and criminality and toward the general study of childhood abnormality outside the court.

Consolidating Mental Hygiene Programs and Philanthropic Funds

At the close of World War I, seven years had passed since the establishment of the Rockefeller Foundation and five years had elapsed since the trustees had employed Salmon as an advisor and consultant in mental hygiene. In January of 1920, Foundation officials and friends gathered at the Gedney Farms Hotel in New Jersey to discuss the future of mental hygiene work and its organization with reference to other Rockefeller projects and philanthropies.

The Gedney Farms Conference

The Foundation had originally considered a separate division on mental hygiene. The hiring of Salmon and support for the NCMH had been a compromise in this regard. Salmon sincerely hoped to convince the Trustees to develop a general division on mental hygiene similar to the General Education Board or the Sanitary Commission. The purpose of the division would be to do research and provide demonstrations in preventive work emphasizing the mental hygiene of childhood, psychiatric studies of delinquency and crime, and the expansion of graduate training facilities, including fellowships for psychiatrists and other related mental hygiene professions. Salmon felt strongly that "the great hour for American psychiatry [was] at hand."[23] Salmon argued:

> The success of a few tentative psychiatric excursions into the field of criminology, the attempts to deal with the roots of mental disease in childhood rather than to devote our efforts wholly to managing them in adult life, the success of psychologists in devising group methods of arranging people with reference to their native intellectual endowment and the distinct tendency on the part of the public to replace by intelligent interest, credulity, and ignorance regarding everything that has to do with mental life, all have combined to open new fields for the practical application of psychiatry.[24]

The participants gathered at the Gedney Farms Conference on the 17th and 18th of January included Rockefeller Foundation President George Vincent, William Welch, Abraham Flexner and Edwin Embree of the Foundation staff along with Salmon. The others at once agreed with the contents of Salmon's proposal and yet remained unconvinced that a separate division on mental hygiene was called for at that time.

This discouraging outcome did not in fact mark a defeat for the mental hygiene movement. Mental hygiene had, in fact, been incorporated into the workings of other previously established boards by the time of the Gedney Farms Conference. The Rockefeller Foundation dominated the fields of public health, medical education and medical research. The General Education Board advanced education in the United States. The International Education Board and International Health Board were designed to take on similar projects without national restrictions.

Significantly, this included health and education in Canada as called for by John D. Rockefeller, Sr. in his 1919 plea for supportive research and educational work in Canada. The Laura Spelman Rockefeller Memorial, founded in this time period in honor of John D. Rockefeller, Sr.'s first wife, was most compatible with mental hygiene and with an international outlook.

The Laura Spelman Rockefeller Memorial was incorporated with a capital of seventy-four million dollars in 1918 with the mandate to "promote the welfare of women and children."[25] The rationale was that through the social sciences:

> might come more intelligent measures of social control that would reduce such irrationalities as are represented by poverty, class conflict and war between nations . . . Through a greater understanding of man and his relation to other men the growing power over the forces of nature would more likely be applied for good than for evil.[26]

The Memorial's work evolved slowly in the years 1919 to 1922. In 1922, Beardsley Ruml was made the director. By 1924, child development demonstration research, which closely followed Salmon's prescriptions, were well underway, and by 1926, it was was the "dominant" activity of the Memorial. In the 1927 report of the Trustee Committee of Review, child study and parent education was central and "virtually the single program of the Memorial for the welfare of children."[27]

The Lakewood Conference

Four months after the Gedney Farms Conference, Salmon was approached by Dr. Max Ferrand, the medical director of the Commonwealth Fund. The Fund wanted advice on potential programs concerning child welfare and delinquency. In July, the assistant medical director, Samuel Fairly, followed up on the initial contact. Salmon was asked to prepare a proposal outlining the ideal project if financing were no object.[28] Salmon's proposal and discussion on it led to the organization by Ferrand of an invitational conference to be held in March 1921 at Lakewood, New Jersey. The topic was to be the prevention of juvenile delinquency.[29] The temporary advisory committee for the conference was composed of Max Ferrand, Thomas W. Salmon, William Healy, Augusta Bonner and Bernard Glueck, as well as J. Prentice Murphy (director of the Children's Bureau in Philadelphia), H. C. Morrison (professor of education at the University of Chicago), Judge Charles W. Hoffman (Court of Domestic Relations in Cincinnati), and Martha Falconer (director of the Department of Protective Measures of the American Social Hygiene Association).

The importance of the conference was reiterated later by Bernard Glueck,

> whatever the vicissitudes have characterized the child guidance movement since then and whatever its future may come to be, nobody can question the fact that this movement had its birth at the Lakewood Conference in 1921 . . . It was Doctor Salmon who contributed most to its deliberations and to the final shaping of the report . . . He was unquestionably the leading spirit.[30]

Salmon had consistently argued for the extension of work in psychopathology to community level investigations on multiple fronts. This approach was illustrated in the Sing Sing Prison study. After the War, he became more adamant on this point not only with the Rockefeller Foundation but in numerous addresses and speeches such as the one in September 1919 at the annual meeting of the American Institute of Criminal Law and Criminology. In this address he gives credit for his ideas to Healy's work, Bernard Glueck's studies and the lessons from his own war experience. His main point was that even though "the children's court is the outpost in the psychiatric study of delinquency" it was necessary in the future to "prevent the first departures from acceptable conduct."[31] From this standpoint, it was necessary to create centers, such as the Judge Baker Foundation in Boston, which did research which went beyond courts and prisons, and, instead, became a part of the "general advance of psychiatry."[32] Further, Salmon claimed, "the study of the abnormal mind" should "extend the frontiers of psychological medicine," which would eventually "repay the debt which the medical criminologist owes to the clinical psychiatrist."[33]

The theoretical focus of the Lakewood Conference did not remain with the juvenile offender. Following Salmon's preventive prescriptions, the medical, psychological, and social aspects of delinquency were to be enlarged in the direction of demonstrations in teaching and treatment, and by the development of new centers of research in strategic locations.[34] The new centers were to concentrate on schools rather than courts, with the idea of expanding the "scientific conception of disorders of conduct and their treatment."[35]

Importantly, this extension of services to the school authorities and teachers were to be carried out through the extension of social casework, visiting teachers, and a variety of specialized school visitors.[36] The resulting program was a very contemporary version of extramural psychiatric services in education, carried out by specialized personnel who concentrated on identifying and remediating individual differences in learning, conduct, and personality. The provision of multiple educational functions inside and outside the self-contained classsroom offered a substantial functional implementation of the progressive educational ideal.

While mental retardation and sexual deviance were cited as contributing to antisocial conduct and insanity, the family was also noted as potentially dangerous influence which could "deprive children of stabilizing influences and subject them to the disadvantages of institutional care or inadequate foster care [which] contributes to delinquency."[37] In general, the phenomenon of delinquency was looked on less as an end goal of study in itself but rather as a symptom of developmental problems in personal and social disorganization.

Additionally, Salmon stressed the need for the provision of adequate personnel. Without properly trained psychiatrists, services were doomed to lag. This reflected Salmon's problems with finding enough psychiatrists to fill the needs of his own programs in the Army. He turned to the practical solution of the development of programs for training in the semi-professional categories of psychiatric social work and public health nursing as alternatives to having all work conducted by what at the time was a very inadequate supply of psychiatrists. His belief in the uses of social workers to provide rudimentary psychiatric services, which he pioneered in the Army and with the Smith program, is evident here. Salmon also spoke adamantly for the development of university facilities in clinics attached to medical schools. These would provide training for medical personnel in psychiatry in conjunction with an opportunity for clinical practice with children.

The mental hygiene prescription for legitimating preventive intervention into child mental and physical welfare came into focus at the Gedney Farms and Lakewood Conferences. Thomas Salmon played a major role in drawing the connection between philanthropic funding agencies and a policy orientation which converged the medical model in problem solving, the new preventive psychiatry, and the preoccupation with children, into a very powerful prescription for social action.

Chapter Seven

Medicalizing Maladjustment: The Child Guidance Movement

The concept of the prevention of delinquency spiraled outward and away from the juvenile courts toward the school, family, and community. Salmon's proposals at the Lakewood and Gedney Farms Conferences for establishing preventive mental hygiene work with children by identifying school age maladaptation, was formalized in the clinical demonstrations organized by the National Committee for Mental Hygiene and the Commonwealth Fund between 1922 and 1927. The child guidance movement, which these demonstrations formed, represents a major subset of the mental hygiene movement as it contributed to the establishment of a psychiatric speciality in childhood disorders.

Child guidance was a unique American contribution to the history of child psychiatry. The demonstrations established a foundation for clinical practice which legitimated an applied psychiatry directed toward identifying and defining abnormal psychological and emotional development in childhood. The transition from a psychopathology of delinquency to child psychiatry also made substantial contributions to the development of school psychology, community psychiatry, and family counseling services. The deliberate intention of disseminating psychiatric perspectives successfully influenced the medicalization of related disciplines in human services including social work, psychology, counseling, and teaching. An unintended outcome, however, was the proliferation of non-medical disciplines which displaced the dominant role intended for psychiatry.

Organizing Child Guidance

The child guidance movement took shape when a five-year program for the prevention of delinquency was mutually adopted by the Commonwealth Fund and the NCMH, and put into operation in December of

1921.[1] The goal of studying delinquency and creating methods for solving the problem of mental disorder was approached in a threefold manner, all of which involved professional training and demonstrations. This included: 1) a bureau of child guidance; 2) a visiting teacher program; and 3) a series of demonstration clinics consecutively organized in specially chosen sites across the country.

The Bureau of Child Guidance

The first division created was the Bureau of Child Guidance directed by Bernard Glueck, under the auspices of the New York School of Social Work. Social workers were trained in psychiatry with field work in demonstration clinics oriented toward community based mental hygiene services in juvenile courts and schools. To encourage enrollment, the Commonwealth Fund provided over one hundred fellowships annually.[2] Over 2,500 classes in social psychiatry, psychiatric social work, clinical psychiatry, and mental testing were eventually offered to an enrollment which totalled 944 students.[3] Over two hundred of these students participated in mental hygiene demonstration clinics as part of their field work experience.

An underlying concern with delinquency persisted for the first two years, however, the therapeutic focus increasingly turned to the parent-child relationship. Glueck emphasized the significance of "the strong emotional qualities" of family interaction on child socialization. A "significant conclusion which a reading of our records leads to," Glueck surmised, "is that we are discovering, and actually putting into practice on a fairly large scale, the means for the eradication of the evil influence upon the life of childhood."[4] One hundred children were treated the first year. Over the next five and a half years, 1,050 children received consultation services, and 822 were received for treatment. Of these, 591 cases were completed.

Lying and disobedience were the most common "symptoms of misconduct" cited. The least common reasons for referral were also the least definitive but seemed to be related to disobedient or disrespectful behaviors. Children were brought in for such reasons as "facial grimaces" and "bunking out," (running away or staying out overnight). Morbid fears, depression, and shyness generally figured more prominently than delinquent status or "conflict with the law." Seriously delinquent behavior was separated from the more frequent referrals for "disorderly conduct in school" and "stealing."

Eighteen public schools were served and cooperative services were organized with four churches, five hospitals, and twenty-three social agencies, as well as private families. According to one survey, the outcome of therapy was appraised as successful in approximately half of the cases.[5]

Porter R. Lee and Marion E. Kenworthy, who succeeded Glueck as director and assistant director of the Bureau, also stressed an applied psychiatry of child life rather than delinquency. Marion Kenworthy developed psychiatric methods for case work utilizing an "ego-libido analysis of case material." The Bureau disseminated psychiatric and psychoanalytic approaches to child health through twelve international conferences which exchanged theories on problem children.

In 1927, at the end of five years, the Bureau was concluded as a demonstration and an Institute for Child Guidance was created, also with Commonwealth Fund support. The training of psychiatric social workers continued with supervisors from the New York School of Social Work and Smith College. The therapeutic emphasis remained on case-based psychiatry focussing on the role of parents and especially mothers.[6]

Funding for the Institute was cut off in 1932 due to the depression. Barry Smith, of the Commonwealth Fund, argued that the function of the Institute in stimulating psychiatric curriculum and encouraging other training centers was complete.[7]

Visiting Teachers: Mental Hygiene in the Classroom

A second section of the Commonwealth Fund/NCMH Program created a National Committee on Visiting Teachers in affiliation with the Public Education Association (P.E.A.). Howard W. Nudd, director of P.E.A. served as committee chairman and Jane Culbert, staff executive of the P.E.A., chaired the section on visiting teachers. Visiting teachers were trained in psychiatric social work and served as on-site trainers and demonstrators in schools such as P.S. 64 in New York City. The work was seen as "educating teaching staff into a different attitude toward children." The goal was to place mental hygiene at the center of classroom exchange.

Visiting teachers extended the concept of preventive psychiatric work into the ideology of public schooling.[8] Classrooms were considered to be "natural" mental hygiene clinics. The ideology of progressive schooling took on an extended meaning directed away from formal learning and toward socializaton. The goal of schooling was restated as a responsibility to adjust children's behavior and personality, and to prepare them for a proper "healthy" style of living. It was implied that a child's character and ambition should be adjusted according to the reality of their circumstances as well as their innate potential. The acquisition of academic knowledge was considered of minor value compared with the acquisition of a well-rounded personality. The pursuit of abstract knowledge was, in fact, considered under certain circumstances to be deterimental to mental health.

This view, as part of the progressive hands-on child oriented approach to teaching, substantially altered the objectives of schooling. The teacher's primary goal in the classroom was not to impart formal knowledge but to impart life skills, monitor personal adjustment and identify aberrant tendencies. If teachers were to become experts in these areas, a different kind of professional training was required. Visiting teachers were to demonstrate the advantage of psychiatric training for educators. At the end of the three year demonstration in visiting teacher services, forty-eight communities in thirty-two different states had initiated a program. It was reported that 15,439 children had received benefits.[9]

Joint Committee on Methods

A Joint Committee on Methods of Preventing Delinquency was established to join the NCMH, Commonwealth Fund, P.E.A. and the New York School of Social Work staff. It was to function as an executive policy making board designed to coordinate the training work of the Bureau and the visiting teacher efforts of the P.E.A. with the creation of demonstrations in child guidance and the proliferation of clinical services.[10]

The committee decided at an early meeting to keep records of "favorable comments concerning the work of the section." This was to be used in evaluations and for "educating" the public.[11] These "favorable comments" evolved into the elaborate publishing program of the Commonwealth Fund, which became fundamental to disseminating mental hygiene and psychiatric literature. The production and publication of mental hygiene literature expanded rapidly with the demonstrations. It was reported that by the first of May 1928 a total of 94,949 informational publications on mental hygiene had been broadly distributed.[12]

The Child Guidance Demonstrations

The establishment of demonstration clinics was the most important part of the Commonwealth-National Committee joint project. The National Committee for Mental Hygiene was to set up and supervise the actual operation of the clinics. The burden of the work was conducted by the National Committee out of a newly formed Division on the Prevention of Delinquency, a Department of Experiment and Demonstration, and a Department of Psychiatric Field Service. George S. Stevenson was made a field consultant and later became the director of the NCMH Division on Community Clinics.

Commonwealth Fund personnel, such as Barry Smith, acted as a consultant and coordinated the distribution of funds. The Commonwealth

Fund originally provided $15,000 a year for the general maintenance of the NCMH Division on the Prevention of Delinquency and $26,000 a year for a field service. The expansion of the work is illustrated by the fact that by 1924 these budgets had increased to total $140,000 a year.[13]

Eight demonstrations were eventually funded. This included projects in: St. Louis, Missouri; Norfolk, Virginia; Dallas, Texas; Twin Cities (St. Paul and Minneapolis), Minnesota; Cleveland, Ohio; Philadelphia, Pennsylvania; and Los Angeles, California.[14]

The objective of the demonstration child guidance clinic was to illustrate, on a community level, the applicability of psychiatry to problems of childhood, specifically delinquency as a symptom of early mental disease.[15] The demonstrations were to serve as models for permanent clinics to be established and operated by local organizations or governmental agencies at the end of a specified time period. Establishing and operating child guidance clinics on a community level made local cooperation, and ultimately the replacement of philanthropic funding by local funding resources, essential if long term success was to be achieved.

The clinical demonstrations were experiments in the implementation of public policy. An evolution can be seen in the program format, organization of the clinic in relationship to patients and community services, and in therapeutic orientation. Early unstable short term demonstrations related to the juvenile court hardly resemble the sophisticated community coordinated services of the later projects. The National Committee for Mental Hygiene and Commonwealth Fund staff and consultants adjusted the ideology and practice of applied psychiatry as the program evolved. Child guidance was shaped by practical consideration of what worked and what did not. Social and economic conditions in the 1920s and 1930s resulted in a boom-bust effect. Several clinics closed in the 1930s. Although widespread clinical psychiatric services for children remained largely inadequate or non-existent in the inter-War period, the spread of the mental hygiene model for social action extended both geographically and temporally well beyond the eight demonstration sites and the permanent clinics that became their legacy.

The First Try: St. Louis

St. Louis, Missouri was chosen for the first demonstration since volunteer psychiatric work had been carried out in the juvenile court there for fourteen years. The demonstration also had the strong support of the president of the Missouri Society for Mental Hygiene, the juvenile court judge, the public health department, probation officer and other social organizations.[16] The demonstration was to last eight months beginning in April 1922.[17]

The St. Louis demonstration established the staff ideal, suggested by Salmon, of a psychiatrist, a psychologist, and psychiatric social worker.[18] Thomas Heldt, a psychiatrist, was hired to direct the clinic with the assistance of a psychologist, E. K. Wickman, and a psychiatric social worker, Mildred Scoville, who later became Barry Smith's executive assistant with the Commonwealth Fund.

Three hundred cases were seen by the clinic during the demonstration.[19] The clinic did not immediately achieve permanent standing after the demonstration but was continued by volunteers with the cooperation of the St. Louis Medical Society. NCMH and Commonwealth Fund executives served in a consultative role.[20] In March of 1923, a city ordinance authorized the establishment of a permanent psychiatric clinic to serve the juvenile court, schools, social work agencies and the public under the auspices of the Department of Public Welfare.[21] However, it quickly became apparent that the clinic did not have enough resources to serve such a broad range of clients.[22]

The St. Louis clinic was not considered ideal in the eyes of the National Committee.[23] Much of the problem was with personnel, including the deficient training of its permanent director, William Nelson.[24] In addition to personnel problems, the St. Louis clinic had problems with an uncooperative governing board and intrusive city politics. The clinic was threatened with collapse in 1925 and 1926. It was not until 1927 that the budget was passed by the city council without a confrontation. Nonetheless, the clinic's budget was severely cut during the Depression and finally closed as a psychological service in child guidance in 1933.[25]

Case study records from the St. Louis demonstration reveal a therapeutic procedure which included a descriptive life history report, physical examination with psychological testing and a psychiatric interview. The results of the clinical examination in court-referred cases were given back to the court, where seventy-four percent of the referrals originated. The outcome of the demonstration supported Salmon's claim that prevention had to occur before the juvenile court stage. Case records indicated that children coming into the court had previous records of misconduct in school or with other social agencies. This insight was significant for it encouraged a preventive framework which concentrated on schools and social service agencies in order to catch pre-court delinquency.

However, examples of the clinical case reports show little evidence to substantiate the sensitivity of the case workers in their identification of predelinquents. The following description is taken from a case report submitted by William Nelson, the clinical director.

> A twelve year old boy was referred to the clinic by an unstated agency for being "disobedient and stubborn." He had recently completed the sixth

> grade. His parents were Greek immigrants. His mother never learned to speak English. There were seven children in the family, one of whom was physically handicapped. His father owned a pool hall and thus had a steady income at what was seen as a dubious enterprise. The "harmony" of the home was credited as "excellent." A physical exam noted that he had flat feet and poor vision in one eye though in general he was "well developed and nourished." During the psychological interview he tended to be "inattentive" and he performed poorly on grammar and abstract vocabulary tests. The psychiatric interview states that he was generally responsive, friendly and honestly answered questions. The report noted that he confessed that he had smoked cigarettes some, but has not gambled. He admits masturbation, but denies heterosexual experiences. He is fonder of his mother than his father. He wants to be a locomotive engineer."[26]

The diagnosis was that the child was afflicted with "borderline feeblemindedness" and had discernable "character difficulties." The fact that he had made average progress in the sixth grade was given less credence than the fact that he scored closer to a fifth grade level in the psychological exam which was probably due to poor grammar and vocabulary caused by his dual language background. Instead of taking into account the case history as a mitigating factor influencing the scores on standardized tests, he was placed at a mental age of nine years seven months, which put him in the borderline category of mental retardation with an I.Q. of seventy-six. The summary of the report emphasized that it was "doubtful" his mental capacity could be stretched beyond the sixth grade, and that vocational training "should embrace the limits of his constructive imagination."[27]

In spite of recognizing the "harmony" of the child's home, Nelson is highly pessimistic: "The tendency to over-indulge him is excessive" and it "is desirable that an Americanization program be introduced." His association with older boys and his mother's lack of English is noted as potentially "emotionally traumatic . . . It is doubtful that much improvement will result in him unless the home situation is changed, and it is recommended that he be placed in a foster home and an attempt be made to rehabilitate [the family]."[28] It is unclear from the report if any recommendations were followed in the case. It is apparent, however, that there were considerable discrepancies between procedural formats and the capability of staff in carrying out recommendations in practice.

St. Louis Follow-up: The Long Term Impact on Child Life

Evidence of the long term impact of this clinic is provided by a 1966 follow-up study done on the St. Louis Clinic. Five hundred twenty-four children seen between 1924 and 1929 were located to determine the kinds of problems they had developed as adults.[29]

The follow-up study drew three conclusions: 1) antisocial behavior in childhood is a "powerful predictor of poor adult outcomes." 2) Social class is not a predictor of adult failure. And, 3) Children with mild disorders, but whose father's were antisocial, had greatly increased chances of a "poor outcome."[30] A loosely constructed control group of children in the public schools who did not get into trouble as children, and therefore were not remanded to the clinic, were found to have grown up to live normal lives relatively free of divorce, hospitalization and crime, in spite of a similar economic standing as children in the clinic group.

It is interesting to note, in relationship to the second conclusion, that factors which correlate with class such as educational level and job level attained in adulthood did emerge as significant predictors of adult mental problems. The children in the St. Louis sample who grew up to be identified as troubled were found to have achieved low educational standing and low-paying and low-status jobs, and, not surprisingly, had a relatively low class standing.[31]

This study tells us something about the long term consequences of clinical treatment in childhood as much as the effects of original predispositions to mental illness. The study underscores belief structures about the life chances of children who come before juvenile courts and whose mental and emotional status came into question in childhood. It is unclear if the child's mental status or a combination of other status related characteristics in social and economic terms dominated the original referral and long term outcomes. The results of this study also demonstrate a poor success rate in preventing adult problems by way of childhood intervention. It remains interesting that individuals once preselected as having had maladaptations to what was considered acceptable behavior remained at high risk for reselection years later.

Demography and Successful Clinics: The Norfolk Lesson

The second clinic opened in Norfolk, Virginia in 1923, and is considered to be the sole failure of the demonstrations. It was concluded that a child guidance clinic was too specialized a service for a relatively small community.[32] The greatest contribution of this clinic was in the development of an early example of a cooperative organization which utilized local facilities and volunteers as well as professionals. The Norfolk Clinic worked in tandem with the central council of social agencies, home and school leagues, various churches and nursing associations, as well as the local Bar Association, Medical Society, Women's Club, and Parent-Teacher Association.[33]

The second lesson of the clinic, especially after similar concerns in St. Louis, was not to rely on local political leadership to assume the financial burden of the service after the demonstration. City politics and localized opposition appeared to create insurmountable political wrangling. For example, the mayor and city council budgeted $12,000 for the continuance of the clinic after the Norfolk demonstration, but the city manager successfully opposed the dispensation of funds. The city manager clearly did not get along with the NCMH staff who described him as "a very unreasonable person, who took pride in saying that he thought all social workers [the mental hygienists] were crooks."[34] The Director of Public Welfare for Norfolk opted for a smaller part-time clinic with a budget of under $9,000, which was strongly opposed by the NCMH. The city council, unable to reach consensus, closed the clinic.[35]

The Community Model for Child Guidance in Dallas

After the failure of the Norfolk clinic, the members of the NCMH decided that advance work was needed before any future demonstrations, and that the site for the next demonstration should be in a community large enough to support it. As a result, Dallas, a city of two hundred thousand people, was chosen. Extensive planning and educational work in the community was undertaken prior to the opening of the clinic in order to avoid the failures of the Norfolk demonstration. Pledges were secured in writing and agreements with organizations and the operation of the clinic specified. The voluntary and cooperative efforts of local professionals and university personnel paved the way for more formal contact between professional training in mental hygiene in related fields and clinical contact in the community. The trend toward community involvement in prevention was to become a permanent feature of clinical practice.

The Dallas demonstration utilized a substantial preventive model based in community resources. Regional support included, for the first time, two local universities, Baylor and Southern Methodist. By 1927, 1,535 children has passed through the demonstration clinic, only 4.9 percent of whom were referred from the juvenile court.[36] The largest number, fully 54.6 percent, were referred from relatives.[37]

Private financing was arranged after the demonstration through the community chest. Minor problems in the operation of the clinic were resolved without damaging its viability.[38] In 1927, the NCMH was able to place E. M. Perry, one of their fellowship trainees in psychiatry, in the position of permanent director.[39]

At the time of the Dallas demonstration, the Minnesota legislature authorized an educational program in preparation for the establishment of a psychopathic clinic in the University of Minnesota Medical School. Minnesota was one of the few public institutions whose program in medical training received a hearty commendation from Abraham Flexner in his *Survey of Medical Education in the United States and Canada*, which he conducted for the Carnegie Foundation in 1910.[40]

The University of Minnesota Demonstration

The University demonstration was to serve Minneapolis and St. Paul as a one year demonstration beginning in November 1923. The clinic was directed by Lawson G. Lowrey with an experienced field staff transferred from Dallas. The clinic staff simultaneously taught in departments of psychology, education, medicine or sociology at the University. Fully thirty-nine social workers spent up to three months in supervised training in psychiatric social work. Three fellows in psychiatry, two psychologists and six social workers, as well as volunteers, provided more than adequate personnel.

This clinic established professional standards for staff and provided training programs to meet these standards. The first training of fellows in psychiatry was pioneered by this demonstration. Also, the clinic incorporated students from other programs, such as the Smith College School of Social Work, to a greater advantage than any previous clinic. This instigated a model for specialized training in localized settings which cooperated nationally to distribute personnel trained in mental hygiene. The demonstration also pioneered the first cooperative agreement with a school district. Lowery was able to take advantage of the interest that public school officials in Minneapolis had expressed in child guidance.

Six hundred and ten cases were studied during the demonstration. Thirty-seven percent were referred from social agencies, twenty-five percent from parents or relatives and nineteen percent from the public schools. The juvenile courts did not refer individuals except through the social agencies.[41] This approach emphasized research and community work rather than an institutional or legal emphasis, which concentrated on identifying and remediating pathological conditions.

Plans for a permanent clinic in Minneapolis were initiated before the end of the University demonstration. The permanent clinic was organized as a part of the public school system rather than the university or the juvenile court system. Joint funds were secured from the public schools, the local department of public welfare, and the community chest, in addition to funds from a local philanthropy, the Amherst H. Wilder Charities.

The Longfellow School Survey

In the year 1924 a school survey was conducted. School children were individually rated by their teachers on thirty-seven personality traits using a descriptive scale with five alternatives. Questions ranged from perceived intelligence to behavioral characteristics and attitudes toward peers and authority figures. For example, one question asked the teacher to rate the child's personality as "repulsive," "disagreeable," "unnoticed," "colorless," "colorful," or "magnetic."[42]

From the results of this survey, problem children were singled out for a physical examination, psychometric testing and extensive interviews including teacher, parent and child conferences. Five boys and one girl from kindergarten and the low first grade were singled out. The most common complaint was for hyperactivity, fatigue, and talkativeness, which translated as "jabbering" on the rating sheet.[43] Two of the boys were seen as seriously emotionally disturbed, with constitutional elements cited by the investigators as contributing to their instability.[44] The essential difference in the reports for these two boys in comparison with the children cited as having mild problems were that they had parents who were typed as overattentive. Both children were recommended for removal from their parents' home if conditions were not improved. One child was, in fact, sent to live with an aunt and uncle as a result of the report. The girl, who was recommended because of stealing, was the only child to be essentially normal. This is the only instance where punishment was recommended. The parents were cited as uncooperative in two cases. One mother refused to come to the school to discuss the report. In another case, the "over attentive" parents of the "worst boy" refused to accept the seriousness of their son's emotional problem.[45]

Clinical Demonstrations in Minneapolis and St. Paul

The staff of the Minneapolis clinic included Smiley Blanton as director and Florence Goodenough as psychologist. Blanton continued in the child guidance field and participated in the Los Angeles demonstration clinic. Goodenough became well known for her psychometric tests for preschool children such as the Goodenough Draw-A-Man Test. The first book on child guidance was written out of the experiences of the Minneapolis clinic. Thomas Salmon wrote a preface for the volume where he explained the importance of mental hygiene work with young populations.[46]

Case studies from the clinic described by Blanton illustrate the psychoanalytic theoretical perspective, which was combined with behavioral therapies involving basic health regimentation and "habit training." Adjustment was explained in terms of a conflict between "ego and the group." Authority structures which elicited "repression and expression" had to be moderated by the clinician to offset influences of the problem parent, especially the mother, on the potentially problematic child. The "nervous child" was the result of unfortunate psychological environments. The effort was to try to avoid removing the child from the home if possible and to concentrate on successfully regulating the parent's behavior. Secondarily, the clinic sought to change the classroom teacher's behavior toward the child and to monitor the child's activities outside of the home without interference from parents.[47] Most of the children were recommended for similar therapies including rigid schedules for eating, sleeping and play. Parent training in child development and discipline, and the solicitation of teacher cooperation in the provision of extra in-class attention was also used. For example:

> one seven year old girl was brought to the clinic as "very anxious and nervous, with marked twitching of her whole body." Her parents said she cried frequently and bit her nails. Teachers reported "a slight stutter when she tried to recite in class." The physical exam cited only that she was "round shouldered" and had "circles under her eyes." Her intelligence test placed her two years above her chronological age. Her family was considered good since her father was a successful lawyer, but her mother was typed by the clinic staff as an "over anxious and nagging parent."

At the clinic the child was placed in a special fatigue study under Dr. Max Seham.[48] Therapy consisted of:

> 1) an "extra feeding at half-past three;" 2) twelve hours of sleep with two rest periods after meals "with a pillow under her back," and thirty minutes rest after school. 3) She could play for one hour intervals only. 4) She was given two minute exercises to be performed twice a day, and 4) eye glasses. 5) Her mother was forbidden to talk to her about lessons or to go to the school. The mother was also given instructions on how to control her "anxiety." 6) The school was to allow the child to pass out papers in the classroom and the teacher was to encourage her to make friends and be confident.[49]

That summer the child was sent to a camp which agreed to follow all of the special instructions for diet, rest and play. She was said to have been cured of her "nervousness" by the end of the year. Another child was given nearly identical therapy to cure her symptoms of "running and never walking" and being so over-talkative that "she was a great nuisance to teachers."[50]

From the interviews in the school survey, teachers often represented stumbling blocks to therapy and potentially caused other problems as well:

> One child recommended for therapy was from a class which had acquired the reputation of being filled with problem children. The teacher who had inherited this group is quoted as saying that she "hates the group" and resents having to teach any of them. Further the child referred for therapy

was one of four over-active children "whom the teacher [especially] does not like." Unable to change the teacher's attitude, the clinic advised that the family "move to a better neighborhood" in order to avoid the school.[51]

In the year 1924, a permanent clinic was also set up in St. Paul, funded by the Amherst H. Wilder Charities. The St. Paul clinic was a less advantageous position than the Minneapolis clinic under Blanton. It was less well connected to the public school system and other community organizations. Additionally, it was financially dependent on the Board of the Wilder Charities which was composed of relatively non-sympathetic business men. The clinic was repeatedly required to justify its funding on a "per capita cost" basis. The Board's insistence on business rather than medical criteria for evaluation was seen as an "educational problem" by Commonwealth and the NCMH leaders. The clinic and its director were criticized by NCMH and Commonwealth Fund officials for not successfully "selling" the idea of mental hygiene to the Board and community.[52]

The director, Dr. Stiffler, tended to resist participating in what he saw as publicity and not education or mental hygiene. Representing the position of the NCMH, Stevenson persisted, suggesting that forty cases from the clinic be used over a year, not only as a case study of childhood problems but also for community educational purposes. Facts on the cases, he argued, could be used as evidence in the argument for the worth of mental hygiene services. Problems could illustrate deficiencies in funding and facilities and the long term cost of neglecting these necessities.[53]

The St. Paul clinic consequently labored under continuous pressure, and was constantly threatened with being disbanded, even though it formally served its designated community function. When compared to Blanton's clinic, Stiffler lacked the ability to exploit the "propaganda" factor which was intimately connected with the success of the mental hygiene movement.[54] Even though the clinical work under Stiffler was considered "good," and the training programs for the University of Minnesota and Smith College "very adequate," the NCMH evaluated Stiffler and the clinic as marginally competent.[55]

Cleveland: The Unified Community Prototype

The Cleveland demonstration unified services which operated to serve the entire city. The solution in this case was to expand the psychiatric service already underway under the auspices of the Children's Aid Society into the broader base of a mental hygiene oriented child guidance. The mental hygiene staff in effect merged with the prior functions of the Children's Aid Society. These services operated in tandem by June 1, 1926, six months before the end of the demonstration. The second year of the demonstration was unusual. The Welfare Federation contributed funding for a continuance which was deemed necessary to refine the techniques effected by the merging of functions of a more traditional welfare service with the mental hygiene staff.

The Cleveland demonstration opened in December of 1924. It accepted 706 clients out of 1,015 referrals during the demonstration. Of these, 533 were given full clinical services and the others were given consultative service. Close to thirty-six percent were referred by social agencies, twenty-four percent by parents or relatives and thirty percent by the schools. The juvenile courts only referred seven and a half percent with another two and a half percent referred by medical personnel and health related agencies. Less than one percent were referred by private physicians. Parent referrals were seen as problematical in that they reflected a high per capita cost to the clinic in terms of time and resources, since there were no cooperating agencies to share services.

The sharing of services among agencies was attempted in fifteen percent of the full study cases, which amounted to a case load of nearly two hundred. This was done by setting aside specific consultation hours for social workers and psychiatrists to meet with outside agencies to consult on specific cases. This approach was seen as effectively carrying educational work, that is the dissemination of the ideological perspective of mental hygiene, into these agencies and into the community through diversified authority structures. The argument followed that this dissemination of mental hygiene "equipped the community to meets its whole problem and to get at behavior problems before they became court problems."[56] The success of this approach is cited in the inclusion of a psychiatrist and social workers in the city day nursery and free kindergarten. The nursery psychiatrist also provided testing services for the Jewish Orphan Home. The local hospital and dispensary extended its psychiatric and mental hygiene program in response to the demonstration.[57]

Additional educational work was done through publications, informal lectures and formal courses at Western Reserve University in the School of Applied Social Science and the School of Education. Special efforts were made to provide psychiatric training for local visiting nurses, probation officers, school attendance personnel and supervisory staff operating welfare agencies. Fellows were trained in psychiatry through Commonwealth Fund and Rockefeller Foundation scholarships, and psychiatric social workers were trained in cooperation with Smith College. The permanent clinic was supported by the establishment of the Cleveland Foundation.[58] This clinic was visited by a traveling delegation from Great Britain in 1928 who found it to be the most "typical" of the child guidance facilities surveyed across Canada and the United States.[59]

Changing Clienteles and New Therapeutic Models: Philadelphia

The Philadelphia clinic reflected larger trends in child guidance characteristic of the demonstrations. In that the ultimate goal of the demonstrations was to establish permanent clinical facilities for children, experience proved that success required longer demonstration periods and the establishment of integrated services. The clientele was also directed away from court referred juvenile delinquents, and toward parent referred middle class children. The therapeutic model retained its underlying moralism even as it became more professional.

Philadelphia was an ideal site for a demonstration. There was a long and sophisticated precedent in clinical services including Lightner Witmer's early clinic at the University of Pennsylvania. The Pennsylvania Hospital for Mental Diseases had a history dating back 170 years. There was active mental hygiene work underway in the Children's Aid Society, Public Charities Association of Pennsylvania and the juvenile court. The first juvenile court law of Pennsylvania dated from 1901. A 1904 revision stated that: "juvenile offenders, [that is, dependent, neglected, incorrigible and delinquent children under sixteen], should be wisely controlled, not imprisoned; and the courts' powers, as to children . . . should be distinct from their criminal law powers."[60]

The demonstration clinic opened in March of 1925 with a projected test period of two years. The longer time period was to provide the clinic with enough stability to survive as a permanent organization. The clinic provided services to a variety of social agencies, on one hand, while it experimented with collecting fees from individual clients for the first time. The majority of cases were referred from social agencies, nonetheless, the number of children directly brought in by parents increased over the demonstration period. Parent referrals were again considered to place a heavier burden on the clinic staff due to the absence of a cooperating agency. A screening process was initiated whereby a simple application to the clinic was not sufficient for acceptance as a client.

Parents who could not demonstrate, in an initial interview, their need and willingness to cooperate were discouraged from participating in the clinic's program.[61] Specific arrangements for appointments and fees were arranged prior to the initiation of clinical examinations or therapy. The idea of fees and a more contractual arrangement with clients was new, reflecting the trend toward more cooperative and affluent patients and away from the early involuntary services characteristic of the first clinics.

Even though the number of children referred by parents increased, social agencies remained the single most important referral source. Of 744 cases accepted during the demonstration, close to forty-six percent were from agencies. Of the 362 full study cases, close to forty-nine percent were handled cooperatively with social agencies.[62] This aspect of child guidance, which was first emphasized during the Cleveland program, was expanded in Philadelphia. Slightly over twelve and a half percent of the cases were referred from the public schools and less than three percent came from the juvenile court system.[63] This latter figure was partly attributable to the fact that the court supported its own psychiatrist, and schools were building up independent facilities.

Community educational work was emphasized as a function of the clinic. The fact that parent referrals increased indicates to some extent the success of this campaign. The effort to educate the public in psychiatric explanations of social behavior became increasingly important as a clinical function from the St. Louis Clinic to this last demonstration. Inter-agency cooperation reflected a measure of the success of mental hygienists in placing psychiatry in the curriculum of related mental health fields. Similar training facilitated cooperative therapeutic approaches and was a final step in this elaboration of curriculum. The clinic supported an active program to reach the general public, including public lecture and course work, as well as published articles. A monthly bulletin was published by the Philadelphia Clinic's Board of Directors.

Clinical training of personnel was carried out through fellowships in psychiatry offered by the NCMH. Fellows in psychiatric social work through Smith College were trained at the clinic. The clinic also helped to train students in psychiatry from the University of Pennsylvania. After a period of independent financing to prove its stability, the clinic was accepted as a part of the Welfare Federation in December 1929.[64]

Case records of the Pennsylvania clinic from 1925 to 1945 reveal three separate orientations in the form of therapy and ideological perspective. Attitudes on the part of clinic staff and the therapeutic orientation toward parent-child and especially mother-child relationships changed dramatically over the course of the demonstrations.[65] Most early therapy was directed toward changing the behavior or attitude of the parent or teacher as a means of solving the child's behavior problems. Between 1925 and 1931, the clinical staff at Philadelpia emphasized a "no-nonsense" form of adult oriented "correction and instruction."

In the 1930s this attitude was altered, on one hand, toward a more flexible form of therapeutic manipulation with regard to the parent where "support and reassurance" were emphasized. On the other hand, the child-patient came under greater scrutiny. Disorders of childhood became internalized in the child as a patient/subject. The child came to be seen as a causal factor in his or her own maladjustment. The search for the etiology of mental illness and therapeutic methods for preserving health attitudes and adjusted behavior turned back upon the child.

Interpretations of troubled family relations gradually expanded. Maladaptations were seen as by-products of either psychological malfunctions or genetic factors, as well as environmental conditions which led to mental pathologies. After 1936, the emphasis became more distinctly "psychodynamic," dealing with attitudes and emotional states.[66]

The increasingly sensitive attitude toward the mother's personality and emotional outlook corresponds to the development and spread of psychoanalytic thought as well as developments in child psychiatry. The idea that the mother was a prime suspect in causing later pathological conditions follows from psychoanalytic theory. Changing therapeutic approaches to motherhood reflected developments in the recognition of the children as a psychiatric subject.

The Two Threads of Mental Hygiene: Orthodoxy and Unorthodoxy in California

The focus on children as active participants in their own maladaptations made substantial inroads into the theory and practice of fields which applied mental hygiene had advanced, especially in psychology and education. This occurred in spite of the attempt on the part of orthodox medical men in mental hygiene to bolster the number of trained psychiatrists in child guidance. Increased training in child oriented psychiatry was intended to assure a vital role for direct medical input into clinical services. Nonetheless, two threads of mental hygiene, in a direct medical (psychiatric) versus an indirect (non-medical but medicalized) orientation, took on separate yet characteristic trajectories.

Illustrating the first case of a mental hygiene service with direct medical input, the California child guidance demonstration in Los Angeles was exemplary as a clinical service. The L.A. clinic, in fact, served as a training unit for physicians specializing in community and child oriented psychiatry. Other clinics in the Los Angeles area were less orthodox in their approach. The State of California also attempted to create a statewide mental hygiene service which fell short of the ideal. Financial cutbacks created unintended variations in the model of mental hygiene services which differed significantly from the NCMH's original model. Unorthodox mental hygiene concentrated in school services no longer required a psychiatrist or social worker trained in psychiatry. The California state program illustrates this second thread of mental hygiene which came to utilize a medical paradigm but operated without medically trained personnel.

Orthodoxy in Los Angeles

The Los Angeles clinic was opened in January, 1924 with three psychiatrists, two psychologists and up to six psychiatric social workers, with an additional four social workers in training. The increased staff numbers also reflected strategies learned from the earlier clinics. It was decided to concentrate in this demonstration on carefully selected cases in order to insure a successful demonstration as a model for other clinics and to serve educational functions in the community. Mentally retarded children and those with known mental illness were excluded from clinical service or given brief work ups and "consultative" services. In addition, the clinic only received 10.7 percent of its 300 cases from the juvenile court and only 8 percent from social agencies. The majority of the cases were referred by parents or relatives. This is in contrast to the Minneapolis clinic which received less than half of its clients from parent referrals and twenty percent from the schools. Parent referrals tended to be younger children who scored higher on intelligence tests.[67] Given the class bias of standardized intelligence scales of the period, this is an indication that this self-selected sample tended to represent families with a higher class status.

Parents with higher occupational and educational levels tended to be more interested in and open minded about psychiatric explanations of behavior. They were also more likely to believe in the therapeutic power of medical science to solve behavior and adjustment problems. These families would be more likely to seek consultation and to cooperate with clinical therapy. The trend toward parent referrals altered the original clinical orientation toward lower class, poor and immigrant families. It reflects a practical recognition that what was termed environmental problems, (often in fact economic and political in nature), persistently defied solution by way of the individualistic therapies offered by the clinic staff. The rationale for encouraging this change in client population was that this decision contributed to a preventive approach to problem children. Studying young difficult children who did not have blatant physical or environmental explanations for their emotional and behavioral difficulties was said to advance therapeutic intervention before the child developed problems subject to school or community referral.[68]

The L.A. demonstration was directed by highly qualified and experienced personnel, with Ralph P. Truitt as director, and Christine Leonard as the chief psychiatrist. Los Angeles served as one of the training centers in psychiatry under the NCMH fellowship program. At the successful conclusion of the demonstration, Truitt was made the director of the National Committee Division on the Prevention of Delinquency, and Leonard was transferred to Philadelphia to assist Frederick H. Allen in that demonstration. The NCMH and Commonwealth Fund kept in touch with the clinic. Their reports and memos cite no fault with its operation nor with its personnel and management, and the clinic seemed to avoid problems which had plagued the earlier clinics in their struggle to achieve permanent status.[69]

The regional aspects of expanding services and encouraging psychiatric education was noticeably less successful. Activities in the Los Angeles area in the mid-thirties illustrate the problems and peculiar success of the model of mental hygiene in that it encouraged psychiatric perspectives but not the use of a psychiatrist. The only true child guidance clinic was the Los Angeles Child Guidance Center which had been initiated with the Los Angeles demonstration. In spite of the fact that a number of activities used the title, "child guidance," and spread a popularized psychiatric perspective, there was only one functional clinic with fully qualified personnel after ten years.[70]

Norman Fenton: Mental Hygiene for the Public School

The proliferation of alternative and unorthodox forms of mental hygiene occurred on the state level. The Commonwealth Fund and NCMH staff, in a review and evaluation of mental hygiene activities, expressed concern over the trends. Mental hygiene, as popularized by individuals such as psychologist Norman Fenton, was viewed as not only "superficial" but "dangerous."[71] Nonetheless, Fenton was successful in simplifying and packaging the mental hygiene paradigm over the objections of the NCMH.

Momentum was gained slowly. The California Bureau of Juvenile Research employed a psychiatrist and social worker from 1929 to 1931 in a traveling clinic which worked out of Whittier State School for Boys. With the financial stress of the Depression, the Whittier program was curtailed, and the positions of the psychiatrist and psychiatric social worker were eliminated. Fenton was put in charge of the truncated program, which he moved to Claremont College where he taught summer courses in child guidance to teachers and psychologists.

Fenton's avowed goal was to assist school districts in the establishment of child guidance services at a negligible cost. His guidance program utilized the services of one half-time psychologist aided by teachers and principals. School or private physicians and the psychologist conducted psychiatric examinations. Recommendations based on the results of the tests were carried out by school personnel or relevant community workers such as probation officers.

Fenton's motives for initiating services, which noticeably lacked professionals in psychiatry or a uniform medical approach to problem children, were considered suspect by the NCMH. Commonwealth Fund officers intimated that he was using mental hygiene for personal gain. The proliferation and apparent success of Fenton's program seemed, to the NCMH, to undermine the spirit of scientific child guidance.[72]

Fenton was not deterred by the criticisms of the NCMH nor by their insistence on the dominance of a psychiatrist in a position of leadership in clinical practices. Such criticisms also did not seem to inhibit Fenton's popularized economical version of child guidance from catching on. In fact, it was a simplified model of mental hygiene services which came to dominate school practices. Psychologists and relatively untrained personnel commonly carry out mental hygiene programs in school settings.

After serving as director of the Bureau of Juvenile Research, Fenton became a professor of education at Stanford University. He published a textbook, *Mental Hygiene in School Practice*, in 1943.[73] Illustrating the popularity of this book is the fact that it was in its sixth printing in 1949.[74]

Fenton built his career on popularizing systematic methods for implementing child guidance in schools. His work was directed toward classroom teachers, school administrators and laymen. As the jacket cover of his text advertises, "send for our catalog of tests and guidance materials" and acquire a complete package "capable of implementing a mental hygiene program in your community." Fenton relied on psychological and educational test batteries such as the Stanford Revision of the Binet-Simon Intelligence Scale. Sample forms and blanks were provided in the appendix, and a second appendix provided hints and categories for classifying children. For an additional fifty cents, those interested could acquire Fenton's school case work manuals, "The Counselor's Approach to the Home," and "The Counselor's Interviews with the Student."[75]

Fenton also helped popularize the notion that mental hygiene could not only be utilized inexpensively but that it was essential for social progress.[76] Fenton argued that mental hygiene contributed to "education, recreation, social security, standards of health, labor, housing and medical care" on a state and national level. It was to contribute to "international morale" and "powerful co-operation for peace and human welfare."[77] Fenton disassociated mental hygiene from delinquency. "Over a period of years this may result," he asserted, but mental hygiene would [better] be described as useful for the improvement of the happiness and effectiveness of all children."[78]

The most serious problem Fenton foresaw in his model of mental hygiene was in the potential personality difficulties and maladjustments in school personnel. Teachers were especially singled out as problematic. Maladjusted teachers presented a serious concern since Fenton's program relied heavily on the teaching staff. Principals as a "parent person" were suggested as possible alternatives.[79] Very similar concerns were expressed by Lewis Terman in his 1913 work, *The Teacher's Health*.[80] Fenton's arguments and programs were especially compatible with, and mutually supported, Terman's professionalization of school psychology (over psychiatry) and the role of standardized evaluation procedures.

Mental Hygiene: A Euphemism for the Field of Child Psychiatry

Even considering the various problems with the demonstrations between 1922 and 1927, the number of child guidance clinics rapidly expended with the Commonwealth program.[81] Only ten clinics opened between the end of World War I and the launching of the Division of the Prevention of Delinquency in 1921. After the creation of the Division, the number of clinics jumped to 72 by 1926 and to 102 by the end of the demonstration period in 1927. In 1930, 500 permanent community clinics were in operation. This figure stood at 617 in 1935 when the first textbook on child psychiatry was published in the United States.[82]

The field of child guidance started as an "excursion of psychiatry into the problems of delinquency."[83] Delinquency was abandoned as a primary focus in favor of a more general fusion of clinical services with a broad connotation of behavior problems. By 1930, the White House Conference on Child Health and Protection declared childhood as "the golden period for mental hygiene."[84]

David M. Levy, in the 1947 Thomas W. Salmon Memorial Lecture at the New York Academy of Medicine, observed that:

> the field of behavior problems actually became a kind of euphemistic name for the entire field of child psychiatry, for in the child-guidance clinic or institute, every variety of neurosis or psychosis, of mental aberration or disease, may be accepted for treatment, as well as so-called "primary" behavior problems.[85]

The establishment of mental hygiene clinics contributed to the medicalization of childhood. They served to disseminate psychiatric perspectives and language into popular culture as well as into contemporary social services directed toward children.

Chapter Eight

The Boundaries of Adjustment: From the Clinic to the Classroom

The challenge of mental hygiene was from the onset preventive rather than remedial. The search for causality led the National Committee for Mental Hygiene, the Commonwealth Fund, and Rockefeller philanthropy to look first at juvenile delinquency and subsequently to concentrate on "predelinquent" behavior. Another alternative was to examine the process of adjustment rather than maladjustment and to seek a better understanding of the dynamics of health rather than the pathology of illness.

This approach became a major focus of the Rockefeller Foundation. The Foundation was predisposed to view mental hygiene as the ultimate objective in preventive medicine.[1] It took a number of years, however, to focus on the study of normal mental processes in clinical observations and scientific research. The promotion of maternal and child welfare was an original preoccupation of the Laura Spelman Rockefeller Memorial, established in 1918. However, the broader related perspective in Rockefeller policy in preventive psychiatry was solidified in a demonstration project in Monmouth County, New Jersey. It was subsequently elaborated in Canada in child study research at the University of Toronto.

The Monmouth County Demonstration

Similar to the Program on the Prevention of Delinquency, the Monmouth County demonstration was an outgrowth of the Rockefeller Foundation Gedney Farms Conference of 1920 and the Commonwealth Fund Lakewood Conference of 1921. The demonstration was a turning point in the establishment of the program protocols which guided inter-War child development projects. At each of these conferences, Thomas Salmon put forth his proposals for the prevention of delinquency as the key to the prevention of a variety of social problems from crime and dependency to immorality and insanity. The Commonwealth Fund subsequently undertook a series of projects directed toward the prevention of delinquency based on Salmon's suggestions. However, the first demonstration of Salmon's ideas concerning the prevention of mental and behavioral disorders in childhood was not supported by Commonwealth Fund money. It was supported by the Rockefeller Foundation. This project in Monmouth County, New Jersey is significant because it is a link between child guidance in the United States, the Rockefeller Foundation's independent support of mental hygiene, and the extensive parent education and child development research projects initiated by the Laura Spelman Rockefeller Memorial in the mid-1920s in Canada and the United States.

The Monmouth County Demonstration was the first experimental project carried out by the National Committee for Mental Hygiene on the prevention of delinquency. It was initiated by a local voluntary association, the Monmouth County Organization for Social Service, which had been in existence for ten years. The leaders of the Monmouth County Organization constructed a proposal with Salmon in the early summer of 1921.[2] Geraldine Thompson, the president of the group, had approached Walter B. James of the NCMH concerning the development of a program to investigate the number of retarded children in the schools of the county.[3] James directed the inquiry to Salmon, who "was very much interested," recalled Mrs. Thompson. He "said that the whole question of mental retardation and the problem of unadjusted children was an integral part of the problem of juvenile delinquency." The final proposal, which was approved by the LSRM Board on the seventh of October 1921, reflected a vision of community and school based preventive work with children.[4]

The LSRM, with Salmon's urging, agreed to a five year demonstration. Twelve thousand dollars a year for two years was appropriated with work to begin in January of 1921 with a reevaluation in late 1923.[5] The Monmouth County project was compatible with the ideologies of both the Commonwealth Fund and Rockefeller philanthropies to the extent that they reflected Salmon's version of extramural psychiatry.

The project did not go smoothly, however. The authority structure for the project became confused partly due to changes in personnel, and partly due to internal contradictions in the philosophy methods, and objectives of the promoters of the project.[6] Salmon resigned from the NCMH to accept a position in psychiatry at Columbia University Medical School shortly after the program was set up. He relinquished management of the demonstration to his former assistant, psychiatrist V. V. Anderson. The Commonwealth Fund also acquired a new director, Barry C. Smith. Smith assumed that the Monmouth County demonstration was to proceed solely within the Program for the Prevention of Delinquency. He conceived of the Monmouth County demonstrations as formally a Commonwealth Fund project distinguished only by the fact that funds were provided by the LSRM. Smith concluded that the project was primarily responsible to himself and the National Committee's staff.[7] Lawrence Frank, as officer of the LSRM, was open to the idea of experimenting with collaborative efforts among philanthropies. Yet, he actively took an interest in the progress of the work and was regarded as an authority by the Monmouth County Organization leadership.

In January of 1922, a mobile clinic serving rural public schools was organized with a prototypical mental hygiene team consisting of a psychiatrist, psychologist and a social worker. The first undertaking was a survey which conducted physical and mental examinations of the school population of twenty-three thousand children. The survey combined clinical pathology in a medical tradition and psychology in the philosophical tradition in that it was intended to

> disclose the presence or absence of mental abnormality, tap the emotional life of the individual, . . . discover pathological personality, . . . excavate for mental conflict, analyze mental content . . . and get a picture of the child as a whole . . . living adjusting personality.[8]

The survey concluded that ten percent of the children exhibited "well defined mental or nervous disorders." Another ten percent showed "conduct disorders or tendencies toward criminal careers."[9] In the first school, only one quarter of the children were found to be normal, and half were found to be mentally abnormal or retarded.[10] In the spring of 1923 a permanent clinic was opened and later subclinics were established for infants from nine months, to children and young adults up to nineteen years of age. These clients were labeled variously as "difficult, maladjusted, predelinquent or delinquent."

The LSRM and the Commonwealth Fund officials pursued independent evaluations of the project's progress. Fundamental disagreements surfaced at a conference attended by top personnel from the NCMH, LSRM and Commonwealth Fund.[11] The most serious disagreements existed between the Monmouth County Organization and the Commonwealth Fund and National Committee executives concerning the structure of the work. Monmouth County officers felt that the original concept of preventive community based services was not being developed.[12]

The original proposal emphasized educational work extending into the community. The traveling psychopathic clinic under Anderson concentrated on testing and evaluating on a case by case basis in a way which tended to emphasize pathology. When confronted with accusations of conducting an esoteric and specialized study which did not have general community impact, Anderson attributed these failings to inadequate funding. With the apparent backing of the NCMH, the Commonwealth Fund requested that the Monmouth County Organization require the LSRM to double the budget of the service. Further stipulations required less local control over personnel, equipment, and facilities.[13]

The Board of the Monmouth County Organization, after consultation with Lawrence Frank where they were assured that funds would not necessarily be discontinued, decided to reject the National Committee's requests.[14] The NCMH was asked to withdraw its services, severing the project's tie with the Commonwealth Fund/NCMH Program on the Prevention of Delinquency.[15]

A revised program, based on a preventive theme, was established which was no longer concerned with research on psychopathological conditions. The revised project was predominantly concerned with parent education and training.[16] Monmouth County mental hygiene projects proceeded to pioneer studies on normal child development and parent education which characterized the work of the LSRM for the rest of the decade. Child guidance, as it contributed to child psychiatry, was severed from what was to become scientific child study with its concentration on early childhood education, clinical and community based reserach on normal development.

The Monmouth County demonstration crystallized the mental hygiene format for both child guidance and child development. It is especially linked with the mental hygiene in child study with its built in educational element. This was critical to the orientation of research at the University of Toronto to which the Rockefeller Foundation, General Education Board, and the LSRM contributed support from 1924 to 1939.

The Psychology of the Normal Child in Canadian Mental Hygiene

In the United States child psychiatry was an outgrowth of preventive efforts with wayward youth in child guidance. This was not the case in Canada, except to a minor extent in Montreal. The major contribution of mental hygiene in Canada between 1920 and 1940 was not the advance of child psychiatry. It is significant that the discipline which was pushed forward during this period was child psychology and that this avenue of research and popular press was directed not toward the pathological child but the normal child. Building and preserving well-adjusted children was a new object of research. This was especially the case at the University of Toronto under the direction of E. A. Bott and William Emet Blatz.

Academic psychology and mental hygiene went hand in hand in Canada. As an academic and applied discipline, Canadian psychology had a slow evolution. The first course in psychology was taught under the auspices of philosophy in 1843 at Toronto. James Mark Baldwin, American pioneer in psychology, introduced scientific psychology when he occupied a chair at the University of Toronto from 1889 to 1893. Baldwin was one of the twenty-six founding members of the American Psychological Association organized by G. Stanley Hall in 1892. In 1893, Baldwin left Toronto for Princeton to initiate the first clinical laboratory at that institution. He published, *Mental Development in the Child and the Race*, in 1895. He went on to Johns Hopkins in 1903.

In spite of a contemporaneous beginning with U.S. psychology, psychology in Canada has only separated itself from departments of philosophy in the majority of Canadian universities since the 1950s.[17] While historically the association of philosophy and psychology was not unique, the differentiation was made much more clearly from the 1880s and 1890s in the United States through the sustained influence of men with a research orientation. The emergent American university with its emphasis on diversified scientific curriculum greatly aided this development.[18]

The emancipation of psychology in Canada was directly connected with the work of Canadian mental hygienists. Baldwin's laboratory did not survive his departure, but the clinical tradition was renewed at the University of Toronto in 1914 by E. A. Bott. Bott conducted an experimental rehabilitation center for soldiers in 1916 which attracted the attention and support of University of Toronto President Sir Robert Falconer.[19]

Bott was a founding member of the Canadian National Committee for Mental Hygiene. His laboratory received official recognition by the university administration under the auspices of C. K. Clarke in 1919, and the department of psychology was formally established in 1920 with E. A. Bott as head. It was the first department of psychology which was separate from philosophy in Canada.[20] Bott was the head of the psychology department at Toronto for the next thirty-seven years, and was affiliated with every major mental hygiene activity which operated out of the University of Toronto until 1957. He was instrumental in establishing the Canadian Psychological Association as independent from the American Psychological Association in 1939. He has been acknowledged as the dean of Canadian psychology.[21]

It was the unique contribution of Bott's department to child psychology which shaped the most well known work of the Canadian mental hygiene movement after 1924.[22] Canadian mental hygiene received international recognition for its contribution to longitudinal research on the development of normal children. While the University of Toronto and

McGill were the two leading institutions in this area in Canada, Toronto was especially noted for studies in normal child psychology.

At the first meeting of the Executive Board of the CNCMH in 1919, a gift of five thousand dollars from Lady Eaton was announced with the stipulation that: "one thousand should be utilized for work in industrial psychology." A subcommittee was formed on educational and industrial psychology whose members included: Lady Eaton, professor J. A. Dale, E. A. Bott, C. D. Clarke, C. M. Hincks, professor J. R. MacLeod, and Mr. Norman Burnette. Professors H. E. T. Haultain, C. B. Sissons, J. R. MacLeod, R. M. McIver and J. G. Fitzgerald became ex-officio members of this group. Dale, one of the first professors of social science at Toronto, was made chair and Hincks acted as secretary.[23]

E. A. Bott agreed to undertake a study and to outline a program for useful research.[24] Bott was interested in the percentage of retarded children among those who left Toronto public schools to go to work, and was especially interested in children under the age of sixteen years. He investigated the history of the first two years of the child's industrial life.

In a survey conducted along these lines, Bott found that eighteen percent of the total school enrollment left school early. These children exhibited an average range of intelligence. Seventy percent were under the age of fourteen and a half and ninety percent were under the age of fifteen and a half. Forty-five percent of children leaving school did not get beyond the senior third grade, which was not sufficient to serve their practical needs in Canadian society. Nearly sixty percent had repeated grades. There was no provision in the Toronto schools to give such children systematic guidance. The children who left school for jobs had unstable work careers, the majority changed their position once or more during their first year of employment. They tended to end up working in factories or shops.[25]

Bott's findings marked an innovation in the thinking of the Canadian National Committee. Previously they had been overwhelmingly concerned with "attempting to solve the problems of abnormality." This study implied a similar lesson to the Canadian Committee as Healy's study of the juvenile courts had for the U.S. Committee in the perception that behavior problems could not be attributed to mental retardation. Bott took his findings one step further. Like Salmon, he saw the need to step in and take preventive measures before the child exhibited signs of maladjustment. Bott refocussed his version of mental hygiene in industrial and educational psychology toward the prevention of maladjustment in the normal child. The subcommittee concluded:

> While the accomplishments of the Committee have been considerable in the past, nevertheless activities have been somewhat hampered because of

> a prevalent opinion that our interests are centered wholly in the feeble-minded and insane. While there is not real justification for such an attitude, nevertheless it seems necessary to safeguard our future by laying emphasis on such work as is contemplated by the Department of Educational and Industrial Psychology. If proposed activities are put into effect there can be little doubt that the Committee will be performing a much greater national service than has been the case in the past.[26]

The main body of the work as envisioned by the committee on education and industrial psychology was to work directly with the public schools in providing psychometric testing, modernizing promotion and grading, and initiating vocational guidance as a means to "bridge the gap between school and industry."[27]

Rockefeller Foundation Support For a Mental Hygiene of School Age Children

In the year 1923, the Canadian Committee faced a severe financial crisis. Clarence Hincks, who had assumed the position of medical director after C. K. Clarke's death, approached the Rockefeller Foundation for support. On trips to New York, Hincks struck up a relationship with Edwin Embree, secretary of the Rockefeller Foundation.[28] This friendship became quite close and personal as time went on since they had a similar philosophical and ideological orientation. Their families were also drawn together as summer neighbors with houses in the same Muskoka region of Ontario. Embree shared Hincks' long standing interest in deviant groups and the possibilities of mental hygiene.[29]

In February of 1924, Hincks wrote Embree to follow-up a conversation they had in New York. He inquired about the possibility of securing a grant for the CNCMH from the Rockefeller Foundation. Hincks wrote a proposal which outlined an experimental demonstration in a mental hygiene program for public school children.[30] At a subsequent meeting of the Board, the Foundation considered the proposal favorably.

The feeling was that the NCMH in the United States had continued to pursue work with children in schools, but it was limited to "delinquency rather than the general school problems of mental hygiene." It was deemed beneficial to "obtain the experience of different groups in different nations." The Foundation decided that it would be interested in pursuing such demonstrations for a sum somewhere between fifty and seventy-five thousand dollars at the rate of fifteen thousand dollar annual installments.[31] The news was eagerly passed along to Hincks.[32]

Hincks also pursued Rockefeller philanthropy by contacting Beardsley Ruml, director of the LSRM. In casual conversations, Hincks introduced the importance of the social aspects of mental hygiene with normal children. Ruml suggested pursuing this subject with Lawrence Frank. Encouraged by the interest, Hincks reshaped his proposal along the lines of parent education. He outlined "an attractive program of mental hygiene information to mothers of Canada who have problems in their own home," as well as school problems.[33] Embree encouraged Hincks to pursue the Foundation on multiple fronts. "By all means make such contacts as you can, either officially or personally with the officers of that organization."[34] In April, Hincks submitted an official proposal to the LSRM for a mental hygiene study of school children in Toronto with similar support for Montreal. Through Richard Pearce, Hincks also hoped to acquire five travelling scholarships from the Medical Division of the Rockefeller Foundation for Canadians to study psychiatry abroad.[35]

On May 27, 1924, the Foundation Board of Directors voted to "make possible studies of the application of mental hygiene to the school system" in Canada. The sum of seventy-five thousand dollars was subsequently appropriated for a five year period to begin July 1, 1924. The sum was to be distributed at the rate of fifteen thousand dollars a year provided that contributions from Canadian sources at least equalled the Foundation pledge.[36] The Canadian press announced the gift shortly thereafter and letters of congratulations from dignitaries and men of prominence and wealth in Canada flooded Hincks' office. Hincks and Embree shared their enthusiasm for the upcoming projects.[37] Hincks observed to the CNCMH members that:

> Before discussing a tentative plan for the conduct of child studies, the Executive Committee should be informed of the interest of the Laura Spelman Rockefeller Memorial in our Canadian work. There is a likelihood of our Committee receiving $20,000 per annum, or some such amount, from the Memorial for our studies of children of pre-school age and for the inauguration of plans for parent training in mental hygiene. This interest of the Laura Spelman Rockefeller Memorial might well be kept in mind in formulating a policy in dealing with the Rockefeller grant, because the administration of monies coming from both sources might well be unified.[38]

The members present followed Hincks advice in resolving to find mutual interests between their own goals and the expressed interest of the Rockefeller Foundation. They especially hoped to advance the two largest population centers in Canada, Montreal and Toronto. Subcommittees for "Studies in the Application of Mental Hygiene to Children," were created toward this goal for each city.[39]

Within a year of the Rockefeller Foundation appropriation to the Canadian National Committee, the Department of Mental Hygiene

Research in Toronto was established in affiliation with the University of Toronto.[40] The Department was charged with applying mental hygiene principles to children in school attendance with the expressed intention of "preventing mental and emotional disorders."[41] Dr. J. G. Fitzgerald was made chairman with committee members to include President Sir Robert Falconer; Hon. Dr. H. J. Cody, chairman of the Board of Governors of the University; Mr. C. B. McNaught; Mr. Vincent Massey; Mr. Hugh Kerr; professors Peter Sandiford, R. S. Brett, and E. A. Bott. Clarence Hincks. E. A. Bott, W. E. Blatz and E. D. MacPhee of the psychology department were to act as research directors.[42] The budget was to be provided by the Rockefeller Foundation with matching funds secured through the Lady Byng of Vimy Fund.

A similar Department of Research was established in Montreal. The McGill affiliated group was to focus on the "prevention and control of juvenile delinquency and to the organization of a demonstration mental hygiene clinic." The Division was to grant assistance and vital statistics to the courts, reform schools, probation organizations. The executive committee was to consist of Sir Edward W. Beatty, president of the Canadian Pacific Railway as chair; Sir Arthur Currie, president of McGill University; medical doctors interested in psychiatry, C. F. Martin, C. K. Russel, G. S. Mundi, A. B. Chandler and Clarence Hincks. The research directors were professors J. W. Bridges and Dr. W. T. B. Mitchell.[43]

Shortly after work under the Rockefeller Foundation grant was begun in 1924, successful negotiations were completed between the University of Toronto, McGill University and the CNCMH with the Laura Spelman Rockefeller Memorial. The Memorial agreed to provide one hundred thousand dollars annually toward the establishment of two university based laboratory nursery schools. The grant had three objectives: 1) the intensive study of preschool children; 2) a demonstration in parent training; and 3) the establishment of standards for child directed services in public agencies.[44] The funds from the LSRM at the rate of fifty thousand dollars per annum to each university were to be matched by Toronto and McGill. The CNCMH was to provide administrative support.

Five fellowships from the Rockefeller Foundation and two additional awards from Lawrence K. Frank of the LSRM were also secured. Two of the fellowships sent teachers to study child development in the United States at Columbia University.[45]

William Emet Blatz and Child Study at the University of Toronto

The project on child study at the University of Toronto was greatly influenced by its director, William Emet Blatz. Blatz acquired his bachelors and masters degree from the University of Toronto, in 1916 and 1917, where he worked with Bott on his rehabilitation program with soldiers. He went on to achieve a medical degree, in 1921, before taking a fellowship in psychology at the University of Chicago where he studied under the champion of functionalist psychology, James R. Angell's student, Harvey A. Carr.[46] A position for Blatz was made possible by the Rockefeller Foundation through a matching grant. The position as director of the Centre for Child Study was combined with a half-time appointment in the department of psychology.[47]

The Regal Road School Project

The first demonstration in Toronto was the Regal Road School Project. Permission was granted in October of 1924 by the Toronto Board of Education to allow the Toronto Research Department of the CNCMH access to the public schools.[48] Regal Road was an experimental public school of 1,400 children. The objectives of the research were to make a longitudinal study of conduct deviations and adjustment of school children, primarily by way of observation; and to work out, through a testing program, the classification of the causes and possible treatment for maladjustments. Treatment included the reorganization of promotion and also "reeducation" with individual cases to incorporate parental practices as well as school practices. The Regal Road Project was supervised by W. E. Blatz in association with E. D. MacPhee, and later with William Line, both of whom remained active in the mental hygiene movement in Canada.[49]

The first avenue of research at Regal Road was to give standardized test batteries. In cooperation with the school's principal, Mr. Richardson, E. D. McPhee experimented with homogeneous groupings by ability according to the test results. The school was put on a tracked promotion system which utilized a classification of children into slow, average or fast moving groups. A control group of a heterogeneous mix of slow to bright children was used to evaluate the effectiveness of this method of insuring proper school adjustment by proper placement. Bright children were also studied separately where they were allowed to skip grades and advance more quickly in some cases.[50] The argument was advanced that maladjustment and behavior problems in school were due to poor classification. Children who continued to exhibit problem behavior were followed up on a home basis. Hincks surmised that:

> upwards of 25 percent of mental and nervous disorders are caused or accentuated by unsatisfactory home and school methods that are now in vogue in child rearing. It is possible that Canada will assume a degree of world leadership in fighting mental abnormality as a result of research studies.[51]

Unlike Clarke's earlier surveys, Blatz attempted therapeutic interventions as well as the compilation of statistics. The behavior studies for example, included a listing of all misdemeanors emergent in a school setting. The figures were listed by grade and years with approximately eleven thousand misdemeanors cited for 1926–27, ten thousand for 1927–28, and nine thousand for 1928–29. Individual cases were selected from the survey lists and studied independently. Between the school years of 1925–26 and 1929–30, close to eight hundred such special cases were reviewed.[52]

A typical and easily solved case included an eleven year old boy who vomited and had crying fits after meals, resulting in poor school attendance. The parents were instructed to ignore the attacks and to encourage recreational activities. Soon after, the child was reported recovered.[53]

Other cases were not so simply adjusted. One girl was first reported in 1925 for disobedience and writing notes in class. The next year she was reported for lying, stealing and truancy at school. She was later caught stealing at Eaton's department store. Soon after, she began to stay out all night. The following year she failed the first course in the High School of Commerce. She was eventually brought before the juvenile court for immorality and placed in a correctional lodge. After running away from the lodge she was again caught stealing and sent to a reformatory. After two years in the reformatory, a position was found for her by Blatz working for ten cents an hour. Blatz and his researchers provided supervision consisting mostly of surveillance over her activities.[54]

Parent Education at St. George's School

The LSRM trustees were especially interested in parent training. To acquire additional support for this aspect of the nursery school project, Mr. A. F. C. Fiske, third vice president of Metropolitan Life Insurance Company, was approached. Fiske was able to procure from Metropolitan Life a grant of two thousand dollars toward a parent education project affiliated with the nursery school. The understanding was that, if "a satisfactory program of parent training" was devised. Metropolitan Life would be forthcoming with increasingly large appropriations on an annual basis. The project devised ways to "make direct contact with fathers and mothers," as well as children.[55]

The St. George's School for Child Study opened in January of 1925. It operated in cooperation with the Toronto Department of Health, the dental services and nursing services of the public schools of Toronto, as well as the psychology department, and schools of public hygiene and medicine at the University. St. George's was organized in two divisions to correspond to its related but dual mandate. The nursery school division, established in January, was followed the next November by the parent education division.

Blatz supervised child study research at the Centre, supported by his colleagues in psychology. E. A. Bott provided administrative assistance in practical affairs and took an active part in designing the play equipment. Helen Bott, his wife, played a significant role in research and in the scholarly work of the parent education division of the nursery school.[56]

Between 1926 and 1938, the two divisions of the nursery school and parent education worked in tandem. Within the first three months of its existence the parent education division enrolled sixty parents. This is not surprising since parents of the children enrolled in the school were required to attend parent classes. Blatz introduced a longitudinal element into the project by having parents register their children for the nursery school at birth so that the children could be observed from infancy. The children were followed regularly after they left the preschool until they were ten years old. Blatz did not attempt to recruit from the middle and lower classes; the children who participated in this program serve as a record of the most prominent families in Toronto society.

The popularity and prestige of the program was furthered by the exclusive clientele and Blatz's recruitment of prominent parents as advocates. Unlike other pioneer mental hygiene efforts in Canada, where trained workers were often imported from the United States or received European training, Blatz utilized and expanded a local constituency. One reason for the success and longevity of the program in its particular form was Blatz's success in inspiring dedication, loyalty, and a team spirit among his students and volunteers.[57] This cohesive quality also had negative aspects. The family-like circle of Blatz and his followers was also grounded in a dogmatic adherence to Blatz's theory of child rearing.[58]

Instructional books for parent education were produced in the first four years of the program by Blatz and Helen Bott.[59] There was very little time lag in general between the clinical studies produced by Blatz and his students and publicizing their content. An in-house quarterly journal, the *Parent Education Bulletin*, produced papers from scientific journals such as the *Genetic Psychology Monographs* and *Journal of Genetic Psychology* as well as Child Centre research. In 1933, the University of Toronto Press established a special Child Development Series, the first edition of which was edited by Helen Bott.

In the 1930s, the productivity of Blatz and his team won recognition throughout North America, a factor which greatly helped surviving the otherwise lean years of the Depression. In the early 1930s, Blatz became the director of Windy Ridge Day School for children aged two to eight. He applied his preschool ideas to primary grades emphasizing attitude formation and moral development in the older children. As his popularity grew, Blatz lectured widely in Canada and the United States. He extended his audience to medical students through a seminar for graduates in psychiatry. He also conducted outpatient demonstrations at a psychiatric hospital which trained medical students.[60]

International publicity was acquired through Blatz's work with the Dionne quintuplets in 1934. For two years, from the time the girls were eighteen months to four years, Blatz planned and directed the daily routine and play opportunities of the children with the approval of their medical management committee, caretakers and nurses. In 1937 and 1938, a collection of the studies on the training program was published as part of the Child Development Series.[61]

Partly due to the collaboration across the University on the Dionne quintuplets, Blatz was able to persuade the administration of the advantage of making the Child Study Centre into an Institute for Child Study. The Institute, which was approved, opened in 1938. It was the first such institute at the University of Toronto. Blatz and his colleagues were well on the way to evolving their own distinctive version of the promotion of mental health in normal children.

Security Theory

Blatz believed that the promotion of mental health should be primarily the outcome of parents and educators working together. His goal was the promotion of "security." Blatzian security was not a static state of safety but a state of mind characterized by serenity, meaning a faith in ones own ability to successfully deal with future events. The key to educating children was to teach them to accept the consequences of their own actions, which he argued was acquired in early experience. First, security dependent on caretakers, built habits of bravery, curiosity and self-esteem. Secondly, the child's sense of independent responsibility was acquired by extending the freedom to make independent decisions and to abide by the consequences of those decisions. Coping with one's own successes and failures were the essence of healthy mental development, according to Blatz.

Blatz's theories reflected his training at Chicago. Blatz, as did Chicago psychologists, Harvey Carr and James R. Angell, championed functionalist psychology as opposed to structuralism or behaviorism. Functionalist psychology at Chicago was influenced by Darwinist theories. Human behavior was correlated with the adaptation of mental states where practical habits of conduct, as biological actions, also reflected emotional patterns. These patterns were said to become ingrained because they were successful in achieving useful ends for the individual. One objective of functionalist research was to elaborate individual variations along every conceivable psychological dimension. Functionalists stressed the testing of human differences and the application of the information gained to educational practices. Most contemporary applied psychology has a functionalist component.[62]

James R. Angell's orientation toward psychology corresponded, in many ways, to the program Blatz developed for child rearing. Angell underscored, as did Blatz, the "problem of intelligence, with special reference to the history of instinct and emotion." He felt that self-control "may be regarded as the basic category of consciousness." Angell, used a concept similar to Adolf Meyer's psychobiology where he emphasized the "psychophysical" aspects of human action which viewed the body-mind continuum as a reciprocal relationship concerned with "the process of habit."[63] Blatz substantively continued along these lines of thought in his own development. Blatz elaborated a perspective which combined a Canadian vision of democratic government which depended on parent education and child training as a keystone of democratic social structure.[64] Blatz's concern in the socialization process was with the development of willful control and conscious thought as opposed to unconscious mental processes or simple habits.[65] His approach distinctly opposed psychoanalytic theory.

Blatz was equally alienated from behaviorist perspectives. Most noticeably he shunned reward systems as undermining self-control. As opposed to functionalism, behavioristic psychology emphasized the manipulation of the environment, rather than mental habits, in order to change behavior. Overt actions became the focus of attention because of their observable and measurable quality. Animal studies were often considered as informative as research on human subjects. While the extremely reductionist argument of behaviorist B. F. Skinner appears diametrically opposed to psychoanalysis, behaviorism and psychoanalysis have fundamental, theoretical points of convergence as opposite sides of a similar argument even where they diverge as therapeutic models. Behaviorism became increasingly influential in the U.S. after 1920. However, neither behaviorism nor psychoanalysis enjoyed such popularity in Canada. Blatz, in opposition to behavioral models, was concerned with the acquisition of human dignity, not a psychology which would move mankind beyond human dignity as in Skinner's thesis.[66]

Blatz's functionalism was also distinct from structuralism. Structuralism was originally derived from Wilhelm Wundt's work brought to the U.S. by Edward B. Titchner. Early structuralism placed an emphasis on laboratory studies of the mind and consciousness using introspective techniques. Just as Blatz disregarded unconscious processes, he opposed introspective methods in the study of human behavior. This introspective form of structuralism was also in disrepute by the 1920s in the United States. A new structuralism combined with functionalism was popularized in the 1930s which emphasized stages of development and cognition as in Arnold Gesell's and Jean Piaget's theories. Blatz's ideas became more dynamic in this way as his research continued and as he developed his "security theory."

However, Blatz's view of mental hygiene involved child guidance and training rather than the uncovering and understanding of innate unfolding stages. Blatz remained distinct in his approach to structural functionalism. The purpose in parent training was not to have parents understand to advantage the developmental stage their child was going through, but to train the parent to manipulate their child's development toward the desired goal of serenity as the ultimate life goal of all living things, according to Blatz. Education was directed toward fostering the acceptance of the consequences of one's own acts. In this way, all education in a Blatzian perspective was ultimately directed toward the attainment of mental health.[67]

Blatz attracted and trained a number of graduate students who went on to dominate child study research in Canada. For example, one of the first to publish was Mary Salter (Ainsworth), who constructed for her doctoral thesis (1940) a self-reporting scale to access the security level of young adults, as opposed to defensive behaviors (insecurity). Much of this research was disseminated through the University of Toronto Press.[68] Other important students and colleagues include Mary Northway, Dorothy Millichamp, S. N. F. Chant, S. R. Laycock, William Line and John D. Griffin.

Disseminating Toronto Child Study

The outbreak of war in 1939 interrupted the advance of clinical research at Toronto, but it contributed to the dissemination of Blatzian theory.[69] In times of full mobilization, a substantial majority of the children were in need of day care facilities and there was a great shortage of trained personnel to staff these facilities. The spread of Blatz's work was facilitated by the need for child care in Britain during the War. Blatz produced his first wartime book in 1940.[70]

Early in the War E. A. Bott consulted with Sir Wilson Jameson, chief medical officer to the Ministry of Health and Board of Education of England and Wales on the problem of child care in Britain. After soliciting the help of President Cody of the University of Toronto and Vincent Massey, Canadian High Commissioner to Britain, the CNCMH was brought in to devise a means of Canadian assistance. Blatz, Hincks, and Stewart Jaffery, of the department of social work of the University of

Toronto, visited Britain in the fall of 1941. Hincks organized the Canadian Children's Service in 1942 which sent three groups of workers to Britain. The first group was composed of elementary school teachers who filled vacancies on the staff of London County Council Schools. The second group consisted of social workers who acted as receptionists in areas where children were evacuated from the inner city. Blatz was in charge of the third and most critically needed group to train nursery child care reservists for the day care facilities.[71]

Blatz established a training school in Birmingham for child care workers in day nurseries, nursery schools and infant schools. Blatz had stressed, in the 1941 visit, the dangers of using untrained teachers with young children. In July of 1942, Garrison Lane Nursery opened in a core area of Birmingham. With assistants from the Toronto Institute, Blatz took forty-two children aged two to five years of age and trained forty student child care reservists. Blatz's teachers were senior members of the Institute of Child Study including: Dorothy Millichamp, Margaret Fletcher, Mary McFarland (Smith), Mary Wright, and Anne Harris (Blatz).[72] Garrison Lane was a full day adaptation of the shorter length preschool program at the University of Toronto. The trainees were taught Institute theory and methods. By the end of the summer the program was well established and Blatz and three of the senior staff returned to Canada. A second contingent from Canada arrived in late August.

Garrison Lane functioned until 1944. A 1944 monograph was directed toward disseminating Institute theory and method throughout Britain, and was reprinted in Canada and the United States.[73]

Blatz's long term contribution to British education is difficult to assess. However, associates maintain that there is good reason to believe that his impact was substantial.[74] Significantly, Blatz's ideas on early childhood education were widely disseminated in Britain during the War years on a variety of levels. Blatz and his followers also set up strong mechanisms for their continuance. For example, Garrison Lane offered week length classes in administration as well as child care training. These classes were fully enrolled, and visits from other public officials were a daily occurrence at the school.[75] Blatz also achieved personal recognition as an authority on early childhood education and was in demand as a lecturer where he was often presented along with other notables such as Anna Freud.[76] It has been noted that the informal early childhood education offered in British nursery classes and schools since the Plowden Report of 1967 have much in common with the type of education promoted by Blatz.[77] Lillian Weber, an American professor of early childhood education at New York's City College, was struck with the similarities between the demonstration and laboratory nursery schools in the United States and British infant schools.

She conducted a survey of fifty-six British schools. In her exhaustive descriptions she noted that educators in these schools often used terminology characteristic of Blatzian views of education, such as "serenity" as an educational goal.[78] Joseph Featherstone, a contributing editor to the magazine, *The New Republic*, and a professor at Harvard, wrote three articles in 1967 describing the post World War II revolution in infant schools in Britain.[79] Lillian Weber and others like her adapted these ideas into a U.S. context.[80] Blatz's contributions to educational theory and practice may have, in the long term, been indirect by way of his contribution to early childhood education in Britain and its subsequent influence on the international open education movement of the 1960s and 1970s.

Although Blatz's contribution may have been subtle in the long term, his influence on nursery education in Canada was decisive. His authority in Ontario was straightforward. By the fall of 1942 there was a growing need in Canada, as there was in Britain, for child care facilities and wartime nurseries. The Welfare Council of Toronto argued that children were left without adequate care when mothers were recruited for essential War work. The provincial and federal government were petitioned for help.[81] In July, a cost sharing agreement was worked out between Ontario and the federal government on day care facilities. Ontario initiated the program and was the only province to take advantage of it on a large scale. This was at least in part due to the presence of the Institute with its vocal contingent of authorities on the subject. Dorothy Millichamp of the Institute was asked to join the Department of Public Welfare to direct the new day nursery project. She recruited Institute trainees to help her. Non-Institute workers who joined the program were not allowed to provide simple custodial care for children but were strictly trained in the teaching role characteristic of the Toronto Institute.

Due to the shortage of trained teachers, emergency training classes were initiated at the Institute of Child Study. The first students received a full pre-War curriculum in research and methods. However, it became increasingly clear that the situation demanded the production of teachers, not researchers. The initial training sequence which lasted for eighteen months was cut to six months and finally to four. A one year bachelors program was formalized in 1943.

Since Millichamp and Blatz were both preoccupied with other activities during this period, psychologists Mary Northway and Karl Bernhardt, who had relatively little experience with early childhood, were pressed into service to teach courses at the Institute. They modeled their curriculum on the precedent set by Blatz. The dominance of the Blatzian formula for teacher education was confirmed. A definable "Ontario traditional early childhood format was established which endured for more than two decades."[82]

It is interesting that when the federal government withdrew from day care after 1945, Ontario continued its assistance to these facilities. In contrast, Quebec eliminated such funding. The Ontario Day Nurseries Act drafted in 1946 was passed in the spring of 1947. This law specificed that day nurseries had to meet specified standards and be licensed. Blatz and his colleagues were asked to set out these standards. Blatz's suggestion was simply to "just tell them to do what we did at the Institute."[83] The final version of the act, in fact, specified that the time table was to conform to the standards of the Institute of Child Study of the University of Toronto. A similar statement was included in every subsequent revision of the act until 1968. The 1946 Ontario Day Nursery Act was an exemplary piece of legislation and one of the first of its kind in the United States or Canada.

The 1968 Ontario *Programme of Studies for Grades 1 to 6* carried on a more subtle version of the Blatzian formula for education in that it describes the practice and goals of education in ways compatible with Blatz's teachings. They also reveal an articulation of the evolving concept of parent education in character training. The primary percept was that children should be educated for social responsibility, service to all, and adaptability to change, including an explicit emphasis on cooperation and getting along with others. The school was to provide "meaningful experiences in situations that require the exercise of qualities of helpfulness, self-direction and acceptance of resonsibility."[84] This is, in a sense, an updated definition of what Blatz meant by schooling as fostering a personal acquisition of security.

Educational reforms based on developmental perspectives in the 1960s and 1970s appear to have been pushed aside by the more current emphasis on educational basics and accountability.[85] However, if a distinction is made between the free school movement and open classroom movement it becomes more apparent that the ideology of structured progressive classrooms more typical of the open classroom has historically been compatible with scientific efficiency. Blatzian psychology can be seen in contemporary forms as the individualization of self-development.

A Normative Paradigm Emerges

While Canadian child psychology made a unique contribution to twentieth century perceptions of normal development, the transition from a preoccupation with abnormal development may not have come about if it was not for the philanthropic support and advocacy of the CNCMH, the Rockefeller Foundation and the Laura Spelman Rockefeller Memorial. Rockefeller Grants to promote the development of mental hygiene and psychiatry in Canada from 1924 to 1937 amounted to well over three hundred thousand dollars.

Although the Foundation consistently provided funding, there was much reflection on the quality and benefit of the research. Alan Gregg pessimistically noted at one point, that:

> the results of these appropriations to the Canadian Committee, November 1939, are difficult to describe . . . Except for the growth of psychological work on children at Toronto where Blatz has become established and much of the work incorporated in the university department of psychology, it would not appear that there is much perceptible residue from this series of collaborations . . . Though the sums expended were used in ways to meet local and temporary needs I can not point to any continuing and conspicuous results.[86]

Gregg was concerned with long term Foundation policy on medical research as well as the impact of specific grants. The Rockefeller Foundation had not reconciled its approach to mental hygiene with other medical and public health work. There was a question whether mental hygiene should be a direct function of the Foundation or relegated to one of the Foundation's affiliates or branches. A less favored view was that mental health research should be a support program handled by other agents such as the National Committees for Mental Hygiene. Gregg momentarily came to the conclusion that:

> It would be my considered opinion that Dr. Pearce was right in holding in 1920 that the Rockefeller Foundation should cooperate directly with medical schools and leaders in medical education in Canada in preference to aiding special programs.[87]

Rockefeller philanthropy, nonetheless, contributed to the development of a normative paradigm of mental and physical growth created in research institutions such as Toronto. The Memorial especially helped distribute these ideas through parent training and professional education. While the specifics of the generalizations about developmental processes have changed, more important than the specific content of the message about normality and abnormality was the institutionalization of the idea that we can scientifically validate standards of normal physical and mental functioning. Blatz, as one researcher, used this criteria in a very contemporary sense to individualize education as a form of self-development.

Chapter Nine

Infancy to Adolescence: Rockefeller Philanthropy and the Mental Hygiene of Normal Children

During the period between the first and second World Wars, Rockefeller philanthropy supported research which established a medical basis for the cultural perception of a sequentially elaborated mental world of childhood and adolescence which was correlated with biological maturation unique from adult mental life. Without this original perception the "terrible twos" and the "teenage monster" of post World War II notoriety could not have become institutionalized in public thought and accounted for in social practice.

Whereas G. Stanley Hall's child study movement initiated a momentum for the scientific study of children, his psychology of youth was largely grounded in biography and philosophy.[1] The mental testing movement, although it correlated mental functioning with age, did not interweave the progress of bone growth, and maturation of the nervous and reproductive systems with mood and behavior changes. The mental hygiene movement integrated these ideas, tying together concepts elaborated by research and related social movements into an identifiable, if amorphous, pattern, ready for public consumption. Much of the current information on growth, development and timing of maturation, which are taken as close to self-evident, are in fact based on mental hygiene concepts which have only recently circumscribed the modern phenomenon of growing up.[2]

The Heritage of the Laura Spelman Rockefeller Memorial

Scientific research on child development was primarily funded by the Laura Spelman Rockefeller Memorial and carried out by other Rockefeller funds after 1929, when the Memorial was merged with the Rockefeller Foundation. The numerous research projects carried out by these funds were given various degrees of guidance by Rockefeller officials, and the projects were diverse. Yet, they all shared an emphasis on medical knowledge, scientific methodology, and the application of research findings to administrative practice. The objective was the remediation of "real-life" problems in families, schools and clinics.

The Laura Spelman Rockefeller Memorial was organized in 1918 to promote parent education and the social sciences in order to better human life. Its mandate was pragmatic, where over the long term the Memorial's major contribution was in applied research with children. The express guiding policy of the Memorial to further practical knowledge shaped the character and direction of scientific child research in the decades after 1920.

> The Memorial had no interest in the promotion of scientific research as an end in itself; its motive was not sheer curiosity as to how various human and social phenomena came to be and all; the interest in science was an interest as one means to an end, and, the end was explicitly recognized to be the advancement of human welfare.[3]

The case-based research in scientific child study was oriented toward middle and upper class families in both the United States and Canada. However, the model for healthy family life which was created pervaded all classes. The popular press and the expansion of visual media contributed to the general dissemination of an ideal type of child as normal, as well as a standardization of what was interpreted as positive child-family environments. The concurrent expansion of professional education insured that teachers, social workers and public health officials acquired the new values and promoted them in public policy, as well as in the public eye.

Rockefeller supported research emphasized scientific methodology. The major difference between the sentimental child study of the Progressive Era was the institutionalization of the scientific bias for validating knowledge about children. Much of the scientific basis for child development was a product of longitudinal child growth research involving anthropomorphic and physiological measurement, psychological testing and systematic observation. The studies began with school age children but encompassed a range from infancy to adolescence by the end of the 1930s. Two major sets of data were compiled: one from the early childhood studies of the 1920s; the second, from the adolescent studies of the 1930s. Literally thousands of children across the country became case histories.

These studies were unique. They established the scientific standards for evaluating physical and mental maturation in human populations. The underlying rationale was an adaptation of the mental hygiene framework. The ultimate goal was to strengthen the body politic by fostering childhood social adjustment and preventive health care leading to as nearly universal standards of mental-physical health as possible.[4]

The Research Centers: Infant and Child Studies

Fifteen projects, including five major research institutions, were created by the Memorial in order to demonstrate the usefulness of systematic studies on infants and children. Similar to the child guidance clinical demonstrations, in order to fulfill its objectives of creating a technology of human relations, the research centers were intended to ultimately become self-supporting. Five major institutions most often cited in Foundation literature include the most distinguished and successful programs such as the Iowa Child Welfare Research Station; the Institute of Child Welfare at the University of California, Berkeley; the Institute of Child Welfare at the University of Minnesota; the Clinic for Child Development of the Institute for Human Relations at Yale University; and the Child Development Institute at Teachers College, Columbia University.[5] Two additional centers can also be considered major LSRM contributors to scientific child study including the University of Toronto (Child Study Centre at St. George's School later renamed the Institute for Child Study), discussed in the last chapter, and the LSRM's funding of home economics and child study under the auspices of the American Association of University Women at Cornell University.

Scientific child study took diverse forms. Minnesota maintained a nursery school laboratory with connections to school age children. Yale University concentrated on infant growth and the determination of norms for mental and motor development. Researchers at Teacher's College, Columbia University, studied nursery school age children and family relations, focussing on personality development rather than growth. In cooperation with the Brush Foundation, physical growth studies from infancy to adolescence were pursued at Western Reserve. At the University of Chicago, the Committee on Child Development maintained a Central Record Bureau which coordinated the departments of psychology, education and home economics in keeping records of children from elementary through high school age. Walter Dearborn at Harvard launched a major twelve year growth study which maintained case records on twenty-seven hundred children through the department of public health. At Johns Hopkins University the department of psychology worked on mental and motor development of preschool children. The department of psychology at Stanford University, under Lewis Terman, concentrated on longitudinal studies of the gifted and the testing of intelligence. The Child Research Council of Denver with the School of Medicine of the University of Colorado, did research on infancy. The Merrill-Palmer School in Detroit studied nursery and school age development.[6]

The first and last projects supported by the Laura Spelman Rockefeller Memorial, respectively in Iowa and California, are described in this chapter as case examples of Rockefeller input into the scientific study of child life. They represent two variations on scientific child study research as the focus stretched from birth to the age of majority.

Iowa Child Welfare Research Station

The Iowa Child Welfare Research Station is unique among the group of research centers supported by the LSRM. It predates the creation of the Memorial and it is the only research institution with a guarantee of its continued existence by a special legislative act of a state. LSRM funding helped focus and shape the research carried on in Iowa, but it did not set up the program or initiate the concerns which started the Station. Iowa is a good example of the relationship between philanthropy in contributing to, and shaping through consultation and support, locally generated advocacy. It was hoped that the connection of the Station with state government backed by public support would become a model for related work in other states. However, the example of Iowa did not become widespread.

The Iowa Child Welfare Research Station was a product of the progressive child saving movement. The original idea for the Station was a response to a successful statewide campaign by Cora Bussey Hillis.[7] After sixteen years of advocacy work for child health, Hillis and her associates were able to acquire the support of key figures in the president of the University of Iowa, Thomas H. MacBride and Carl E. Seashore, first chair of psychology and dean of the Graduate College.[8] The legislative statute was approved on April 21, 1917.[9] It created the Station as an integral part of the state University with its object

> the investigation of the best scientific methods of conserving and developing the normal child, the dissemination of the information acquired by such investigations and the training of students for work in such fields.[10]

The "Fitter Families" Movement

The successful propaganda and growing concern in Iowa over the health and welfare of children was encouraged by related popular movements such as that advanced by the Iowa branch of the National Congress of Mothers. Mother's Congress activist, Mary T. Watts of Audubon, Iowa, pioneered in the "better babies" movement and was an originator of another movement termed "fitter families." Watts' concern was with eugenic family fitness. She set up a program at the Iowa State Fair, beginning in 1911, which provided a "competition" for families involving genetic classification.

As one newspaper article reported: "That coveted blue ribbon with which owners of prize livestock are rewarded at the state fairs will be duplicated at the same fairs for whole families who prove, after various tests, to be one hundred percent healthy and sound."[11] Watts managed to get publicity for her campaign and to give mental and physical examinations to hundreds of children and parents through her work at state fairs in Iowa and Kansas.

The Iowa project was a part of the larger trend across the country, not only in eugenics but in child health. On a national basis, the Children's Bureau had been waging a battle since its inception in 1912 for child health and welfare. In the year 1914, children's advocate, George B. Mangold, wrote, "Health is no longer a purely individual matter; it has become the concern of the community." In this view, "preventable infant mortality was a social crime."[12] The federal Sheppard-Towner Act of 1921 was the legislated success symbol of the campaign for public intervention into the protection of the health and well being of infants and mothers. During its span of enactment from 1921 to 1928, seven million dollars were released for grants-in-aid for state governments to promote the conservation of child life.[13] The Sheppard-Towner Clinics provided supportive services for the Iowa State Program of Parent Education.[14]

The Iowa Child Welfare Research Station's priority was the discovery of a sound knowledge base with which to improve child health and welfare. The legislature provided twenty-four thousand dollars annually for research, but as early as 1920, Bird T. Baldwin, the first director of the Station, was actively pursuing an expansion of the research with the financial assistance of the LSRM. Psychology, nutrition, eugenics and a study of "social betterment" were the topics of early studies. Baldwin cooperated with the medical and dental colleges, college of education, the extension division, school of public health nursing, department of speech and home economics. He published a book on the *Physical Growth of Children from Birth to Maturity*. Baldwin hoped to be able to provide clinical and laboratory services for the state of Iowa in such a way as to become a national clearing house for child welfare research.[15] Baldwin emphasized that Iowa occupied both the geographic and spiritual heartland of the nation.

Child Study and Parent Education

The Child Study and Parent Education Division was organized in June of 1924. The LSRM contributed to extension work in child study and parent education.[16] One hundred thousand dollars over five years was appropriated to "supplement and extend the research program."[17] In 1925, the State Board of Education designated the Station as the coordinating center of all of its child welfare research and public education for the state.

This act unified the work of the university, the Iowa State College and Iowa State Teachers College into a single project format. After a lengthy period of negotiation the LSRM agreed to a ten year commitment to child welfare research in Iowa beginning in 1928. These funds allowed for the provision of new laboratory facilities where the "all round problems of child growth and behavior" were taken up.

The Iowa Station emphasized nutrition studies, physical growth and anthropometry where psychology was broadly interpreted to include infant behavior, mental development, motor development, musical development, social and personal adjustment and mental hygiene. The studies began at birth in a laboratory for newborns maintained by Dr. Orvis C. Irwin, who conducted experiments with early reflexes and learning in infants.[18]

The ten year mark of the Station was a transition point. Baldwin died in 1928 and George D. Stoddard became the director. The year 1928 also signaled the first installment of the ten year LSRM grant and the Station's maturity as a multiple functioning state-wide service which developed a new knowledge base through research. Stoddard cites the "wise council" of the new University President Walter A. Jessup, Dean Carl E. Seashore, Beardsely Ruml and L. K. Frank of the LSRM as contributing to the success of the work.[19]

The nutritional studies with the advent of the new biochemical laboratory took up metabolic functioning and the physiological effects of too little food. While children from orphanages and private homes were used as case studies other clinical research was performed with laboratory animals. Results of the research in 1938 received awards from the Borden Milk Company and the American Home Economics Association for determining that the "average" child's diet was deficient.[20] Related physical growth studies began with Baldwin's own work. Data was synthesized from anatomic, anthropometric and statistical material over a ten year period. H. V. Meredith collected ninety thousand values for eighteen anthropomorphic measures on 1,243 males and a similar number of females over fourteen years. This type of data was used to create charts on estimated child growth and maturation. C. H. McCoy and his associates formulated a packaged program so that the relatively uninitiated could evaluate the physical status of an individual child. This type of material was developed for use in public schools across the nation.

The Station sought to increase its effectiveness by disseminating its research findings in terms of practical educational material. The Station was extremely successful in its educational campaign. As of December 1938, 1,534,062 standards and testing materials had been distributed to appropriate social and educational agencies, 898,738 popular bulletins and pamphlets had been provided for public consumption, and 41,756 technical monographs had been published for a professional audience. Of the 896 publications of the Station, 225 contributed to child psychology and child behavior, 137 were in the form of popular bulletins, 125 dealt with parent education, 101 with preschool education, 69 with physical growth, and 64 with nutrition. Others dealt with allied fields, general development, methods and reviews and abstracts.[21]

The Station cooperated with and found "a bridge between the work of the Station, viewed as a whole, and the citizens of the State." The list of cooperating agencies was extensive and diverse including: the American Association of University Women, American Legion Auxiliary, Iowa Congress of Parents and Teachers, Iowa Farm Bureau Federation, Iowa Federation of Women's Clubs, Iowa League of Women Voters, Iowa State Association of Social Welfare, Iowa State College, Iowa State Department of Health, Iowa State Department of Public Instruction, Iowa State Medical Society, Iowa State Physical Education Association, Iowa State Teachers Association, Iowa State Teachers College, Iowa State Tuberculosis Association, the University of Iowa and the Women's Christian Temperance Union of Iowa.

The Station's research in child psychology took on a distinguished trend for which it became well known. This was to emphasize environmental factors in understanding the physical and mental capacities of children. Studies on the influence of environment over genetic heritage were carried out from infancy through school age using the University laboratory preschool, and community data in city and rural school settings.[22] Research conclusions in work such as that of Harold Skeels, supported the premise that: "illegitimate children of dull and feebleminded mothers and out-of-work or laboring fathers, if placed in good homes in early infancy, will turn out to be bright children as measured by the best tests now available."[23] Beth L. Wellman's research supported a similar conclusion with findings that children attending the preschool laboratory gained twenty I.Q. points.[24] Kurt Lewin, a German gestalt psychologist known for his field related work, contributed significantly to the development of group therapy techniques and to new strategies in "action research." Lewin was added to the Iowa staff in the 1930s under the auspices of a three year General Education Board grant.[25] The Iowa Child Welfare Research Station advanced the nurture side of the nature-nurture controversy through its relationship between intelligence and environment.

Iowa and the Nature-Nurture Debate

The "nature-nurture" controversy was a product of long standing discrepancies in interpreting the meaning of evolution applied to human populations.[26] The mental hygiene movement was informed by the evolutionary theory of Social Darwinism and the development of experimental biology and its application to preventive medicine and public health.[27] The position that mental retardation, mental illness and social disorders from immorality to criminal behavior were grounded in hereditary tendencies had been spread by mental hygienists since the inception of the movement. Mental hygiene has also increasingly served to moderate these views in light of its preventive orientation. The extremist position of segregating and isolating the unfit and abnormal, in an effort toward their elimination, was reconstructed by the emphasis on prevention with the young, and on the nurturance of normality.

By the 1930s, the emphasis on preserving normality was well developed in mental hygiene. The LSRM concentrated its funds on elaborating preventive models of mental health which tended to emphasize developmental and environmental factors over genetic determinants. The effort to identify life adjustments which would conserve and promote ability was in direct conflict with the underlying assumptions of the eugenic oriented leaders of the mental testing movement.[28] The controversy rested on the contention that I.Q. represented an unchangeable biological fact. This latter position was advocated by proponents of mental testing such as Henry Goddard, Lewis Terman and Robert Yerkes.[29] The notion that intelligence was subject to social and environmental factors was viewed as heretical by these individuals, and especially by Lewis Terman and his followers at Stanford University. The views of the Iowa Child Welfare Research Station were seen as dangerous. This ill will was mutual.[30] The arguments and counter arguments were often stated as a question of which side could claim scientific validity and which was most unscientifically biased.[31]

The debate over concepts of intelligence can be followed in the three yearbooks published on the subject by the National Society for the Study of Education in 1922, 1928 and 1937.[32] The Iowa-Stanford debates from the 1920s through the 1940s illustrate the flexibility and diversity of the mental hygiene paradigm. In spite of the apparent dissension caused by the controversy, mental hygiene's psychobiological paradigm is compatible with both sides of the argument. The mental hygiene movement advanced the practice of mental testing with the reification of I.Q. scores as scientifically verified, even while as a therapeutic model its case based orientation encouraged researchers to look toward the impact of developmental conditions.[33] It should also be noted that the environmentalism characteristic of Iowa rested on a medical paradigm as much as the Stanford position.

The University of California Studies

In the year 1921, California volunteers attempted without success to enact, as had Iowa, a state funded institute for child study.[34] Similar 1923 legislation elicited the support of Stanford President David Starr Jordan, Lewis Terman and psychologist Olga Bridgman of Berkeley, along with prominent religious and social leaders.[35] A bill was passed, but "conflicting schemes for control of the proposed station" by the Berkeley faculty led to the rescission of the legislation.

Unlike the Iowa Child Welfare Research Station, the LSRM's support for the Institute of Child Welfare at the University of California came largely after the formative period of Rockefeller philanthropy in its orientation toward child study and parent education. Similar to Iowa, the Memorial took advantage of an ongoing interest in child study and parent education which may not have prospered in the same way without the advantages of the funding and supportive collaboration of the staff of the LSRM, General Education Board, and the Rockefeller Foundation.

The LSRM was willing, in 1923, to step in and provide supportive funding for child study in California, but as Lawrence Frank noted there was little to do "but wait until such time as the consolidation scheme has been developed, when the plan thereof will be submitted informally for our consideration."[36] A plan was developed and legislation enabling the establishment of an Institute for Child Welfare was passed four years later in 1927.

The Berkeley Institute was the last major research center initiated with LSRM funds. In 1927, the officers of the Laura Spelman Rockefeller Memorial and the officers of the other Rockefeller philanthropic funds were in the process of reorganization. The LSRM was nearing the ten year mark, the designated period of its trust, and the Rockefeller Board set about evaluating the progress of child study and parent education research.

Serious questions were raised. One critic concluded that instead of building facts much of the research was "silly twaddle."[37] Foundation officials did not question the efficacy of their belief in the potential of a technical science of human behavior. They did question the success of their methods of promoting social science. They addressed the issue of whether or not "the demonstration work has gotten far ahead of the field covered by research" and that to some extent at least the Memorial had put "the cart before the horse."[38]

Edmund E. Day, director of the Division of Social Sciences for the Rockefeller Foundation, emphasized the distinction between "child study as fact finding and parent education as fact-using . . . the action for the present would seem to be to turn the Memorial's energies primarily to the promotion of fact finding projects and agencies."[39] It was agreed that child study research was of vital importance and no one seriously questioned the validity of applying this knowledge, the emphasis on relatively short studies and propagandizing findings, however, was questioned. The Berkeley research came on the heels of this internal soul searching. The research priorities and conservative approach to publishing material at Berkeley are reflective of the more serious tone.

The more painstaking design and longer time frame of the research proved costly. It is important to note that it probably would not have been sustained, especially in the depressed years of the 1930s without large external grants. The first grant was initiated in 1927. The Laura Spelman Rockefeller Memorial appropriated three hundred thousand dollars to be distributed to the University of California for the Institute for Child Welfare at the rate of fifty thousand dollars annually for six years, expiring June 30, 1933.[40]

The Berkeley Institute for Child Welfare

Lawrence Frank of the LSRM was active in the development of the Institute at Berkeley.[41] He influenced the two usual components in planning which determine the character and progress of research; the choice of personnel and the structural design of the research organization.

Herbert Stoltz, a medical doctor with a degree from Stanford and Oxford, who had been assistant superintendent of public instruction in California in charge of parent education, was appointed director of the Institute.[42] Stoltz contributed widespread legitimacy as a medical doctor, researcher, administrator and state level bureaucrat. He continued in these diverse and helpful roles throughout the inter-War period. In 1932, Stoltz accepted a position as assistant superintendent of Oakland Public Schools. He maintained his affiliation with the Institute acting as a go-between as the Institute's research increasingly focussed on the Oakland Public school system. He joined the Oakland Public School administrative staff full time in the late 1930s. Stoltz continued his research into physiological processes in adolescence which served to summarize and publicize this most important aspect of the Institute's child study research. His research and writing was also complemented by his marriage to Lois Meek [Stoltz], a Stanford professor in child study who had previously been director of parent education at Columbia University. Stolz and Meek collaborated on articles and monographs based on the Berkeley and Oakland data.

Stoltz's successors at the Institute, Harold Jones and Jean Walker MacFarlane, were also influential in shaping the Berkeley and Oakland research. Harold Jones, a psychologist educated at Amherst and Columbia came to Berkeley with a part time appointment in psychology and as director of research at the Institute. He was an able successor when Stoltz officially left the Institute directorship. Jean Walker MacFarlane, a Berkeley graduate, had dual appointments in psychology and at the Institute where she was director of child guidance. MacFarlane became increasingly powerful and influential as the longitudinal child guidance and Oakland adolescent studies were expanded in the 1930s and 1940s.

There were three organizational aspects of the Institute for Child Welfare for the first six years from 1927 to 1933, as developed with L. K. Frank's help. The Institute was to include a nursery school, child study center and research facilities to be used cooperatively between several departments of the university.

The Berkeley Studies: Nursery School, Survey and Guidance

The establishment of a nursery school provided one hundred children for study whose progress was monitored over time in order to collect cumulative data on cognitive and physical development. Secondly, sixty babies were enrolled in an infant growth study. Each of these children were also given systematic examinations and their anthropometric measurements charted. Two-thirds of the original infants in this study were still being examined, at least monthly, six years later.

Perhaps most important in the long term, was the Berkeley survey and child guidance experiments, under MacFarlane's direction, which began rather modestly and developed into a model for future long term cumulative data bases. The work began as a sutdy of child development and parent training which, for the first time, used two groups of children, one being a control. The efficacy of clinical intervention into child life and family practices were monitored by this technique. This project was expanded in 1930. It became the definitive study of later childhood and adolescence which coincided with a study of paired adolescents conducted in the public schools of neighboring Oakland.

Foundation officials encouraged the Institute to expand its research agenda into the adolescent years. Although separate from the adolescent study which was independently funded, the longitudinal and guidance studies in Berkeley set up a demonstration for the later study just as it supplemented the adolescent data from the Berkeley group as the original subjects aged.

The Oakland Adolescent Study

The Oakland Public Schools adolescent study, like the Berkeley MacFarlane survey and guidance project, grew out of modest beginnings in

1930 to substantial size and importance. Researchers from the Institute for Child Study and Oakland Public Schools followed the original group of ten and eleven years olds through their high school years. Follow-up investigations tracked this group into adulthood. The goal was to capture the physical and mental reality of child growth by way of systematic scientific data.

Adolescent research in Oakland began in 1930, with a pilot study group of one hundred boys and an equal number of girls selected from sixth grade classes in Claremont Junior High School. The effort was to develop a sample for a long range study of normal adolescent development. The children selected were not necessarily representative of either the schools or Oakland in general, but were apparently normal children from families who were expected to remain in the area long enough to be studied without interruption. The area in the northeastern portion of Oakland was middle class and the children selected for study voiced an intention to go to the academic high school rather than to the alternative technical high school. University High School, the secondary education institutional goal, functioned as a part of the Oakland Public School system.

In addition, a second, slightly larger group, who were already in high school, were selected to be used for exploratory studies and testing.[43] In the spring of 1931, with LSRM funds under the direction of the Rockefeller Foundation, ninety-one thousand dollars was appropriated for the use of the Institute of Child Welfare and Oakland Public Schools for the study of adolescents. The appropriation became effective July 1, 1931 and was disbursed at the rate of thirteen thousand dollars a year for seven years.[44]

The method included anthropometric, photographic and medical record taking twice a year at the Institute. These examinations charted skeletal proportions, sex characteristics, dentition, muscular strength, and subcutaneous tissue. A physiological battery of tests were performed once a year on basal metabolism, respiratory rate, blood pressure, body temperature, and pulse rate. More unusual tests included 'vital capacity', and auditory, visual, olfactory and association word stimuli as related to skin resistance and other physical changes.

Individual and group psychometric tests were conducted to determine general intelligence, as well as specific reading, math and learning skills. Clinical observation, and parental, teacher, peer and self ratings were used to determine a range of personality traits indicative of attitudes toward peers, teachers, school activities, home and civic responsibilities. While attitudes toward sex and academics were stressed, suggestibility levels, ambitions and leadership aptitude were also studied. The group tests alone took over thirty hours using the Terman group intelligence scales which were supplemented by individual Stanford-Binet intelligence tests. Three visits to the children's homes were made by psychiatric social workers where medical histories were compiled and noted.

Support for Longitudinal Research

The exhausive testing was time consuming and expensive. The first two years found the study $13,000 over budget.[45] A strong vote of confidence from University President Robert Sproul and Oakland Public School Superintendent William A. Givens appeared as proof, however, of the worth of the research. L. K. Frank, of the GEB, argued for the value of the scientific content and justified the expanding cost on the basis of a need for systematic research. The General Education Board subsequently renewed its commitment to the project in 1934. The Institute was to receive $10,200 in 1934–5 and $7,900 in 1935–6. The Oakland Public School administration was to receive $13,900 for the first year and $13,200 the second.[46] The slow pace of the longitudinal studies and the fact that their results often appeared arcane was interpreted as a testimony to their validity. The research was seen as painstaking and exact. The systematic cumulative methodology, the emphasis on medical and physiological data, the use of standardized tests and apparatus in collecting information were at the forefront of the technologies of the day.

The systematic methodology employed by MacFarlane and even more the topic of research in detailed scientific longitudinal data on human mental and physical development impressed Foundation officials. Lawrence Frank felt that the research was

> unique both in the wealth of cumulative material on child and family situations and in the use of an adequate control group to test the desirability of guidance procedures. If these children can be kept under observation by the clinic until they move into the adolescent years and then followed in their personality development and social adjustment, the full length study will provide something that has never before been attempted but is of the utmost value for the future of psychiatry and mental hygiene.[47]

Alan Gregg, director of the Rockefeller Foundation Division of the Medical Sciences was also impressed with the cumulative data on "anthropometric, medical, psychiatric and psychological" grounds.[48] Robert Havighurst, who took over the responsibility for overseeing the grants to the project after Lawrence K. Frank resigned to take over the presidency of the Josiah Macy, Jr. Foundation, pointed out that: "This is the only grant the General Education Board has made to extend over such a long period [twenty years] in connection with its support of research in human development . . ."[49] Havighurst argued that the research:

> must be carried on patiently over a relatively long period (ten years?) before sufficient data will be available for the testing of various conclusions and hypothetical conclusions, and that the work of the Institute is being conducted in a very cautious, conservative spirit.[50]

He emphasized the importance of continued funding citing the contribution of longitudinal adolescent research in particular and the complexity of "this field." Long term Rockefeller support for adolescent research continued to 1950. In 1940 the General Education Board appropriated two hundred thousand dollars for ten years in order to complete studies and disseminate research finding accumulated over two decades.

The intention of the related adolescent studies was to capture biological and psychological adaptations to physical development. This was reflected in the major findings of the research. Researchers sought an ultimate reality in human growth cycles. The proposals and research summaries omit the comments on social, political and economic questions. Harold Jones, for example, summarized the making of adolescence as "basically a biological phenomenon . . . The general hypothesis may be offered that the anthropomorphic and physiological changes of adolescence affect an individual's behavior through four channels of psychosomatic relationship."[51] The channels included: 1) "physiological equilibria" which required behavioral adjustment; 2) changes in intra-organic stimulation or physiological "drives," indicated by "lowering the thresholds to stimulation related to sex;" 3) quantitative growth in abilities and patterns of abilities such as muscle strength; 4) finally, changes in group status manifested in a "pressure system" which necessitated critical adaptation. This was seen as causing a transformation in activities, attitudes and interests.[52]

Stoltz's work is a good example of the conclusions drawn from the Berkeley/Oakland data sets. Stoltz argued that adolescence was not a chronological category but a physiological category. He developed growth charts, one hundred and eighty of which were published in the four hundred pages of his work on somatic development. Unlike Wingate Todd of Western Reserve who worked on a similar problem. Stoltz did not want to rely on one measure such as skeletal development. Stoltz combined skeletal data, sexual maturation and metabolic changes.[53] His treatise on adolescence illustrated the prototype of normal adolescence to be disseminated to teachers, university faculty in departments of education including inservice training, medical schools and schools of social work. A strong emphasis on the biological underscored the "human animal's developmental characteristics."[54]

Biology while dominant was, however, considered to be offset by cultural expectations and pressures of home and community. Statistical and standardized measures of physical development and mental processes in learning and intelligence were reflected in social adaptation and adjustments to social class, culture and peers. Problems of adolescence were seen as pressures from society as well as internal problems stemming from early childhood. Schools were especially responsible for identifying the stage of growth of the individual and aiding in the individual's adaptation to cultural values, including social and political attitudes.

The identification of problems incorporated the relationship between parent and child in the adolescent's search for independence, sexual identity and vocational orientation. The ability to get along with others including popularity, leadership training and the development of skills figured as a significant stage in adolescent growth. Adolescence was clearly projected as physiological fact which presented a severe challenge for parents, teachers and for school administration.[55]

Publishing Research in Human Development

While Rockefeller Foundation officials were concerned with the premature distribution of studies, they were also mindful that to contribute to the continuation of good research and to provide for the improved welfare of the public, valid findings must be effectively disseminated. Efforts in preventive medicine had proved this point well, and the task at hand was to produce similar results in the area of social and mental well-being. The continuation of the various projects in child and adolescent research in the late thirties represented twenty years of work. It seemed time to seriously provide for the dissemination of the research results.

Robert Havighurst and Alan Gregg felt that the Berkeley and Oakland studies were a major contribution to available knowledge on child growth. As a consequence, they sought multiple forums to put this information before other researchers, professionals and the public. The funds which had been transferred from the LSRM to the Rockefeller Foundation Division of the Medical Sciences in 1929 were taken up by the General Education Board Program on Child Development in 1933. The GEB extended support of the Berkeley related projects to mid-century in order to complete the compilation and analysis of data. Publication funds became an increasingly dominant portion of the continued appropriations.[56] The provision for publication was due, as Havighurst states, to the fact that "we have come to accept the fact that much of the publication of results of this research must be subsidized. Many of the most valuable studies cut across the conventional lines dividing psychology, physiology, anatomy and sociology, and consequently cannot be easily published in the journals of particular sciences."[57] Havighurst noted that other influential figures on the Foundation staff agreed with him as witnessed by the fact that the day after an inter-office memo was sent to President Raymond Fosdick requesting six thousand dollars to publish the Berkeley data, the sum was approved.[58] In 1938 four theses and two monograph series including six publications, eleven articles and seven other abstracts or papers on Institute research were published from this fund.[59] Additional funds produced a *Yearbook on Adolescence*, and Herbert Stoltz and Lois Meek Stoltz's work on adolescent growth titled, *Somatic Development in Adolescent Boys.*[60]

The National Research Council: Professional Knowledge for The Public Good

The dissemination of child study research proved to be a problem similar to the early problems of mental hygiene in Adolf Meyer's concern over the proliferation of propaganda and impromptu legislation before adequate research could be conducted. The problem was how to screen information presented to the public and to make sure that it went to legitimate professionals. The issue was complicated by the tendency to have scientifically validated knowledge twisted by unwarranted assumptions, over simplifications, and blatant prejudices of lay audiences. One attempt to secure professional leadership over the distribution of information was the creation of the National Research Council.

The creation of the NRC Committee on Child Development and the Monograph Series on Child Development and Abstracts did not, however, prove sufficient to distribute and synthesize the volume of research produced over the years of support for scientific child study. Further, it seemed abundantly clear that a coordinating body should be created as a further quality control over extraneous propaganda. To this purpose, Robert Havighurst, who had been instrumental in coordinating funding in child study research after Lawrence K. Frank, took a position at the University of Chicago as secretary of the Committee on Human Development. Havighurst directed the Collaboration Center in Child Development, which was created with GEB funds in 1943.[61]

This project was an outgrowth of the Center of Documentation and Collaboration for the Study of Human Development and Behavior at the University of Chicago which had operated since 1930. It also continued the work of the Commission on Teacher Education of the American Council on Education set up in 1938 under a GEB grant of $250,000.[62] It was specifically to "synthesize knowledge about human growth, motivation, learning and behavior" in light of the "implication for the education of teachers." The fifteen collaborators representing the major research centers in child study developed out of the work of the LSRM. As experts in their fields, the collaborators were to state the "scientifically validated generalizations of principles" from the "research findings in the biological, psychological, sociological, and medical sciences." Further, they were to select from these generalizations the concepts which should be distributed to professionals working with children and youth. A sequence of undergraduate course work was to be developed, as well as minimum standards of knowledge which would "permit a person to make valid judgments" as to which of the generalizations "apply to that child in a particular situation."[63]

The results were to be distributed through committee reports. A newly organized subcommittee on Standards of the American Association of Teachers Colleges was to relay information to over 175 institutions concerned with professional education, and to college administrators, curriculum committees and professors of psychology and child development.

The Waning of Psychiatry in Child Study Research

Mental hygiene in scientific child study, as did child guidance, tended to expand without direct psychiatric input. While the primary objective was to assure normal socialization, the criteria of adjustment were not based on social factors so much as according to clinical measures of mental and physical changes. Foundation staff was aware of the problem and attempted to include psychiatry and the formal social sciences in the 1940s.

Alan Gregg and Lawrence Frank were especially interested in having the longitudinal data collected in the Berkeley research analyzed by a psychoanalyst. Throughout 1937 and 1938, various ways were discussed to provide this kind of perspective.[64] Eventually a five year grant was offered to Erik (Homburger) Erikson from Yale.

Erikson was unhappy at Berkeley and refused to cooperate with an integrated approach to data collection typical of the Berkeley projects. His style of research and eclectic interests especially did not fit well with MacFarlane's views.[65] During this period, Erikson completed a monograph he had begun at Yale, and in collaboration with anthropologist, Alfred L. Kroeber, did summer studies on the impact of culture on socialization and mental development with Indian children. He also devoted considerable time to the observation of children's play. In fact much of the data for Erikson's monograph, *Childhood and Society*, which was not published until 1950, was begun during this period.[66]

Nonetheless, the experiment with psychiatry at Berkeley was not considered successful for the purpose intended by MacFarlane or Alan Gregg of the Rockefeller Foundation.[67] The effort to create a model for psychiatric research in an interdisciplinary child study setting failed partly because of a personality conflict between MacFarlane and Erikson. Erikson's psychoanalytic approach, subject-oriented methodology, and interest in cultural phenomena was ill suited to supplement MacFarlane's more rigid systematic clinical approach to data gathering.[68] On a more fundamental level, the shortage of trained psychiatrists and the underdeveloped state of child psychiatry in the medical profession made it difficult or impossible to acquire and maintain psychiatric personnel in child study, just as it had been in child guidance.

Similar to the experience with psychiatry, the project did not employ until very late, and then only briefly, someone trained in social science. Foundation staff noted the lack of a systematic analysis of the social and environmental factors in the adolescent experience. In an effort to remedy this situation, a fellowship was belatedly awarded in 1940 to Buford Junker, a student of Lloyd Warner, a sociologist at the University of Chicago. Junker was to do social placement charts for each child, and for parent and child interviews. He spent very little time on the case study material. Even though Junker's fellowship was renewed in 1941 he acepted another position before the data was complete. Warner noted that a proper analysis of the community would have taken another two to three years research.

The extraneous information on social factors gathered in Oakland allowed for a reinterpretation in a study published in 1974 on childhood in the Depression.[69] This later study by Glen Elder is remarkable in that it addresses the questions which remained unasked in either the Berkeley or Oakland projects. The fact that Elder was able to reevaluate the data illustrates the massive amount of detailed information collected by the longitudinal studies in Berkeley and Oakland. Research affiliated with the Institute for Child Welfare did not address the impact of class, race, or socio-economic factors on family life. Considering that the research was conducted prior to, during, and after the economic crisis of the 1930s, and in the face of the second World War, these factors in hindsight were clearly significant. The orientation of the research as based in a medical paradigm downplayed or ignored historically specific conditions as irrelevant to the creation of a universal science of the the psychobiology of man.

Similar to child guidance, scientific child study advanced a medicalized outlook with minimal direct input from medical fields. Instead, clinical psychology, public health and welfare personnel, and teachers were initiated into the mental hygiene field. While psychology rather than psychiatry dominated the research agenda in Berkeley and Oakland, the underlying format was rooted in a version of psychobiology recognizably compatible with Adolf Meyer's use of the term. In this way, mental hygiene interpreted as the ultimate goal of a science of human behavior was applied to the betterment of human life. The search for truth, as properly revealed through science, looked from the infant toward the adolescent encased within a medical perspective.

By 1940, the General Education Board and Rockefeller Foundation trustees wanted to change the focus of their philanthropic interests. Following the early policy imperative that no effort was to take on a permanent status, child-oriented research was expected to become self-supportive or to acquire permanent funding from governmental or other granting agencies. The Rockefeller Foundation had hoped that this point had been reached in the mid-thirties with the establishment of the National Research Council on Child Development. By mid-century, Rockefeller support for child research turned toward integrating and analyzing findings rather than the gathering of primary data.

– Part III –

The Estate

The Legacy of the Paradigm

The nations of our time cannot prevent the condition of men from becoming equal, but it depends upon themselves whether the principle of equality is to lead them to servitude or freedom, to knowledge or barbarism. (Alexis de Tocqueville, *Democracy in America*, New York: Mentor, 1956, p. 317, first published 1835).

Is not this poor child without knowledge, strength or wisdom, entirely at your mercy? Are you not master of his envirnoment so far as it affects him? Cannot you make of him what you please? His work and play, his pleasure and pain, are they not, unknown to him, under your control? No doubt he ought to want to do nothing but what he wants, but he ought to want to do nothing but what you want him to do. He should never take a step you have not foreseen, nor utter a word you could not foretell. (Jean Jacques Rousseau, *Emile*, trans. B. Foxley, London: S. M. Dent, 1957, p. 84–5, first published 1762.)

Chapter Ten

Mental Hygiene and the State: Formalizing a Psychiatry of Childhood

The 1940s have been called the "age of anxiety." Shaped by the second World War, it was a decade of harsh realities and stubborn transcendent idealism concerned with collective "morals, national identity and character." After 1949 there was a modification in this orientation where the search for personal identity became paramount.[1] The mental hygiene movement contributed to this transition. The institutionalization of the medical model was accelerated during the War. The transition in the mental hygiene movement to the contemporary mental health movement contributed to the popular perception of the identity crisis of post War children and adolescents.

The National Committees for Mental Hygiene served, from their origins, to mediate between professional organizations, government, general purpose philanthropy and the public. After World War II the roles of the philanthropies and the Committees changed significantly in response to the expansion of the public sector in governmental regulations and agencies. Secondly, organizations such as the American and Canadian Psychiatric Association became actively involved in overseeing and monitoring standards for research and professional growth. These events were connected with increased general publicity on mental hygiene and the popularization of medical perspectives in the decade between 1940 and 1950. These trends usurped the former role of the U.S. National Committee, Rockefeller philanthropy, and the Commonwealth Fund in mental hygiene work. In the United States, the National Committee reverted to a less powerful national force, with its major role taken over by more official and powerful agencies. The Canadian Committee retained a formal position as an agency which cooperated with and advised government and the public in a semiformal symbiosis between public and private realms.

Children in a Democracy: The White House Conferences

The White House Conferences on children record the formalization of ideas on the child's relationship to the state. Mental hygiene was of increasing importance in the programs of the conferences, and Canadian as well as U.S. delegates attended and participated. Although Canadians did not necessarily draw the same conclusions, they were influenced by the perspectives and social mandates which came out of these gatherings.

A long standing precedent for governmental concern over children's welfare was set by the first White House Conference on the Care of Dependent Children in 1909. Increased public interest in social welfare followed the trend in the secularization of charity to scientific philanthropy to government function.[2] In the 1940s, the perceived need for children to be treated according to their age and developmental psychological status was incorporated into the standards of professonal organizations, and mandated in the practices of government agencies. These ideas were made generally available to the public through the popular media, where they were gradually incorporated into everyday knowledge.

The first White House Conference in 1909 concentrated on family preservation. The next conference emphasized the child within the family circle. The White House Conference of 1919 signaled the completion of a year long campaign for child welfare, the "Children's Year," sponsored by the Children's Bureau. The White House gathering was the first of a series of Bureau sponsored mini-conferences which spread the perspective of psychiatry and mental hygiene that had been brought to the attention of policy makers by mental hygienists during the first World War. The "mental hygiene of the child—the care of the instincts, emotions, and general personality, and of environmental conditions," over the first seven years of life were emphasized as critical to adult health, education, morals and habits.

Training teachers and social workers in mental hygiene was given great priority.[3] The emphasis on the medicalization of the helping professions was reflected at the National Conference of Social Work (which also represented Canadian social workers) where the first section on mental hygiene was initiated in 1917. The National Conference of Social Work was dominated by mental hygiene related concerns by the 1920 annual meeting. Psychiatric social work had been successfully encouraged by the National Committee for Mental Hygiene through expanded training programs fostered by Thomas Salmon during the first World War. A concentrated effort for auxiliary mental health training occurred in Canada after the second World War.[4]

The White House Conference on Child Health and Protection of 1930, called by President Herbert Hoover, reflected a research demonstration in mental hygiene conducted by the National Committee for Mental Hygiene and philanthropies in the 1920s.[5] The White House Conference on Child Health and Protection was dominated by medical personnel and a whole-child approach which stressed mental hygiene. The Conference also emphasized the need for elite professional leadership in government and private philanthropy in order to bring about reforms.[6]

On April 26, 1939 the planning committee for the 1940 Conference met in Washington.[7] It was to be the fourth such conference hosted by a president of the United States, at this time Franklin D. Roosevelt. It was the third conference organized by the U.S. Department of Labor, Children's Bureau. The General Education Board provided a grant of $47,000 which was disbursed by the American Council on Education to meet the Conference's expenses.[8]

The theme of the family "as the threshold of democracy" was similar to that of the first Conference in 1909.[9] The preservation of the economic well-being of the family was declared as the heart of the "conservation of the greatest of all our resources—our children."[10] As Francis Perkins, secretary of labor and chairman of the Conference noted, the 1940 gathering came upon the similar problem of conserving children and family life from degradation as in 1909 but "with the advantage of thirty years of experience and a greater sense of public responsibility."[11]

The White House Conference on Children in a Democracy took place in January 1940 at the end of a depression and at the beginning of a devastating war. It addressed the disjuncture between democratic ideals and the social reality of U.S. society as systematically stratified. The Conference addressed the evident problems of economic and political disorganization in relationship to public responsibility for child mental health. Delegates to the convention clarified the rationale which became the basis for federal mental health policy after the War. It represented a turning point where mental hygiene took a formal place within the ideology of American individualism as a modification in the relationship between the democratic state and the child.[12]

The exposition of Conference ideals in 1940 added the political issue of mental and physical well-being as the basis for democracy and "brotherhood." This was to be accomplished by following the prescription of validated scientific research on the basic needs of children.[13] This view also reflected the Canadian perspective as represented at the Conference by Charlotte Whitton.[14]

The 1940 Conference coalesced the issues of previous Conferences. It moved child mental and physical health, educational opportunity and social welfare within the realm of entitlement, rather than moral obligation extended by benevolent reformers. The Conference members further addressed the "scientific research" conducted in child development in the 1920s and 1930s by incorporating distinctions between age groups by identifying specific needs for preschool, school age, youth, and young adult categories. Restrictions and benefits were recommended according to age-related criteria with regard to family income, housing, labor, education, handicapping conditions and health care.[15]

The 1950 Mid-Century White House Conference on Children and Youth took these prescriptions one step further than the 1940 Conference. For the first time personality development was the major topic of discussion which pervaded the technical papers and work group discussions. No aspect of the Conference was unmarked by the importance of the issue of mental health and the specifics of age-graded statuses spanning infancy and early childhood through young adulthood.[16]

Mental Hygiene to Mental Health

The Mid-Century White House Conference was a sounding board for forty years of formal mental hygiene organization. From Clifford Beers' first Society for Mental Hygiene in Connecticut in 1908 and the National Committee in 1909, the movement had changed and grown, dramatically fulfilling, in many ways, Beers' dream. The state societies grew rapidly from the second society in Illinois in 1909. New York joined in 1910; Massachusetts, Maryland, North Carolina, and Pennsylvania in 1913. Over fifty state and local societies operated by 1930. By the 1940s, an amorphous group of approximately two hundred state and local societies existed in a loose coalition with organizational characteristics which varied from support groups to those which carried out clinical services. Membership was honorary and by invitation, reflecting an individual's previous record in mental hygiene work. The local and state societies and the National Committee, served, at minimum, as publicity agents spreading the word of mental hygiene. Mental hygiene moved toward increased popular support and organizational specialization in the 1940s.[17]

During World War II, mental hygienists worked closely with the Canadian and U.S. Armies. William Line of the CNCMH served as head of the Directorate of Personnel Selection and Social Services of the Canadian Army and the Canadian National Committee formed a civilian advisory council to the Service.[18] In the U.S., conscientious objectors were assigned by the

Selective Service System to work in mental hospitals. A group of these individuals began to publish a mimeographed bulletin called "The Attendant." This publication utilized articles, photographs and such popular media as cartoons to describe conditions and seek reforms concerning the treatment of mental illness. The Canadian National Committee sponsored a similar booklet titled "The Attendant's Guide," which it distributed to every mental hospital in Canada.[19] Supported by the American Friends Service Committee, a Civilian Public Service organization was initiated in the United States which drew up an informal "mental hygiene program." This was subsequently formally recognized by the Selective Service as the Mental Hygiene Program of the Civilian Public Service and placed under the direction of the National Committee for Mental Hygiene. After the War the program was renamed the National Mental Health Foundation.[20] It was merged with the National Committee in 1950.

During the War, in collaboration with the NCMH, the Mental Hygiene Program of the Civilian Public Service published fourteen hundred reports on conditions in mental institutions, including photographs which they made available to journalists and writers.[21] This publicity was part of a general public awareness campaign concerning mental health. In the year 1942, the New York State Committee on Mental Hygiene and the State Charities Aid Association collaborated in producing a series of dramatic sketches on mental illness through the American Theatre Wing Victory Players (later called the American Theatre Wing Community Players). The popular press joined the voluntary associations in furthering public concern over mental illness. *Life* magazine published an expose of mental institutions called "Bedlam, U.S.A." in May of 1946. *Readers Digest* published "The Shame of Our Mental Hospitals," in July. Albert Deutsch's *Shame of the States* was first published in the New York daily newspaper *PM* in a series in 1945. Deutsch testified before a U.S. Senate committee: "The institutional care of psychotics has been traditionally mainly a state responsibility. It should remain so. But the job of getting preventive devices and using them is a national responsibility."[22] Deutsch's classic, *The Mentally Ill in America*, which was commissioned by Beers and the American Foundation for Mental Hygiene in the mid-thirties and published in 1937, was revised, enlarged and reissued in 1949.[23]

Television and radio were utilized as well. A series of eight programs on mental illness titled, "For These We Speak," was distributed to one thousand stations in the United States and Canada. Twentieth Century Fox dramatized Mary Jane Ward's *The Snake Pit*, in a 1946 film. The Columbia Broadcasting system produced an hour long documentary in 1949, narrated by Surgeon General William C. Menninger, called "Mind in the Shadow," which relayed the inadequacy of mental institutions. The National

Film Board of Canada produced a similar group of related programs called the "Mental Mechanisms Series."

Popularizing children's needs predated the War. Lawrence K. Frank published a monograph, *Fundamental Needs of the Child*, which first appeared in the NCMH journal, *Mental Hygiene*, in 1938. That same year the American Council on Education published *Emotion and the Educative Process*. The National Committee sponsored a quarterly journal for teachers called *Understanding the Child*, edited by Carson Ryan published with help from a grant from the Carnegie Corporation. In the 1940s popular media items on mental hygiene and child development expanded. Catherine Mackenzie produced a weekly column for the *New York Times Magazine* called "Parent and Child." Virginia McMullin produced and Jessie Stanton moderated a thirty-five minute talkshow called "The Baby Institute" in 1943–1944 on the Blue Network, forerunner to the present American Broadcasting Company. In Canada, S. R. Laycock, director of mental hygiene education for the Canadian National Committee gave workshops on child guidance at Home and School Clubs (an organization similar to the Parent-Teachers organizations in the U.S.). Laycock also gave addresses to the Ontario Education Association and wrote popular articles for *School*, *Canadian Home Journal*, *Food for Thought*, and the *Canadian Nurse*. He produced a chart entitled "Child Needs." Over 150,000 copies were distributed by the Canadian Broadcasting Company. Copies were mailed to teachers by every provincial department of education.[24] Benjamin Spock's popular *The Commonsense Book of Baby and Child Care* was first published in 1945. In 1949, the American Theatre Wing Community Plays and the National Committee for Mental Hygiene developed "Temperate Zone: Three Plays for Parents about the Climate of the Home." In 1950, the Mental Health Film Board produced a series, "Angry Boy," which depicted the motivations behind a child's delinquent behavior and the work of a child guidance center in curing his problems. Erik Erikson's *Childhood and Society* was put together as a working paper for the Mid-century White House Conference and published the same year.[25]

The combination of the War, popular publicity, and the appeals of the National Committee for Mental Hygiene by mid-decade brought about federal legislation the Committee and its philanthropic mentors had long sought. The passage of the U.S. National Mental Health Act in 1946 and the creation of the National Institute of Mental Health (NIMH) in 1949 culminated the NCMH efforts to expand governmental responsibility and financial assistance for research and mental health care services.[26]

The collaborative work of the U.S. NCMH and philanthropy was coming to a timely transition point in 1950. The National Committee for

Mental Hygiene, the National Mental Health Foundation, and the newer Psychiatric Foundation were merged in September of 1950.

The Psychiatric Foundation was the fund raising arm of the American Psychiatric Association. It was put together under the direction of the National Committee for Mental Hygiene and the American Neurological Association in order to solicit funds for a hospital survey to be conducted by the APA. The Psychiatric Foundation served as a repository for the distribution of funds.

The coalition of the three groups, the Psychiatric Foundation, the NCMH, and the Mental Health Foundation, became the National Association for Mental Health. Owen Root was made president and George S. Stevenson continued as medical director, the position he occupied since Clarence Hincks resigned to return to Canada in 1939. The newly constituted Association accepted a mandate to serve as an umbrella organization for fund raising and public education concerning mental health primarily on a state and local level.[27]

From 1915 to 1943, the Rockefeller Foundation had contributed over a million dollars to the NCMH. In January 1947, fifty thousand dollars were appropriated for general expenses for the Committee. However, half of this amount lapsed in December of 1949, because the condition of matching funds was not met.[28] After the reorganization of the National Committee, requests were made to the Rockefeller Foundation in order to launch a new program highlighting the establishment of the National Mental Health Association.[29] The Rockefeller Foundation agreed to a final general purpose dispensation of one hundred thousand dollars to the new association. Consultation with other philanthropies disclosed similar appropriations from the Carnegie Corporation for seventy-five thousand dollars and the Commonwealth Fund for fifty thousand dollars.[30] Alan Gregg explained:

> we have stressed the importance of getting the Association independent of the large foundations. Though the present recommendation is a complete reversal of my previous attitude I think we cannot refuse to contribute anything, and that our position in the future will be better protected by a generous final grant than in any other way.[31]

The impact of the National Institute of Mental Health is witnessed in the expansion of mental health funds and services after its creation. By 1963 the modest NIMH budget of $8 million had expanded to $144 million. The NIMH had sponsored three thousand research programs and instituted fifteen hundred teaching programs in psychiatry by that same date. The number of psychiatrists went from three thousand in 1944 to seventeen thousand in

1964. Mental health auxiliary workers increased by thirty percent during this same period.[32] Over the next five years the NIMH budget more than doubled to $361.5 million. The NIMH spent twenty-nine percent of its funds on manpower research, twenty-eight percent on research, twenty-six percent on state and community programs. The remainder went to service activities and program management.[33]

In 1955, *The Mental Health Act* created the Joint Commission on Mental Illness and Health to report to Congress on the state of psychiatry.[34] A report was submitted in 1960 and published the next year. The *Community Mental Health Centers Act* was signed with strong presidential support in 1963.[35] This legislation signaled, in the U.S., the formal end of the asylum and the institutionalization of the idea that psychiatric practice belonged in the community hospital, clinic, or private practice. Canada also followed the trend to place mental health care within the human services system. It has been pointed out that public mental health care extended the range of the welfare system as it performed functions of control, surveillance and normalization. Public services came to rely increasingly on psychology as a strategy for therapy and social order.[36]

After 1950, the Canadian Committee retained a position closer to government than the U.S. Association. In 1945, Clarence Hincks, as medical director of the Canadian Committee, became an advisor to the Department of National Health and Welfare formerly the Department of Pensions and Welfare. He outlined a plan for a national institute for mental hygiene. The Canadian National Committee recommended that the government provide mental health grants totaling $6,250,000 with $4,000,000 to provinces on a per capita basis, $2,000,000 to improve existing facilities and $250,000 for research and training.[37] Dominion Mental Health Grants were created along these lines in 1948. The grants did not directly benefit the Canadian National Committee. However, unlike the establishment of the National Institute of Mental Health in the United States, the Canadian grants substantiated the continued position of the Committee in the guidance of public policy and mental health leadership.[38]

In the 1940s, the Canadian Committee not only contributed to government programs and increased its educational publicity, but initiated major surveys and research oriented organizations and demonstrations. For example, in 1946 the Toronto Mental Health Clinic was created. This was the first child guidance center to conform closely to the U.S. child guidance demonstrations using the services of a psychiatrist, psychologist and psychiatric social worker. In 1952, the clinic was renamed the Hincks Treatment Centre with in-patient and out-patient facilities for children and young adults. Originally a cooperative effort between the CNCMH and Toronto Welfare Council with funds from the Community Chest and the

University of Toronto School of Social Work, the clinic became an independent agency with its own board of directors that same year.

Hincks retired and John D. Griffin took over the medical directorship of the Committee in 1947. A major school survey was undertaken which assessed mental hygiene teaching practices. The Canadian Education Association and the Canadian Public Health Association utilized the CNCMH for consulting services on mental hygiene. The second of these reports was an explication of "a mental hygiene approach to education," with detailed descriptions of child mental health problems and their remediation in clinical settings.[40] The school surveys led to projects in teacher training and demonstration pilot projects. One of the major demonstrations was the Forest Hill Village Project initiated in 1948 which did "psycho-social research in community mental health."[41] A liaison officer project which trained eighty teachers by 1960 combined academic child study, psychiatry, social work and education. An emphasis in the demonstrations, similar to the U.S. committee, was to initiate permanent projects to be taken over by official bodies, university faculties and school boards.[42]

As early as 1946, the Canadian Committee began to discuss expanding into a popular movement by encouraging the growth of provincial and local societies.[43] While local expansion had characterized the U.S. movement, from the beginning the Canadian movement had remained national and exclusive in its membership. In 1949, a new organization was proposed which would operate on three levels. The national level would essentially remain the same. It would continue with its technical staff to provide liaison and consultative services including task force surveys and public forums. It would be a major policy innovator for government. The provincial level of organization would provide liaison services between the local communities and the national organization, assist branch work and offer an information service. The local level would provide grassroots services and gather information to pass on to the higher levels on community needs.[44] A similar organizational format exists to the present. The Canadian Association for Mental Health is the largest provider of non-public mental health services in Canada. The Association in this way serves as an official public consultant, as a private provider and as an advocate for mental health policy.[45] The Committee was renamed the Canadian Association of Mental Health in 1950. The first provincial division under the new "white cross" symbol was created with the help of S. R. Laycock in Saskatchewan in November 1950. Divisions were subsequently established in all ten provinces.[46]

Canada as the first international committee retained a close connection to the international mental hygiene movement. The international growth of mental hygiene expanded over this period beginning with the

Canadian affiliation in 1918. The first International Congress on Mental Hygiene was held in Washington D.C. in 1930. The Congress gathered more than three thousand participants from fifty countries. The international movement also changed significantly in the 1940s. A second International Congress was held in 1937 in Paris, however, the international exchange was practically nonexistent for the next decade due to the War. The movement was reactivated in 1947. In August of 1948, the Third International Congress on Mental Health was held in London.

In 1948, the World Federation for Mental Health was established in response to a recommendation by the United Nations World Health Organization (WHO) and the United Nations Economic, Social and Cultural Organization (UNESCO). The first director was Canadian psychiatrist, Brock Chisholm, former general director of the Canadian Army Medical Services. The current World Federation has official consultative status with the United Nations and continues to work closely with the WHO and UNESCO.

Children were an early and major consideration for the World Federation. English child psychiatrist, John Bowlby, became a consultant in 1950. His monograph, *Mental Health and Maternal Care*, was prepared under the auspices of WHO. Bowlby emphasized the importance of mother-love in the development of the child's character and personality.[47] Child mental health surveys were conducted on a world wide basis in 1960 which related these areas of concern to education, industrialization, migration and cross cultural attitudes toward mental disorders, professional training and research.[48]

The Rockefeller Foundation also participated in the internationalization of mental hygiene. Part of the world wide campaign for public education on mental health was the issue of professional training strongly endorsed by the Rockefeller Foundation as it extended programs in medical and psychiatric education around the world. Research activities were initiated in the United States, Canada, Great Britain, France, Holland, Belgium, Germany, Sweden, Norway and Switzerland.[49]

The state of psychiatry, in general, was discussed through the Foundation's network of inter-office correspondence in the 1940s.[50] Enthusiasm over advances in psychiatry was mixed, however. Problems within the professional associations in psychiatry reflected the continuing lag effect of the mental health field in comparison with the natural and medical sciences. Rockefeller staff observations on the psychiatric profession were three fold. The Foundation questioned the gain in prestige afforded psychiatry by its role in the second World War on the grounds that it was not based on scientific breakthroughs. The Foundation was becoming increasingly disturbed by the fact that psychiatry and psychiatrists failed to scientifically validate clinical procedures. Related to this, the Foundation staff had misgivings about the capability of psychiatry to become scientific. "Tested scientific knowledge" had to come out of laboratories and individual research. Instead, as Robert S. Morison of the Rockefeller Foundation noted, "There have been several times recently when I have felt that the leaders of American psychiatry are trying to establish truth on the basis of majority vote. This is, of course, quite contrary to the usual scientific procedure of submitting evidence which can stand on its own merits in a candid world."[51]

In 1948, President Chester I. Barnard of the Rockefeller Foundation, after reviewing documents on the Foundation's support for psychiatry, came to the conclusion that there was an underlying fundamental "criticism of psychiatry generally" implied in the record. Barnard admonished:

> Isn't there any way to blast this situation? Doesn't a continued and general refusal to permit or attempt validation of psycho-therapeutic methods put everyone concerned, including ourselves, in a position of promoting or carrying on a social racket? How can the charlatans be dealt with if the good men will give no validation but their own individual say sos?[52]

The Professionalization of Psychiatry

The advancement of psychiatric education and leadership was a problem in the United States, which was even more acute in Canada. The Group for the Advancement of Psychiatry (GAP) was established in the mid-forties. It was affliated with the American Psychiatric Association, the professional organization of both Canadian and United States psychiatrists through the 1940s. GAP illustrates the political process where professional psychiatric perspectives and mental health protocols were encouraged by the leadership of philanthropies. Similarly the establishment of an independent Canadian Psychiatric Association in 1951 is instructive of the changing relationship between advocacy, psychiatric professionalism and government.

From the early Association of Medical Superintendents of American Institutions for the Insane (1844–1892), to the American Medico-Psychological Association (1893–1921), and the American Psychiatric Association, psychiatrists had sought legitimacy and recognition for their field. Major movements toward organizational changes were occasioned by lay reformers, first by Dorothea Dix (1840s) and then Clifford Beers.[53] Prior to 1900 there was no systematic instruction in psychiatry. In the 1920s, Thomas Salmon and the NCMH urged psychiatric education, as did C. K. Clarke in Canada. The need for certification by an outside board became a major issue in the 1930s. The National Committee organized a Division on Psychiatric Education in 1930. The American Medical Association conducted a survey of mental hospitals which was resented by the APA as reducing the autonomy of psychiatry. The NCMH played a strong role in trying to gain autonomy and status while integrating psychiatry into medical curriculum. The American Board of Psychiatry and Neurology was not formally organized until October of 1934. The discipline was still in a dire state of flux in 1942. The Group for the Advancement of Psychiatry was organized in this juncture. Its role was to professionalize psychiatry as medical doctors, whose clients were in outpatient clinics, child guidance clinics and private practice, and as public consultants on a wider basis in human services.[54]

The Group for the Advancement of Psychiatry was a product of philanthropic encouragement. Before World War II ended, Barry C. Smith of the Commonwealth Fund initiated discussions with army personnel and his own staff and the National Committee for Mental Hygiene staff over the organization of a planning conference for mental hygiene. The major concern was "psychiatric planning for personnel, training and service."[55] William C. Menninger, surgeon general of the U.S. Army in charge of psychiatry, concurred with the need for the professionalization and training of psychiatrists and support personnel.[56] As the conference format evolved, it was determined that participants were to be carefully picked. The exclusive group was to be confined to top government and civilian representatives of medicine and psychiatry, as well as Foundation staff members. Those invited included Alan Gregg, director of the Rockefeller Foundation Medical Division, who had served as an aid to Menninger during the War; Frank Fremont-Smith, medical director of the Josiah Macy, Jr. Foundation; Lawrence S. Kubie of the National Research Council; Commonwealth Fund executive assistant, Mildred Scoville, and medical associate, Lester J. Evans. Other individuals were chosen because of their clinical experience or the "importance of their perspective or stragetic position."[57]

The Hershey Conference, so named for its location in Hershey, Pennsylvania, took place February 1–3, 1945. Nine recommendations came out of the conference, including a call for: a continuation of psychiatric training and facilities in the military; continued research by the Veterans Administration on soldiers; the expansion of non-hospital facilities for mental hygiene; "intensive efforts to arouse and inform" public forums on mental hygiene in churches, schools, industry and labor through the NCMH; expanded medical education in psychiatry, especially as serving education and industry; comprehensive undergraduate medical education in psychiatry directed toward outpatient clinics and wards; graduate training in psychiatry, combined with pediatrics and internal medicine; and the training and increased use of auxiliary personnel such as social work and psychology in "community services for mental health."[58]

The Hershey Conference timing was conducive to change. At the next meeting of the American Psychiatric Association in Chicago the standing committee from the Conference discussed active steps for furthering professional training in psychiatry and the certification and reorganization of clinical facilities. Funds were sought from the Commonwealth Fund and two immediate steps taken. The first was to nominate and elect members of the committee to the council of the American Psychiatric Association. Secondly, a semi-independent organization was created called the Group for the Advancement of Psychiatry.[59]

GAP was exclusive from the onset, and was limited to 150 members who had to "pass a rigid scrutiny as to serious interests, professional soundness and willingness to give promptly and freely of their own time and money."[60] In the words of William Menninger, who became the first chairman, GAP operated as a "small mobile striking force for American psychiatry."[61] Committee members saw themselves as a forward action group within a conservative field. They tended to view the APA and the American Medical Association as not having kept "abreast of the times." It was "too protective," "too cautious" and lacking in "aggressive leadership."[62]

By 1948, GAP had reached its anticipated membership of 150. The group worked through fifteen functional committees. Fall and spring general meetings, interim committee meetings, the circulation of reports and "circular letters" for approval and revision kept members in close contact. The pace of the group is witnessed by the fact that from July 1947 to March 1948, five reports and forty-nine circular letters were published and distributed. The reports were mailed to researchers in the area and also to "many persons whom the committee believed could or should profit from the report." The social work report, for example, was sent to every member of the APA, every member of the Association of Psychiatric Social Workers, and was made available for students in the field and "distributed to every state hospital and Veterans Administration Hospital." Requests for orders of fifty to one hundred copies were "not infrequent." First printing of some reports, in anticipation of their demand, ranged from seven thousand copies on shock therapy to ten thousand on social work.[63]

GAP attempted to gain "spheres of influence." It circulated information through the National Committee for Mental Hygiene to the scientific and lay press. GAP made major endorsements on social policy such as the President's Committee on Civil Rights, and also made recommendations on military training. It encouraged other organizations such as the World Health Organization, created in 1948, which subsequently became a vehicle for the international mental health movement through the World Federation for Mental Health.

GAP's rapid rise in power and influence was due to the personal positions of its members. This reflected the policy decisions of the original Hershey Conference committee in choosing to include only strategically influential members, whose mutual support would serve to cross institutional and disciplinary boundaries. As Menninger pointed out in his report to Mildred Scoville: "Through its committee on Federal Agencies, GAP has had a definite and direct influence on the psychiatric work in various government agencies, not only of the United States, but through Canadian members, on the Canadian government."[64] Members were in the mililtary services, public health administration, veteran's administration and the office of the surgeon general. Other GAP members included consultants to the Federal Security Agency, Joint Research and Development Board, National Research Council, Federal Medical Services Committee and the Mental Health Advisory Committee (U.S. Public Health Service). Robert Felix, head of the federal Division of Mental Hygiene, who was made director of NIMH, was active in GAP.[65] Strategic recommendations from GAP were funneled to government and to professional associations by members who routinely served on major policy making boards.[66]

GAP's direct influence on the American Psychiatric Association was dramatic. "Extensive reorganization plans" were made for the structure of the APA with eleven of fourteen members on the reorganization committee GAP members. A full time medical director was hired for the APA who was also a GAP member. Even though the GAP membership of 150 was dwarfed by the APA membership of 4,500, they "turned out full force" to nominate and elect members to three of four available seats on the APA council in 1947–1948. GAP members then totaled five of the eleven council seats. They chaired thirteen out of twenty-six standing APA committees, and by 1948–1949, held the positions of president, secretary and treasurer, seven out of twelve council positions, and chaired twenty of the twenty-six standing committees of the APA.[67]

Criticisms of GAP are instructive in that the organizational character of the group proved more problematical for the American membership than for the Canadians. This was the case in spite of the fact that GAP addressed U.S. issues and appeared to be successfully advancing the status of psychiatry in U.S. medical circles. The Group for the Advancement of Psychiatry was accused by U.S. members of being an elitist political body which had attempted to take over an egalitarian association of professionals. It was accused on one hand of serving propagandistic purposes outside the realm of science, and conversely, was questioned on the basis of the self-proclaimed over scientistic standards it upheld in psychiatry.[68] One critic wrote:

> GAP is a small, self-contained body which has to a very great extent presumed to speak authoritatively for American psychiatry . . . The continuance of GAP in the manner it is and has been functioning is a serious threat to the unity of the American Psychiatric Association.[69]

Another member of GAP in a letter of resignation noted that: "One would not expect a self-elected 'leadership' group, especially while subsidized, to recognize spontaneously the appropriate time for relinquishing its functions to a more broadly representative organization."[70] Another APA member who refused to join GAP resented the

> inference which the GAP tries to convey that it has a monopoly on the psychiatric knowledge of this country. [Further, the political and manipulative nature of the group was seen as undermining psychiatry in that] the vast majority of the members of the Association . . . by inference are not considered to be competent enough psychiatrists to belong to the inner circle.[71]

Some of these allegations were simply correct. GAP members consciously saw themselves as an elite vanguard. Members pushed a distinctive view of science and professionalism. As an elite group within the APA, it followed a hierarchical model in its internal structure. On one hand, the officers and membership of the committee were inflexible. Yet, members were obliged to participate and committees were obliged to produce position reports for general discussion among members. The reports were circulated and a consensus was reached by having the report revised to conform to the dissenting opinions. The executive steering committee made decisions as to which reports would be published and circulated and to whom. These procedures resemble the internal dynamics of the foundations with their divisions and committee structures, with the exception that the foundations delegated authority to various levels and did not require general consensus. GAP, like the discipline of psychiatry itself, was riddled with contradictions. These included equally problematic elitist and democratic tendencies. The emphasis on the need for basic scientific research and standardization of training and practices before propagandizing results also contradicted the active campaigns to popularize psychiatric perspectives in affiliated disciplines and in the minds of the lay public.

Some members ignored the demanding work schedule for GAP. For example, even an important GAP circular on the aims and objectives of the organization, written to clarify their position vis-a-vis the general APA membership, was answered by only two thirds of the GAP members.[72] Many members found the paper work demanded in the committees to be overbearing. Consequently, external criticisms were matched by internal dissension.

The Canadian psychiatrists found less fault with the elite structure of the organization and its dual sense of obligation to work for the whole. This conformed with the Canadian view of the role of leadership and its obligations. The problem was that the purposes of the APA and GAP were increasingly directed internally and toward problems typical of the United States. Not surprisingly, financial issues overshadowed the ability of GAP to become independent or to expand its specific interests internationally. This also was brought to a head in 1949, in that the Commonwealth Fund, which had supported GAP, was to withdraw January 1, 1950. No other funds appeared forthcoming.[73] Canada, at this time, was concerned with issues in its own national development. Psychiatry in the United States and Canada was in different stages of growth. Each context required new and innovative solutions. Canadian psychiatry was less advanced than in the United States, but it was not just a matter of catching up but of being structurally different in its relationship to the Canadian government and to the Canadian Medical Association.

Reassessment of the relationship between Canadian psychiatrists and the APA contributed to the formal establishment of an independent Canadian Psychiatric Association in 1951. The CPA was founded after four years of discussion. Similar forces which had led to the creation of GAP occurred in Canada at the end of the War. The Canadian Psychiatric Association was in a sense the equivalent of GAP in the U.S. The Canadian Association was a product of a small group of Canadian mental hygienists who contributed to the collaboration of a self-identified vanguard contingent of Canadian psychiatrists, the CNCMH and the Canadian Medical Association.[74]

The Canadian National Committee for Mental Hygiene and William Line, Directorate of Personnel Selection and Social Sciences of the Canadian Army, initiated an Inter-Service (military) Conference on Psychiatry in April of 1944. Psychiatrists and representatives from the Department of Pensions and National Health attended.[75] The committee consisted of Clarence Hincks, William Blatz, J. C. Meakins of McGill University and G. Humphrey of Queens University. They initiated an internal educational campaign that January. Clarence Hincks convened a meeting of seventy-two Canadian psychiatrists to discuss the future of psychiatry at the close of the war. It was noted that psychiatrists who had worked in the cooperative Canadian program for evacuated children in the British Isles would return to Canada, enlarging the group of qualified personnel in psychiatric-related disciplines and moderating to some extent the shortage of trained personnel.[76] A second conference of the inter-service psychiatrists was held headed by J. D. Griffin, Brock Chisholm and D. Ewen Cameron in 1945. This meeting took up the question of the advancement of post graduate training in psychiatry, the professional status of psychiatry, and an increase in provincial services. A survey contacted every psychiatrist in Canada trying to draw them into "partnership with [the] National Committee to promote progress."[77] Partly as a result of these meetings and inquiries, a Section on Psychiatry was established in the Canadian Medical Association in 1945.[78] By 1948, there was growing interest in creating an association independent of the Canadian Medical Association and American Psychiatric Association, neither of which were truly representative as spokesmen for the interests of Canadian psychiatry.[79]

The incipient association of Canadian psychiatrists took advantage of existing organizations since they lacked funds to establish independent meetings. At the 1949 Montreal meetings of the APA, an Interim Committee was formed. A new survey of Canadian psychiatrists showed support for an independent organization. At the April 30, 1950 APA convention in Detroit, the group of Canadian psychiatrists formally voted approval. At the Canadian Medical Association meetings a month later in Halifax, a committee which included J. D. Griffin of the Canadian Mental Health Association, was instructed to draw up a constitution and to apply for corporate status under Canadian law.[80] The organization was incorporated June 1, 1951 and the first formal meeting was held June 20, 1951 in Montreal, coinciding with the Canadian Medical Association meetings. Its original membership totaled 143.

The Canadian Psychiatric Association remained weak in membership and, consequently, weak in funds since it was supported by members' dues. The bulletin of the CPA (later the *Canadian Psychiatric Association Journal*) was initiated in March of 1952. It was distributed under the aegis of the Ontario Health Department. Membership in 1952 had only grown to 182 of the 685 psychiatrists in Canada, and in 1956 the 437 members still only represented 56.8 percent of all Canadian psychiatrists.[81]

The establishment of professional standards, certification of mental institutions, and expansion of psychiatric curriculum in medical schools has been a priority since the mid-fifties.[82] It was not an issue easily solved. The Ontario Psychiatric Association in 1973 still emphasized the need for training in psychiatry.

In 1958, a contingent of Canadian psychiatrists interested in children created a committee to gather information. A report, in 1961, revealed a very uneven distribution of services. Outside of Quebec and Ontario, services concentrated on adult oriented facilities which carried heavy case loads involving children.[83]

In the United States, the increase in the number of psychiatrists coincided with the emphasis on child mental health. In Canada the small number of practicing psychiatrists retarded the development of specializations, including child psychiatry. The Laidlaw Foundation funded a workshop in techniques of teaching child psychiatry in 1974, but the number of professional child psychiatrists did not dramatically increase, even under the pressure of expanding child and family oriented community services in mental health. Toronto and Montreal remained the major training centers in Canada. Child psychiatry, while a two year component in medical education at the universities of Toronto, McGill and Queens, remained an informal subspecialty in the Canadian Psychiatric Association. The Royal College did not initiate separate examinations for child psychiatry to correspond to the American Boards in Child Psychiatry.[84] Canadian psychiatrists found the push for psychiatric leadership in community level services a difficult or impossible challenge to meet. Similar to the U.S., one solution was to endorse the use of auxiliary personnel and to rely on public health education, using the services of medical doctors, teachers, psychologists, social workers and public health nurses.[85]

The Clinical Classification of Abnormality in Childhood

The classification of mental diseases was an important aspect of the effort to substantiate the medical validity of psychiatry. It was also a way of making psychiatry more readily accessible to auxiliary professions. In a series of reports on child mental health dating from 1951, GAP contributed to this enterprise.[86] The Group for the Advancement of Psychiatry set the classification of mental diseases, especially in children, as a major objective. In 1957, GAP produced a report on child psychiatry from its newly formed Committee on Child Psychiatry.[87] In 1966, the GAP Committee produced a monograph on the *Pathological Disorders in Childhood: Theoretical Considerations and a Proposed Classification*.[88] This document presaged the introduction of children into the official nosology of mental pathologies. Up to this time childhood mental pathology did not have separate classifications and was not formally singled out from adult mental illness.

The GAP Committee on Child Psychiatry contributed to the creation and expansion of categories identifying infant and child-related mental illnesses, which have grown exponentially in the Post World War II period. One third of the categories of mental disorders were cited as either "evident in infancy, childhood or adolescence," in the *DSM–III–R*, the latest diagnostic and statistical manual of the American Psychiatric Association, which is used by both U.S. and Canadian psychiatrists.[89] In addition to the thirty–six age related coded categories there are 182 additional mental disorders specifically noted as "appropriate for children or adolescence."

Since the late 1940s, young children and adolescents have been the fastest growing segment of the population of patients with mental disorders.

The number of children and adolescents in mental institutions in the United States increased by 150 percent between 1962 and 1973. By 1973, there were twenty-six thousand children in mental hospitals with admissions predominantly for "personality disorders," "adaptation reactions" and "behavior problems" as well as mental retardation.[90] In the United States, in 1966, there were 149 clinical centers specializing in childhood and adolescent mental disorders treating ten thousand juveniles.[91] By 1974, 340 centers had opened which treated thirty-thousand children.[92] Overall, the number of patients under twenty-five years of age tripled between 1955 and 1972 when the number of adult patients most rapidly declined, due to the new emphasis on community and out-patient mental health facilities and the closing of state hospitals.[93]

The major trends in hospitalized mental health care in the United States and Canada include increases of up to sixty-five percent for: 1) social misfits and deviants who are considered dangerous but not necessarily clinically mentally ill; and 2) the so called "revolving door" patient. Both of these designations are dominated by minors.[94] The revolving door for children is created by the chance nature of the referral process. Children, depending on the referral source, their geographical location, and their individual symptomology, can end up in the "correctional, social service, special educational or mental health" system.[95] Further, the follow-up and coordination of services with children has generally been poor.[96]

Class plays a large factor in the identification and type of therapeutic intervention of mental disorders of all ages. This may be most decisive in the case of the young. Wealthier families can pay for therapeutic educational or psychiatric settings. They can solicit private consultations with highly trained medical professionals.[97] "Less favored" families may be swept, involuntarily, into the correctional and social welfare system. Due to the prevailing lack of child psychiatrists, the dominant professional intervention, in most cases by necessity, relies heavily on medicalized, but not medical, professions in education, social work and psychology.[98]

One of the legacies of the formalization of categories of mental disorders of infancy, childhood and adolescence has been the increasing presence of a medical paradigm applied to the lives of all children.[99] As the dividing line between normal and abnormal is more frequently and rigorously examined, it has become more instead of less, meaningful. The refinement of categories of definition, and selective methods of identifying abnormality tend to be self-justifying and self-perpetrating. This "surveillance" function of rewarding normality and identifying potential deviance, is part of the essence of mental hygiene as preventive public health work. The object of eliminating mental disorder and promoting mental well-being through early identification divides and subdivides the potentiality of any given circumstance or characteristic for its potential for causing maladjustment. It becomes an a priori warning system for deviant development.

Chapter Eleven

Private Knowledge Brokers and Public Policy: U.S. and Canadian Style

By mid-century mental hygiene advocates felt they had successfully established scientific standards for preventive mental health practices focused on children. "Ideas which were once strange," in the words of the chairman of the Mid-Century White House Conference on Children and Youth, had "achieved the high success of becoming . . . commonplace." Included were the birth right of all children to "a fair chance for a healthy personality;" "a right to childhood;" and, the observation that "what is good for any child is good for all children."[1]

The paradigm of preventive mental health contributed to the criterion by which modern social institutions identify and judge the normality of any one individual's experience of growing up. Mental hygiene legitimated public scrutiny into the private sphere once reserved for family and close kinship relationships. This happened to different degrees and for different reasons in the United States than in Canada. Mental hygiene supported the political ideology of the United States as grounded in the doctrine of individualism and equality of opportunity. Mental hygiene in Canada substantiated the traditional role of elites as overseers of social policy, government, and order.

Social Values, The Politics of Individualism, and National Character

Just as mental hygiene was an aspect of the public health movement from its earliest stages, public policies in mental health care are a fundamental aspect of what is termed the modern welfare state.[2] The ideology of welfare services in the United States and Canada differ in comprehensiveness and intent to serve. In general, Canadian policy has evolved toward the attempt to provide comprehensive public health services.[3] The United States tends toward the provision of residual services of basic needs for those who cannot provide for themselves on a personal basis, or public care for those who fall extremely low on social scales developed for the purposes of comparison. Supplemental services are provided to help individuals out of particular life crises. Both countries developed and expanded social security measures as a result of the Depression.[4] Canada had developed prior examples of governmental support such as minimum wage legislation, mothers' pensions, and workman's compensation stemming from the first World War, and the Old Age Pensions Act of 1927.[5] Manitoba, Saskatchewan, and Alberta, in 1916, 1917 and 1919 respectively, were the first provinces to establish mothers' pensions.[6] The Canadian Parliament had expressed interest in family allowances since 1929.[7] By the end of the second World War, Canada had children's allowances and unemployment insurance in place. National health legislation, on a cost sharing basis between the federal and provincial governments, came into effect in 1958. By 1963, 98.8 percent of the population was covered by hospital insurance. In 1961, the Royal Commission on Health Services recommended a comprehensive, universal health service administered by government and financed by provincial and federal funds. The Medical Care Act was passed in 1966.[8]

The expansion of public welfare was not smooth in either Canada or the United States.[9] There were similar sources of opposition to the expansion of the public sector in the provision of welfare in both the United States and Canada. For example, family allowances, as a solution to poverty affecting young children, were opposed by Charlotte Whitton, the executive director of the Canadian Council on Child and Family Welfare.[10] Whitton feared an undermining of parental responsibility and favored a rise in real wages rather than governmental support.[11] Private charity organizations in both countries opposed public sources of relief to families on the basis of poverty. The argument was that public authority should be restricted to the provision of institutions for criminal, delinquent, mentally ill and mentally deficient groups, leaving noninstitutional relief to voluntary agencies. Underlying this perception was an individualistic interpretation of poverty.[12] This perspective was supported by the ideological stance of mental hygiene where poverty was interpreted as an indication of personal pathology and inadequacy. The provision of relief from this standpoint needed to be provided on the basis of a therapeutic medicalized relationship.

Mental hygienists, in both Canada and the United States after World War I, argued for the legitimacy of publicly supported welfare which included therapeutic relationships.[13] This was part of the push for the professionalization of mental hygiene related disciplines in the social sciences. Professional social work, public health nursing and psychology were in the process of taking over the traditional roles of voluntary charity.[14] In the United States, the successful control of professional medicine in the

American Medical Association and the concurrent interests of the rising business of insurance created powerful lobbies which restricted the rapid advance of the public domain into their economic jurisdictions in health and welfare.[15] In the United States, the provision of welfare advanced with professional civil service. An individualistic perspective on poverty was institutionalized. In Canada, the coverage was more comprehensive, and a paternalistic perspective prevailed as civic authority expanded into public welfare. Volunteeristic organizations remained important in civic services as professionalization occurred more slowly than in the United States.[16]

Canada's goal of universal access to medical care as a social minimum in health services remains unparalleled in the United States.[17] Federal support programs in the United States are generally funded on a categorical basis with grants designated for specific utilization within limited program boundaries. While federal programs have consistently expanded in the United States they also have consistently proven inadequate to meet needs, and increasingly costly, in spite of attempts to limit government responsibility. Federal spending for mental health services, largely by indirect means as opposed to direct grants, expanded from less than five billion dollars to ninety billion dollars in the twenty-five years between 1945 to 1970.[18]

More recent developments in the 1980s attempt to reduce federal spending through the initiation of block rather than categorical grants.[19] Although this has not occurred in health care, it has in education.[20] Chapter two of the Education Consolidation and Improvement Act of 1981 combined twenty-eight categorical programs which had attempted to equalized educational opportunity by providing funds targeted for specific problem areas to serve those most deprived or disadvantaged by current policy. The replacement block grant distributed funds to state and local recipients regulated only by broadly defined objectives, sidestepping issues of need. In its efforts to decentralize government, and to increase efficiency and family choice, this policy may in fact increase costs on local levels where the need is greatest. The policy also has the potential for decreasing efficiency, defined as providing for the general good, and in the process, depriving those most in need of the basic provisions while supporting those who have already met basic standards.

The idea of solving social problems by preventing them from developing in childhood seems, in hind sight, at once self-evident and incredibly self-righteous. Perhaps it is understandable that the effort to put this ideology into practice made children into a social problem. In the United States, it made the state's role in providing for children in a democracy a source of major ideological discrepancies in the practice of the American dream.[21] De Tocqueville, who criticized the oddities of democracy one hundred years earlier, found the source of discrepancies in democratic ideals and practice in unfettered individualism.[22] Political leaders of the twentieth century utilized the concept of individualism as a rationale which moderates the social ideals of democratic equality by the acknowledgement of human differences and the "natural" inequalities between men.[23] This resolution to the ideological dilemma gained scientific legitimacy from the medicalized perspective of mental hygiene.

Individualism, with its rationale in mental hygiene, has not meant so much to Canadians. Canada lacks the strong "charter myth" present in the U.S. Constitution and Bill of Rights which supported universal values and the existential right to individual freedom. Individualism had no preconstructed ideological niche for Canadians. One argument for the function of ideological concepts and ideological systems of thought is that they constitute a public rationale for the legitimacy of the state. Both the United States and Canada, in popular media, formally identify themselves with egalitarian values over authoritarian values. Neither society supports a formal aristocracy or aristocratic institutions.[24] To this extent both societies need to conceal or minimize the existence of inequalities and the basic structure of power and distribution which supports systematic uneven gains.[25] This is significantly more important for the United States than it is for Canada. The United States has formulated a vigorous self-image, derived in part from its revolutionary heritage, as a free people united in a democratic and egalitarian society. Individualism is part of this image.

Canada, on the contrary, has an anti-revolutionary heritage. W. L. Morton has noted that the character of Canadidan institutions have been shaped by an historical and psychological allegiance to monarchy. Allegiance means that the state has an objective reality embodied in the succession of persons designated by parliament with hereditary rights.[26] Freedom and democratic participation in this view are guaranteed, not diminished, by the presence of a political order based on public rank and personal honor. Elites are seen as acting within a framework of larger interests which sustain a diversity of customs and rights under law in a way that the rational scheme of abstract principles in a republican democracy can not.[27] Republican institutions based in popular sovereignty require the formation of a consensus on the part of citizens. The state exists subjectively in that it must be given assent by popular vote in periodic reviews. This places a premium on conformity and homogeneity not called for or considered desirable in Canada. The allegiance to social order and a moral respect between political factions take precedent as values over individualized notions of freedom as a political issue. While the United States, with its republican institutions, validates by law the right to life, liberty and the pursuit of happiness, traditionally Canadians have looked to peace, order and good government to do the same. Until recently the basis for Canadian rights was not in any one act but in an historical continuum.[28] Individual freedom, in this view is not a prior condition, but proceeds from moral consensus and social order. Class structure is viewed traditionally as a source of order and, therefore, a source of freedom and democracy.

Canadians have tended to refrain from asserting any national *idée fixe* about their society.[29] Comparative studies have identified, nonetheless, national characteristics which strongly differentiate the United States and Canada. The characteristics focusing on values and belief systems are necessarily relative in that they reflect comparative differences rather than absolutes. This is not to say that there are not wide ranges of opinion and diversity of beliefs and values in any one society. World views which contribute to the perceived "rightness" of the social order must, nonetheless, be consistent enough to maintain a value system. As John Porter has pointed out, any working hypothesis on Canadian national character must begin with the recognition that "Canadians are a conservative people."[30]

The shape of Canadian conservatism has much to do with Canadian as opposed to U.S. support for mental hygiene. For example, the Canadian public is more consistently conservative in their appreciation for the maintenance of the status quo and traditional values in multiple cultural forms, less committed to republican institutions, and more tolerant of paternalistic leadership than U.S. citizens. This is not to say that the U.S. does not have its collegial relationship between groups who share elite status and power or lacks appreciation for wealth and class status.[31] The American value system, however, demands that such configurations be systematically justified. This has been done on the grounds of individualism described as personal talent, wits and ability. As a culture built of immigrants who have also learned to use the resources of a new land, Canadian values reflect an admiration for fortitude, wit and talent but do not necessarily see power, prestige and material wealth as a natural outcome or evidence of such qualities.

Canadians have been characterized as more law-abiding, less suspicious of governmental authority and more collectivist in orientation than Americans. Canadians are also more "particularistic," or tolerant and protective of cultural and group variations, whether regional, ethnic, religious, linguistic or social.[32] In the United States the emphasis on individual achievement and competition serves to mediate what are otherwise viewed as suspiciously unequal variations in power relationships and class structure in American society.[33]

Canadians have tended to view social differences in terms of ethnicity, language and religion. Policy questions have centered more recently on balancing the power and status of Canada's traditional dual French and English cultures and the relative position of immigrants with alternative traditions. Mental hygiene in Canada in its earliest phases tended also to concentrate on group differences and to rationalize such variations as contributing to social and economic problems. Yet this particularistic view of mental hygiene with its eugenic overtones was disruptive in Canadian culture, which is fragile at this level.[34] Eugenics gradually became less important as a rationale as mental hygiene turned to more positivistic aspects of public health. This transition also had the support of American philanthropy. Public health had less ideological implications and was compatible with a collectivist orientation directed toward the public good. It also had the basic support of both French and English factions, even if state supported public health had to mediate with traditional charitable and church authority in this area, especially in Quebec. The mixing of public and private spheres in paternalistic intervention by either charitable organizations or the state was not as problematical in Canada as in the United States.

The secularization of charity, the interrelationship between scientific philanthropy and government, and the intermixing of public and private spheres has been described in the U.S. as synonymous with the problem of the separation of the church and state.[35] In Canada the integration between public and private spheres is more readily conceived as beneficial to the common good. Using the church and state example, the Canadian issue is not to delineate separate spheres, but to promote general allegiance to the state while accounting for pluralistic interests. In the United States pluralism is interpreted as best represented by independence of action. In this view the consolidation of public and private interests that are not subject to popular review represent monopolizing practices which constitute a policy dilemma. To the extent that mental hygiene is accepted as a scientific and, therefore, neutral decision-making criterion, it alleviates the policy dilemma in the United States.

Mental hygiene is useful in Canada to the extent that it justified demands for conformity against those who did not exhibit the minimal allegiance to Canadian institutions required for peaceful social continuity. Yet, the mental hygiene input to national identity has never been as conceptually useful to a Canadian perspective as it has in the United States. A unified "national identity" has been elusive in Canada for a number of reasons, including its dual French-English heritage combined with anti-revolutionary and ecclesiastical traditions. So too, the demographic flow of immigration and emigration has contributed to Canadian multiculturalism and particularism.[36] Because of the cultural impact of the larger and more powerful United States, a resistance to U.S. values has also been a source of Canadian identity.[37]

The divisiveness of Canada's dual heritage was also a factor in Canadian continuity.[38] Historically, English and French Canada, for all their cultural friction and incompatibilities, agree in their disagreement with the republican values of the United States.[39] The necessity of mediating the French-English dualism contributed to a pluralism or multiculturalism in Canada which makes an American style "melting pot" ideology impractical or impossible. Social change or mobility has been much more readily conceived in ascriptive terms which do not impinge upon particularistic values. The Canadian viewpoint, at least up to the post-World War II era, found little advantage in individualistic interpretations of social realities. Canadian mental hygiene also tended to focus on the pattern of balancing groups rather than a conforming, unified lifestyle.

On the other hand, Americans with their more insistent grounding in democratic and egalitarian ideals found individualism an increasingly important explanation for discrepancies in social and economic power. The medicalized version of individualism argued that differences between social and economic statuses were products of scientifically accountable classless criteria. In the United States the distinctions drawn by mental hygiene reinstated by way of individualism a universalistic orientation toward equality, the right to be unequal. The idea of inequality as innate, and, the necessity to deal with this fact, formulated the basis for an apolitical view of state policy. A stratified class structure was justified as providing for able leadership. Supposedly, the most qualified advanced to the top, and conversely, the least able settle into positions compatible with their lesser abilities and talents.[40] Individual fulfillment, personality, and ability were central concepts in this version of the mental hygiene prescription for progress.

Canadian development did not foster an apolitical view of the state but a consensual politics of accommodation. The obsession was with national unity and identity in a society which has remained, in a sense, infinitely divisible. Traditional leadership with a benevolent orientation was not seen as a danger to demographic government, but a key to its functioning.

The American melting pot ideology favored universal values and also depended on personal criteria to explain mobility. The value structure emphasized achievement, and legitimated success and failure on an individual basis. Mental hygiene, with its individualistic emphasis, contributed to a process which masked the ascriptive advantages or disadvantages of ethnicity, class, race, gender or other group characteristics. This is in contrast to the more eugenic orientation of Canadian mental hygiene.

Mental hygiene, as a set of ideas popularized and articulated by voluntary associations and private interests, was increasingly articulated and made available in this century to policy decision-makers in both the United States and Canada. One outcome was the medicalization of normality and legitimation of clinical abnormality. Mental hygiene has been more important in the United States in legitimating scrutiny into private life.

Transitions: Merging the Public and Private

The mental hygiene paradigm, to the extent to which it is institutionalized formally in legislation and informally in social practices, directly intervenes into the dynamics of public-private relations. Mental hygiene necessarily, in its assumption about the individual as the primary social unit, defines private relations as public. This assumption has achieved great influence due to its stature as a belief grounded in scientific truth. Warren Weaver, who was director of the Division of the Natural Sciences of the Rockefeller Foundation from 1932 to 1952, noted the importance of the faith in scientific knowledge to solve social problems. He identified this faith as underlying "practically all the activities of the great general purpose foundations." Weaver warned that "a critic who is not prepared to recognize, credit and share this faith is bound to misunderstand and underestimate many of the activities of philanthropic foundations."[41] The underlying issue concerning the relationship between philanthropy and the power to legitimize knowledge is not a question of the truth or untruth of science. The question behind the scientific orientation of philanthropy is the question of power and the politics of knowledge in decision-making. The boundary is between science and scientism which places technological methodology above politics. This is a question of distributive justice and the mechanisms of democratic control and legitimacy in modern industrial capitalistic states which value democratic political processes.[42]

The ideological importance of the argument that science is value-free, which in turn justifies the role of philanthropy in public policy, is illustrated by the struggle of the Rockefeller Foundation over its policy in promoting psychiatry. The Rockefeller Foundation in the 1940s attempted to find ways to make psychiatry scientifically verifiable and productive as an applied medical speciality. The psychological and social sciences of human behavior, however, consistently eluded the grasp of hard science. For all of the research dollars, institutes and conferences, there was little reason to believe that an empirical body of knowlege had been developed after more than twenty years of work. The historical record seemed to mock any other contention. The economic and social deterioration of the Depression years, culminated in the political upheaval of war, is a case in point. The Committee on Medical Education of the Group for the Advancement of Psychiatry put it bluntly, "The problem of medical education is not simply to train more doctors, but to train doctors who can help men and women to understand and live with themselves at a time when man's lack of understanding of himself and his misuse of his own powers has become a threat to civilization."[43]

The value and ultimate truth of scientific discovery seemed redeemed in other fields of scientific research. For example, the International Health Division had scored a major victory in 1937 with the discovery of a vaccine for yellow fever; in 1939 it brought a malaria epdemic under control in Brazil, and in 1940 it scored major battles against a potentially devastating outbreak of international typhus. The forties was not only a decade of war and social reconstruction but a major transition period for philanthropy, which seemed justified in areas outside of psychiatry. The World Health Organization was established in the United Nations in 1948. This organization served a very similar purpose to the International Health Division. The International Health Division was merged with the Rockefeller Foundation in 1951. It had successfully demonstrated effective procedures and organization, justifying its advisory role in public policy, which, Foundation officials felt, was rightfully taken over by government. However, the formula did not seem to work for psychiatry.

Seven years of major funding for psychiatric research and medical education in psychiatry from 1933 to 1940 had not reaped a similar victory for a happier healthier population. Instead, it seemed like humanity was embroiled in a flight from reason in a world gone mad. No scientific breakthrough seemed at hand. The evaluation of the program did not question the underlying premise of the applicaton of scientific principles to the field of human behavior. To the contrary, the Rockefeller trustees reaffirmed their commitment to the ideals and purposes of preventive psychiatry. The lack of strong scientific gains, however, indicated a need for reorganization. Part of this reorganization included a cut in funding for less research oriented endeavors such as the National Committee for Mental Hygiene. The Foundation had not yet ceased to hope that the social sciences would attain the status of the natural sciences, that somehow its knowledge would prove cumulative, and that the theories would become social laws.

The role of American foundations in this century can be characterized by a consistent intervention into public affairs. In the first two decades of the century, the emergent general purpose philanthropies developed projects directly concerned with public health, education and welfare. The Rockefeller Foundation's work in the southern states through the General Education Board and Sanitary Commission are a case in point.[44] In the 1920s and 1930s, the philanthropies concentrated on the production of knowledge through research. Foundation personnel saw themselves as disinterested and objective facilitators of science as an impartial means of problem-solving. During this same period government expanded its own participation in social welfare.

In the 1940s, government, to a significant degree, adopted the advocacy role of philanthropies in knowledge production. While foundations had organized activities on an international scale since their inception, after 1945 a network of intercommunication developed between philanthropy and government in domestic and foreign relations.[45] The tendency to interface private and public funds was also a tendency to inter-link foundation support for projects.[46] Spokesmen for "modernist" philanthropy in the post-War era have argued that the active role of foundations in guiding and shaping public policy is beneficial. Scientific philanthropy, in this modernist view, is argued to offer a value-free, non-political perspective which productively contributes to domestic policy and international relations. This argument rests on the assumption that "value-free" science can be translated into a "value-free" social policy. Historically, this goal appears to be not only over ambitious as an objective but illusory in practice.[47] The underlying prejudices ingrained into scientific "problems" may arise precisely due to the dependency of scientific knowledge production on decisions which are not value-free.

The NCMH played a strong role in the transition from policy advocacy as a private concern supported by philanthropy to a public function of government. The 1940s was the decade of transition. In the U.S., the National Committee for Mental Hygiene was instrumental in the formalization of public mental health policy. In the mid-forties, the National Committee lobbied Congress and drafted federal laws designed to expand the Mental Hygiene Division of the Public Health Service. The National Mental Health Act, passed in 1946, ultimately accomplished this goal. The National Institutes of Health were established in 1949. The Mental Hygiene Division of the Public Health Service was reorganized under Robert Felix as the National Institute of Mental Health (NIMH). The National Institute of Mental Health took over the supervisory and funding functions which the Rockefeller Foundation and Commonwealth Fund had occupied in connection with the National Committee for Mental Hygiene. NIMH became the major funding agency for research, fellowships, construction of academic facilities, and the development of research efforts in the mental health field. In the United States the Mental Health Act made substantial federal financial resources available for mental health research. From 1947, funds were provided for the development of clinical psychology. In the early 1950s, funding for psychology was expanded to include all of the social and behavioral sciences.[48]

The Rockefeller Foundation advocated governmental support for mental health research and development. The creation of NIMH signaled the accomplishment of the Rockefeller Foundation objective in the acceptance of federal responsibility for what had been the Foundation's projects. The U.S. government was now the provider of research grants for mental health and manpower training through program development and educational fellowships.

The Commonwealth Fund also experienced direct organizational changes during this period. Edward S. Harkeness died in 1940. Harkeness had led the philanthropy initiated by his mother since 1918. His increased interest in medical education and public health in the 1930s was acknowledged by his successor, Malcolm P. Aldrich; yet, the orientation of the Fund changed. Rather than cooperative programs and support for other agencies such as the NCMH, the Fund began to work directly with medical educators. An interest in psychiatry and community health was retained only until the retirement of Barry C. Smith in 1947, when Aldrich took over the general directorship. The Public Health Division was eliminated and the Mental Hygiene Division dropped shortly thereafter. The advance of the public sector into what had been the preserve of philanthropy was a stated factor in the decision to drop some aspects of public health and mental hygiene work, which was subsumed by government. For example, the Commonwealth Fund public health program emphasized upgrading rural medicine and community services in the years between 1933 and 1946. The Hill-Burton Act (Hospital Survey and Construction Act) of 1946 provided large federal grants precisely for this purpose. Similarly, the National Mental Health Act covered the Fund's traditional area in mental hygiene advocacy.[49]

After World War II, not only government but the number and diversity of philanthropic funds directed toward professional medicine and medical research increased. The Rockefeller Foundation and its associate funds spent approximately $152 million on scientific medicine between the First World War and the late 1960s. The Commonwealth Fund spent $110 million on public health, of which $8 million went directly to mental health. While the RF and Commonwealth Fund continued to support medicine, other philanthropies joined in. The Ford Foundation, which assumed national stature in 1950, was the largest. Ford spent nearly $350 million on medical schools and hospitals in its first fifteen years. In one year, 1956, Ford contributed $100 million to private medical schools.[50] Other funds such as the New York Foundation, Josiah Macy, Jr. Foundation, Joseph P. Kennedy, Jr. Foundation, W. K. Kellogg and Max F. Fleishmann Foundation also contributed millions of dollars to medicine in the first few decades after the second World War. The 270 major foundations, which controlled eighty-seven percent of the total philanthropic funds, spent up to ninety-six percent of their appropriated resources on scientific research.[51]

The expansion of government in the World War II era resulted in a symbiotic relationship between the public interest, as represented by government, and philanthropic interests. Private money and philanthropically devised policy formats were subsumed within the auspices of public bureaucracies. The philanthropies have continued to support and to devise protocols for future developments, in this new capacity, in the expanding public realm, and in the private mental health industry. The outcome, in terms of access to services, the relative position of professionals as policy makers, and cost effectiveness to the general public is, at best, mixed.[52]

Governmental expansion into health was modeled on the formats laid down by philanthropy. This has been critical to the shape of developments in public health through the 1950s and 1960s. Federal funds, in the U.S., established cooperative governmental agencies by encouraging state and local level programs through the use of incentive grants. These grants were enormously more comprehensive than the demonstration project grants in the inter-War period. The distribution of the governmental grants were not selective. They were made available to all governmental agencies meeting the Federally determined criteria.

In spite of the effort to institutionalize new programs rapidly, the results were marginal. The mixed result of these projects is illustrated in the effort to establish community based services. In 1955, the Health Amendments Act (Title V of the Public Services Act) provided short-term grants to encourage demonstrations in the area of community services. These grants, similar to the grants of the National Committee for Mental Hygiene, Commonwealth Fund, and R.F., were designed to stimulate local and state governments to assume the cost burden of these services. The 1955 legislation also provided for the creation of the Joint Commission on Mental Illness and Health. This Commission was designed to undertake the survey and analytic services which the National Committee for Mental Hygiene had provided with philanthropic funding for the past four decades. The comprehensive report, *Action for Mental Health*, published in 1961, laid the basis for the adoption of the *Community Mental Health Centers Act* of 1963. This act was designed to eliminate large scale public institutions for the mentally ill and to encourage local, state and private sources to develop community level services for preventive, clinical, diagnostic, consultative and acute care psychiatric services. This legislation contributed to the deinstitutionalization of patients in mental hospitals. it has not been as successful in stimulating adequate community level care, which was its original intention. The community service idea is a long-term formalization of public policy protocols, evolved out of the collaborative programs of philanthropy and the National Committee for Mental

Hygiene.[53] The first models for the community services were the clinics and child guidance projects.

The Political, Social and Economic Fortunes of Preventive Psychiatry

Medicine has been called the stepchild of philanthropy because of the support it has received from these sources. If we interpret the stepchild metaphor to mean that the story of medicine has been a Cinderella story from rags to riches, then psychiatry is "Cinderella's Cinderella before the glass slipper."[54] Rockefeller Foundation President Charles Barnard's frustration with psychiatry in the late 1940s encapsulated the problems the Foundation had with its broad and fundamental belief in the usefulness of psychiatry, and its inability to transform this field into an infallible scientific format.[55] The Foundation sought the break-throughs that bolstered the spirit of public health work at the turn of the century.[56] Approximately three-fourths of the Foundation's appropriations for medical science had gone into projects in psychiatry or related fields over the ten year period between 1933 and 1943. In 1943, Alan Gregg reflected on the Foundation's progress in advancing psychiatry as a science. He was probably accurate in his observation that "it was always pioneer work and pathfinding. We didn't add to what was already a substantial nucleus; our gift created the nucleus complete or provided an indispensible fraction of it."[57] Yet, psychiatry seemed constantly to be facing the same crisis which had initiated the Foundation's concentration in the area in the early thirties: 1) the enormous economic loss attributable to nervous and mental diseases; 2) the "backward" state of the field; and 3) the need for improvement of general medical education which had neglected psychiatric considerations.[58] Professionalization was consistently put forward as the key to success from the time of Thomas Salmon.[59]

Support for the Group for the Advancement of Psychiatry was an example in the 1940s of an attempt to provide psychiatry with an internal professionalising team similar to the purpose served in the first half of this century by the advocacy of voluntary associations such as the National Committees for Mental Hygiene and the philanthropies. The Foundation passed along this aspect of what has been called its gatekeeping function.[60]

The main work of the Foundation was initially, however, more than gatekeeping in that the staff of the Foundations were active participants and planners. The Foundation's function in charity work can be interpreted similarly to the operating principles their creators once advocated in the business world. The major general purpose foundations, such as the

Rockefeller Foundation, were created by funds derived from wealth associated with power over distribution. In a sense this was the original meaning of scientific philanthropy. The new charity work was to distribute knowledge about social practices as the businessman in a distributorship of manufactured goods mediates between the manufacturer and commercial outlet. Distributors disperse goods, create markets and control supplies between wholesale and retail outlets. Similarly, foundations have served to regulate the flow of knowledge. In addition to the distribution of goods or knowledge is the production of the pathways upon which the products flow. In business this includes the roadways, rail and shipping networks. In knowledge systems this communication function includes support for conferences, fellowships, publications and correspondence. The creation of policy making boards and professional organizations are like branch offices in the business of ideas. The overview of funding agencies can enlarge developments in one sector and make links between selected sectors. Since World War II, this function of philanthropy has become more complex and more conservative precisely because of the increasingly amorphous interface between government and philanthropy. In a large sense government assumed the role of philanthropy, taking over its mandates and overwhelming the market with even larger resources.

To what extent does contemporary philanthropy continue in its function as an agent of control? In both the United States and Canada, humanitarian motives aside, mental health programs are sanctioned in the community because they are fundamentally agencies which foster social continuity.[61] The role of preventive mental health was ultimately to ensure citizens who were not disruptive to the continuity of societal functioning.

The mental hygiene movement originated in voluntary organizations, and was perpetrated by communities of elites in two countries. In both instances the elites were interested in moderating social change and in conserving either traditional values or social configurations, or both. in the United States mental hygiene eased the tensions between democratic ideals and practices by validating inequality. The individualistic therapeutic model inherent in mental hygiene's medicalized perspective was relatively incompatible with Canada's particularistic orientation. Canadian democratic values depended less on rationalizing political, social, and economic inequalities. Instead, public health aspects of the mental hygiene movement became widespread. In Canada, medicalization was a functional rationale for progress, but not the key to equal opportunity as it was in the United States. The mental hygiene movement took different paths in the U.S. and Canada as it reflected values which were products of divergent histories.[62]

Chapter Twelve

The Legacy of the Childhood Gaze: The Institutionalization of Childhood and the Formalization of a Social Problem

The purpose of this study has not been to determine the correct relationship between the ideological content of mental hygiene and scientific truth, as elaborated in the practices of mental hygiene in the medicalization of childhood. The goal has been to historically search back through events in the effort, in Michel Foucault's words, to "detach truth from its forms of hegemony, social, economic and cultural with which it operates."[1] It is only upon this basis that we can determine the relationship of public policy to the emergent structures of social organization.

Knowledge and Power: Mental Hygiene and Philanthropy

The relationship between twentieth century philanthropy and mental hygiene can be understood in terms of the interaction between advocacy, enforcement, and knowledge. This relationship is complex.

Relations of power and knowledge are shaped by their ethnographic and cultural context, as illustrated by the examples of the United States and Canada. Knowledge exists within social institutions which serve as structures for the exercise of power. This fact is illustrated in schools, courts, child guidance clinics and child research institutes. Finally, knowledge and its configurations serve as instruments of control which shape social interaction. Mental hygiene protocols in public policies shape child rearing. They legitimate definitions of health and illness.[2]

Knowledge and power are inseparable in that the relationship is integrated into social structures and interpersonal relations, as well as into formal definitions of normative behavior. The subject of this study in the history of concepts of normality and abnormality in childhood, and what has come to be considered reasonable and unreasonable in the progress of human biological and psychological development, are cases in point. What is rational or irrational depends on the structure of society. Normality can be considered an adaptation which assures survival in a particular context. This observation supports the mental hygiene notion of the importance of adjustment while it questions the very psychobiological notions of childhood upon which mental hygiene is based. Norbert Elias in his *History of Manners* notes that:

> The psychological problems of growing people cannot be understood if the individual is regarded as developing uniformly in all historical epochs. The problems relating to the child's consciousness and instinctual urges vary with the nature of the relations of children to adults. These relations have in each society a specific form corresponding to the peculiarities of its structure.[3]

If the example of adolescence is used, "the specific problems of puberty in our civilized society—can only be understood in relation to the historical phase, the structure of society as a whole, which demands and maintains this standard of adult behavior and this special form of relationship between adults and children."[4]

If reason or unreason, normality and abnormality are adaptations to a particular society and to survival within it, then the mental hygienists' frontal attack on maladaptations represented an accurate appraisal of a weak point in modern social organization. Their efforts to control the individual coincided with a search for mechanisms which would assure social order and continuity. Civilization is, certainly, dependent on interweaving social interactions and on creating an interdependence between individuals that includes coordinated social adaptations which reflect different configurations of dependent statuses.

As bourgeois social organization and the modern nuclear family evolved, increasing distinctions emerged between the public sphere with its formalism, external legal sanctions and emphasis on status and power, and the cushion of the personal and internalized haven of the private sphere. The potential break down of former mechanisms of conformity encourages public control into the hidden sphere of the individual psyche and the institutions in the family and school. The twentieth century has, not surprisingly from this standpoint, placed great emphasis on the socialization of children. Professionals, and their expanded role as public entities with esoteric knowledge, were well placed to penetrate and exert social constraints and pressures to conform on the loose structure of the private sphere.

This change in the "drive mechanisms" of society or "steering" and the basis of its legitimacy has had far flung effects, witnessed in the growth of bureaucratic institutions concerned with social welfare, health and education which have characterized U.S. and Canadian twentieth century life.[5] It is important to note that the interaction between the professional and the client, or parent to child, reflect interdependent statuses where the least powerful must acquiesce and provide approbation for the more powerful. Particular paradigms, habits and orientations, such as with mental hygiene, legitimize and sanction the forms of acquiescence. We can interpret the mental hygiene model as an "instrument of power" which organizes, explains and legitimizes interdependent relationships. The spheres in which mental hygiene functions in the courts, clinics, and classrooms, serve as structures where rules are enforced.

One of the major transitions, since the end of the court societies of the seventeenth and eighteenth century, has been the transition to civil governments. This has included the advance of centralized authority from sacred-monarchical rule to the rule of secular formalism. Again this is a transition both in the "drive mechanism" of society in its organization of power, and in its "steering" or structure of legitimacy.[6]

The industrial revolution and growing strength of the money sector in Great Britain, Canada and the United States down graded monarchical forms of government based on ascriptive statuses. In the United States successful industrial captains were elevated to great power and authority. The institutionalization of compatible ideas in social policy reinforced the emergent power structure in professional elites, based on the underlying philanthropical support of the money sector. In the mental hygiene movement financial advocacy was derived from surplus resources, which were by-products of the industrial revolution encouraged by nation building and technological development.

Industrial monopoly led by individual tycoons grew into structures of corporate financial power as resources were accumulated in the nineteenth century by men such as John D. Rockefeller, Sr. In the twentieth century, this power was extended to specific groups represented by the secular institutions of philanthropies and cooperative private and governmental agencies. These agencies contributed to the rationalization of knowledge in the social sciences according to a medical model. This occurred just as it became more important to assure the continuance of the body politic by normalizing individual behavior and rationalizing common ideologies across a broad range of societal levels. The transition from the private power of individuals to the collective power of semi-public contemporary elites marks a shift from the simple dominance of economic financial power to a complex intersection of political, corporate and social authority.

In states such as Canada with relatively low levels of interindependence among its constituencies, the social functions of private monopoly tended historically toward oligarchy rather than individual dynasties as it did in the United States. Canada retained interdependence between private and public spheres based on is monarchical past which weakened the private-public distinctions. However, recent changes constitutionally and in the formalization of the relations between Canada's diverse cultural heritages, have increased the interdependence of the Canadian social fabric. Consequently, the divisions between public and private interests have increased and may undermine the tradition of *noblesse oblige* which has fostered Canadian social institutions. If so, the traditional benevolent role of elite leadership, which has served to mediate the use of ideologies, may also weaken. This may encourage formalized individualistic paradigms such as mental hygiene which appear universalistic and detached.

In the United States, high levels of interdependence support a growing dominance of structured leadership in professional elites. Mental hyiene serves as an important supporting instrument legitimating the increased vigilance on the part of the public into the private life of the child and family. The United States has been dominated by formalism in the relationship between power and knowledge, where mechanical, external controls, standardized tests, and legal sanctions have supported the primary relations of status and power. Hence the mental hygiene paradigm's rationalization of stratification and inequalities continues to prove useful as a protocol for public policy.

While Canada has used the mental hygiene paradigm to confirm the legitimacy of traditional leadership, the "power of science" also proved useful as a device which justified policy decisions as objective rather than self-serving. Canada remains, despite trends which would bring it closer to the U.S. prototype, a nation concerned with mediating particulars where the building of consensual unity in the face of diversity is a political necessity. The exigence of the U.S., which seeks to operationalize the boundaries of normality, are less of a concern.

The Legacy

The knowledge secured by private foundations in their support for child study research and parent education has in large measure standardized the cycle of human growth and development as currently understood. The impact from the pioneer investigations into child life lasted for the next fifty years, as a 1930s General Education Board report projected. With minor alterations it has brought us into the 1980s. The GEB's presumption that "significant insights with important educational implications will be secured," also proved prophetic.[7] The coordination of child rearing with scientifically verified age related biological and psychological traits did not free children from stress and anxiety. Nor did it avoid adult failures. It coincidentally produced age specific pressures and cultural adaptations. The definition of the psychobiological basis of adolescence, for example, in practice added unforeseen demands on teenagers, parents and social institutions. The psychobiological understanding of the child derived from scientific child study in the inter-War period has persisted. Based in quantitative data and bolstered by the authority of science, it is a paradigmatic undergirding of modern social life. Child study research and parent education has, to a profound degree, shaped modern institutions such as family, school, and community public services. It has hardly left untouched our own self-concepts and age related anxieties, much less our attitudes and behavior toward children and parenting as personal and collectively experienced phenomenon. Inter-generational relations are a part of the production of social continuity. In so far as children become the future, changes in their status and emphasis on their socialization represent fundamental changes in social organization.

As W. I. Thomas has so pointedly described in his studies on children in America in the 1920s, the ongoing disorganization and reorganization of the definition of any situation, including expectations of children, determines to a large extent the social reality collectively experienced. Further, societies are more or less successful to the degree that mutually recognized definitions of situations are considered valid and passed along as such by a majority of the people. Thomas' observation of social interaction remains a case in point, the extent to which "men define situations as real, they are real in their consequences."[8] From age graded schooling to retirement, the social consequences of the age specific norms are among the most fundamental aspects of the process of cultural determination.

Afterthought

What is the legacy the twenty-first century will inherit from the mental hygiene movement of the twentieth century? Has mental hygiene reduced social problems or produced them? Research in mental hygiene has articulated life stages in terms of biological and cognitive maturation. It has brought about the recognition that poor environments, inadequate health care and negative experiences in childhood can cripple a child's life prospects. We have recognized that severe emotional and mental problems are not just an adult phenomenon, but that children are also afflicted with mental and emotional problems. We can agree that mental health problems in childhood are perhaps more treatable if their problems are dealt with early and effectively.

Both the United States and Canada have tried to develop policies to address these issues and to nurture and protect children as future citizens and leaders in democratic social institutions. Nonetheless, in spite of increased services for mental health, the problem of mental health disorder has increased, along with the underlying social problems which mental hygiene sought to eliminate. Just as surely as child guidance did not do away with delinquency, we can argue that paternalistic public policies have in fact created the social phenomenon of the maladjusted and mentally disordered child.

Social problems, such as delinquency and abnormal behavior, are social constructs attached to social institutions and derived from socially produced conditions.[9] Mental disorders as a social problem are causally related to the society which produces both the disorder and recognizes the disorder as a problem.

The irony of this perception was not lost on Lawrence K. Frank of the Laura Spelman Rockefeller Memorial, who did much both to identify social problems, and to provide for their solution. He comments that trying to solve a social problem is like "trying to cultivate a flower without the fruit."[10] The dilemma for reformers who wanted to solve crime, disease, poverty, delinquency, and war by way of mental hygiene was that they did not want to change any of the structures that had caused the problems. The effort was to make social institutions "work better" without altering their basic character. Separating the problem of mental illness from mental disorders, as a symptom of other problems, was increasingly unclear. Mental hygiene became a catch-all for problem solving through prevention. Even with the emphasis on correcting underlying causes the therapeutic model singled out symbols grounded in an individualistic psychobiological framework. Mental hygiene became a way of exercising humanitarian values without addressing social structural considerations of an economic or political nature, except in the most benign context of environmental issues.

Willard Waller in the 1930s noted that the shift from economics to psychiatry in the field of social work solved what was an inherent professional conflict between "humanitarian and organizational mores."[11] Waller's discussion on the realtionship between values and the maintenance of organizational mandates is relevant to an understanding of why mental hygiene as a humanitarian ideology did not solve social problems, but in fact contributed to their construction and maintenance:

> organizational mores produce conditions which call the humanitarian spirit into activity; at the same time humanitarianism takes care of certain exigencies in such a way as to decrease the probability of sudden, violent changes in the organizational mores.[12]

The question revolves back to the issue of who has the power to define the context in which a social understanding of what is a problem is agreed upon, that is, the relationship between power and knowledge. The past century has witnessed an increase in the number of professional knowledge-makers who have acquired the power to construct social definitions of situations. The establishment of social policies based on formal knowledge, whether their scientific validity is real or imagined, has cumulative outcomes in social practices. The mental hygiene movement has effectively contributed to the transformation of the family, school context and family court in the United States and Canada over this century. Regardless of its reflection of the "truth" of science, mental hygiene has become integrated into our cultures as common sense material, grounded in established authority structures.

Scientific truth in this sense is to be understood in a circular relationship to power; the power, in this case, to produce new knowledge and to regulate and distribute systems of ideas such as preventive mental health policy. In mental hygiene, the focus has been on the proper public stance vis-a-vis the nature of childhood, that is, the establishment of professional knowledge defining the proper personal and collective behaviors to be followed by parents, teachers, social workers and counselors in order to conserve normality.

The power to establish knowledge as scientific in mental hygiene evolved from private spheres to increasingly public but still elite circles. The ability to manipulate the procedures for the circulation and development of knowledge was directed by the National Committees for Mental Hygiene, general purpose foundations, professional organizations and public agencies. Private monopolies over knowledge-making were gradually made public.

This study has followed the cumulated actions of individuals and organizations who were a part of the mental hygiene movement. The biographies of these individuals and organizations in their national context were interconnected and interdependent. Over the long term there emerged three major recurrent structures and processes: 1) the professionalization of knowledge; 2) the trend from private to public hegemony over the system of ordering knowledge, and 3) the emergence of elaborate categories of human differences applied to young children.

If we can learn from the mental hygienist's search for truth through the scientific examination of the child, it is that the uniqueness of any one situation or individual occurs within the framework of re-occurring patterns. Control over centralized and monopolized resources in mental hygiene research and training passed from the hands of a few individuals into interdependent groups of elites. The mental hygiene paradigm was structured by these expanding hegemonical units of elite advocacy organizations, that is, elite voluntary advocacy, general purpose foundations and growing state bureaucracies. The leadership of philanthropies or the National Committees was far from absolute. Power was distributed first among individuals and then among networks of participating groups. Nonetheless, social practices bolstered by conservative ideological perspectives tended to first construct, then to reproduce, new organizational structures with similarly placed elites. The free competition of ideas, which first sought to establish the authority of medical science, progressively qualified the criteria for competition so that only legitimated scientists in interdependent units could participate. Within the interdependent networks, such as the committees for mental hygiene, the university based research centers, the funding organizations, and professional associations, there were a number of competing struggles. The competitions on a personal and ideological level, such as the I.Q. and nature-nurture controversies, did not transform the underlying structural relationship between the particular form of legitimate knowledge in science, nor the structural hegemony of the interdependent organized monopolies over knowledge-making. Mental hygiene and the twentieth century *childhood gaze* obscured the boundary between private and public spheres in that it elevated selective leadership in the public interest while it reduced popular access to knowledge-making. Due to the historical character of each society this was more of an ideological problem for social policy in the United States than in Canada.

It is unclear what alternative patterns could have evolved in the mental health field without the input from large scale general purpose philanthropy with its emphasis on science. Informal theories and practices based on tradition and shared experience concerning child life also have a substantial impact on social thought. Nonetheless, accredited agencies have assumed the role, over this century, of legitimating certain practices and perspectives over others. The professionalization of ideas and the formalization of compatible public bureaucratic and legal structures have served to legitimate standards of normality and abnormality, health and illness. The medical paradigm for problem solving and individualistic values expressed in the mental hygiene movement have become widespread and perhaps even an inescapable aspect of contemporary social thought.

Notes

Introduction

1. Adolf Meyer to Abraham Flexner, 20 April 1927, Adolf Meyer Papers, Series III, cited in Gerald N. Grob, *The Inner World of American Psychiatry, 1890–1940, Selected Correspondence* (New Brunswick, N.J.: Rutgers University Press, 1985), p. 177.

2. "The Speculative part of Medicine is threefold: to wit, Physiologia, Hygiene and Pathologia," Salmon, *Syn Med* III, i (1671): 322, cited in *Oxford English Dictionary* vol. 8 (Oxford: Oxford University Press, 1971, 1981), p. 493

3. Ellen Keys, *Century of the Child* (New York and London: G. P. Putnam's Sons, 1909); Peter B. Neubauer, "The Century of the Child," *Psychiatry in American Life* ed. Charles Rolo (Freeport, N.Y.: Books for Libraries Press, 1971), pp. 133–41.

4. Giovanni B. Sgritta, "Childhood: Normalization and Project," *International Journal of Sociology* 12, 3 (Fall 1987): 39–57; Sol Cohen, "The Mental Hygiene Movement: The Development of Personality and the School, The Medicalization of Education," *History of Education Quarterly* 23, 2 (Summer 1983): 123–50.

5. Philip J. Greven, Jr., *Four Generations: Population, Land and Family in Colonial Andover, Massachusetts* (Ithaca, N.Y.: Cornell University Press, 1970); Tamara K. Hareven, ed., *Transitions: The Family and Life Courses in Historical Perspective* (New York: Academic Press, 1978); Tamara K. Hareven, "Modernization and Family History: Perspectives on Social Change," *Signs* 2 (August 1976): 109–206; Christopher Lasch, *Haven in a Heartless World: The Family Besieged* (New York: Basic Books, 1977); Michael B. Katz, *People of Hamilton: Canada West, Family and Class in a Mid-Nineteenth Century City* (Cambridge: Harvard University Press, 1975); Peter Laslett, *Family Life and Illicit Love in Earlier Generations: Essays in Historical Sociology* (Cambridge: Cambridge University Press, 1977, 1978).

6. Philippe Ariès, *Centuries of Childhood: A Social History of Family Life* trans. Robert Baldrick (New York: Random House, 1962); also Lloyd de Mause, ed., *The History of Childhood* (New York: Psychohistory Press, 1974); R. L. Schnell, "Childhood as Ideology," *British Journal of Educational Studies* 27 (February 1979): 7–28;

Arlene Skolnick, ed., *Rethinking Childhood: Perspectives on Child Development and Society* (Boston: Little, Brown & Co., 1976); Chris Jenks, ed., *The Sociology of Childhood: Essential Readings* (London: Batsford, 1982); Bernard Wishy, *The Child and the Republic: The Dawn of Modern Child Nurture* (Philadelphia: University of Pennsylvania Press, 1968); F. Musgrove, *Youth and the Social Order* (Bloomington: Indiana University Press, 1964, 1965).

7. W. I. Thomas, *The Unadjusted Girl: With Case Studies and Standpoints for Behavior Analysis* (Boston: Little, Brown & Co., 1923); W. I. Thomas and Dorothy Swain Thomas, *The Child in America: Behavior Problems and Programs* (New York: Knopf, 1928, reprint New York: Johnson Reprint Corp., 1970).

8. Hareven, *Transitions*; Hareven, "Modernization and Family History;" Lasch, *Haven in a Heartless World.*

9. Mary O. Furner, *Advocacy and Objectivity: A Crisis in the Professionalization of American Social Science, 1865–1905* (Lexington, Kentucky: University of Kentucky, 1979); Thomas Haskell, *Emergence of Professional Social Science* (Chicago: University of Chicago Press, 1977); Andrew Abbott, *The System of Professions: An Essay on the Division of Expert Labor* (Chicago: University of Chicago Press, 1988), pp. 280–314.

10. Lloyd Taylor, *The Medical Profession and Social Reform, 1885–1945* (New York: St. Martin's Press, 1974); Paul Starr, *The Social Transformation of American Medicine: The Rise of a Sovereign Profession and the Making of a Vast Industry* (New York: Basic Books, 1982).

11. Magali Sarfatti Larson, *The Rise of Professionalism: A Sociological Analysis* (Berkeley: Univ. of Calif. Press, 1977); James Leiby, *A History of Social Welfare and Social Work in the United States* (New York: Columbia University Press, 1978).

12. Michel Foucault, *The Birth of the Clinic: An Archeology of Medical Perception* trans. S. M. Sheridan Smith (New York: Random House, 1975), p. 68.

13. See Andrew Scull, "Humanitarianism or Social Control? Some Observations on the Historiography of Anglo-American Psychiatry," *Rice University Studies* 67 (1981): 21–41; Samuel Bowles and Herbert Gintis, *Schooling in Capitalist America* (New York: Basic Books, 1976); Stanley Aronowitz and Henry A. Giroux, *Education Under Seige: The Conservative, Liberal and Radical Debate Over Schooling* (Massachusetts: Bergen and Garvey, 1985); Anthony Platt, *The Child Savers: The Invention of Delinquency* (Chicago: University of Chicago Press, 1969, 1972).

14. Seymour Martin Lipset, "Historical Traditions and National Characteristics: A Comparative Analysis of Canada and the United States," *Canadian Journal of Sociology* 11, 2 (1986): 113–55; W. L. Morton, *The Canadian Identity* 2nd ed. (Madison: University of Wisconsin Press, 1961, 1962).

15. Lawrence K. Frank, "Social Problems," *The American Journal of Sociology* 30, 4 (Jan. 1925): 462–73; Willard Waller, "Social Problems and the Mores," *American Sociological Review* 1, 6 (Dec. 1936): 922–33.

16. Michael B. Katz, *In the Shadow of the Poorhouse: A Social History of Welfare in America* (New York: Basic Books, 1986), p. 290.

17. Sol Cohen, "The School and Personality Development: Intellectual History," in *Historical Inquiry in Education: A Research Agenda*, ed. John Best (Washington, D.C.: A.E.R.A., 1983), pp. 109–37; Sol Cohen, "The Mental Hygiene Movement, the Commonwealth Fund and Public Education, 1921–1933," in *Private Philanthropy: Proceedings of the Rockefeller Archive Center Conference*, June 1979, ed. Gerald Benjamin (Rockefeller Archive Center Publication, 1980), pp. 33–46; in the same volume see: Steven L. Schlossman, "Philanthropy and the Gospel of Child Development," pp. 15–32; and Robert J. Havighurst, "Foundations and Public Education in the Twentieth Century," pp. 5–14; also, Elizabeth Lomax, "The Laura Spelman Rockefeller Memorial, Some of its Contributions to Early Research in Child Development," *Journal of the History of Behavioral Science* 13 (1977): 283–93.

18. Sol Cohen, "The Mental Hygiene Movement and the Development of Personality: Changing Conceptions of the American College and University," *History of Higher Education Annual* 2 (1982): 65–101; Jacques M. Quen, "Asylum Psychiatry, Neurology and Mental Hygiene in Interprofessional History," *Journal of the History of Behavioral Science* 13 (1977): 3–11.

19. The main work is the autobiography which kicked off the movement in 1908, Clifford Beers, *A Mind That Found Itself: An Autobiography*, (New York: Longmans, Green, 1907, reprint Garden City, N.Y.: Doubleday, 1965, most recently with a preface by Robert Coles, Pittsburgh: University of Pittsburgh Press for the American Foundation for Mental Hygiene, 1981); also, Earl D. Bond, *Thomas W. Salmon: Psychiatrist* (New York: W. W. Norton, 1950); Nina Ridenour, *Mental Health in the United States: A Fifty Year History* (Cambridge: Harvard University Press for Commonwealth Fund, 1961); Alfred Deutsch, *The Mentally Ill in America: A History of Their Care and Treatment From Colonial Times* (New York: Doubleday, Doran & Co., 1937). All of the above are more or less in-house histories with the exceptions, Norman Dain's excellent biography, *Clifford W. Beers: Advocate for the Insane* (Pittsburgh: University of Pittsburgh, 1980); Barbara Sickerman, *The Quest for Mental Health in America, 1880–1917* (Ann Arbor: Michigan, 1967); Fred Matthews, "In Defense of Common Sense: Mental Hygiene As Ideology and Mentality in Twentieth-Century America," *Prospects* 2 (Winter 1979): 459–516; Kathleen McConnachie, "The Mental Hygiene and Eugenics Movement in the Inter-War Years," paper presented at the History of Education Association Meetings, Vancouver, B.C., October 1983.

20. Ellen Condliffe Lagemann, "The Politics of Knowledge: The Carnegie Corporation and the Formulaton of Public Policy," *History of Education Quarterly* 27, 2 (Summer 1987): 205–220; and William R. Johnson, "Empowering Practioners: Holms, Carnegie, and the Lessons of History," *History of Education Quarterly* 27, 2 (Summer 1987): 221–245.

21. Donald Fisher, "American Philanthropy and the Social Sciences: The Reproduction of a Conservative Ideology," in Robert Arnove, ed., *Philanthropy and*

Cultural Imperialism (Bloomington, Indiana: University of Indiana, 1982), pp. 233–68; Donald Fisher, "The Role of Philanthropic Foundations in the Reproduction and Production of Hegemony: Rockefeller Foundations and the Social Sciences," *Sociology (UK)* 17 (1983): 206–33; Donald Fisher, "The Impact of American Foundations on the Development of British University Education, 1900–1939," (Ph.D. Dissertation, University of California Berkeley, 1977); Donald Fisher, "American Philanthropy and the Social Sciences in Britain," *Sociological Review* 28 (1980): 277–315; Ellen Condliffe Lagemann, *Private Power for the Public Good* (Middletown, CT.: Wesleyan University Press, 1983); Edward Berman, *The Influence of the Carnegie, Ford, and Rockefeller Foundations on American Foriegn Policy: The Ideology of Philanthropy* (Albany, N.Y.: State University of New York Press, 1983); E. Richard Brown, *Rockefeller Medicine Men: Medicine and Capitalism in America* (Berkeley: Univ. of Calif. 1979); Lewis A. Coser, "Foundations as Gatekeepers of Contemporary Intellectual Life," in Lewis A. Coser, *Men of Ideas: A Sociologist's View* (New York: Free Press, 1970), pp. 337–48.

22. Harold W. Stevenson and Alberta E. Siegel, eds., *Child Development Research and Social Policy* vol. 1 (Chicago: University of Chicago Press for the Society for Research in Child Development, 1984), pp. ix–xiii; Orville G. Brim, Jr., *Education for Child Rearing* (New York: Free Press, 1959, reprint 1965), pp. 329–46; Raymond B. Fosdick, *Adventure in Giving: The Story of the General Education Board* (New York: Harper & Row, 1962), pp. 259–65.

23. Alfred Cobban, *The Myth of the French Revolution: An Inaugural Lecture Presided Over by His Excellency the French Ambassador* University College, London, 6 May 1954 (London: H. K. Lewis, 1955, reprint, The Arden Library, 1978).

24. The idea of the body, the mind and the estate was conceptualized out of the "field of inquiry," in George Duby's, *The Three Orders: Feudal Society Imagined* trans. Arthur Goldhammer (Chicago: University of Chicago, 1980, 1982), study of the three orders or estates general of France: the Clergy, the Nobility, and the Third Estate (meaning both estate and state in French), pp. 1–9.

Chapter One

1. George Rosen, *Preventive Medicine in the United States, 1900–1975 Trends and Interpretations* (New York: Science History Publications, 1975), p. 20.

2. Simon Flexner and James Thomas Flexner, *William Henry Welch and the Heroic Age of Medicine* (New York: Viking Press, 1941), p. 341, fn. p. 234; Donald Fleming, *William H. Welch and the Rise of Modern Medicine* (Boston: Little Brown & Co., 1954), ch. 10, "The Birth of an Influential," pp. 131–151.

3. Jens Qvorthrup, ed., Special Issue: The Sociology of Childhood, *International Journal of Sociology* 17, 3 (Fall 1987), see especially Jens Qvorthrup, "Introduction," pp. 3–37.

4. David Rothman, *The Discovery of the Asylum: Social Order and Disorder in the New Republic* (Boston: Little, Brown & Co., 1971); Leroy Ashby, *Saving the Waifs: Reformers and Dependent Children, 1890*–1917 (Philadelphia: Temple University Press, 1984); Barbara Brenzel, *Daughters of the State: A Social Portrait of the First Reform School for Girls in North America, 1856–1905* (Cambridge, MA.: MIT, 1983); Michael B. Katz, *In the Shadow of the Poorhouse: A History of Social Welfare in America* (New York: Basic, 1986); Walter I. Trattner, *From Poor Law to Welfare State: A History of Social Welfare in America* (New York: Free Press, 1974, 1979).

5. See the American Psychiatric Association, *Diagnostic and Statistical Manual of Mental Disorders* 3rd ed. rev. (DSM-III-R) (Washington, D.C.: A.P.A., 1987), pp. 27–97.

6. Ivy Pinchbeck and Margaret Hewett, *Children in English Society* 2 vols. (Toronto: University of Toronto, 1969, 1973); Patricia Rooke and R. L. Schnell, *Discarding the Asylum: From Child Rescue to Social Control in English Canada, 1800–1950* (Landham, MD: University Press of America, 1983).

7. Robert M. Mennel, *Thorns and Thistles: Juvenile Delinquents in the United States, 1825–1940* (Hanover, N.H.: University of New Hampshire, 1973), pp. 12–13.

8. Mennel, *Thorns*, p. 10–1; Joseph M. Hawes, *Children in Urban Society: Juvenile Delinquency in Nineteenth-Century America* (New York: Oxford University Press, 1971), pp. 27–29.

9. Grace Abbott, *The Child and the State* 2 vols. (Chicago: University of Chicago, 1932), II, 345–6.

10. U.S. Census Office, *Report on the Defective, Dependent, and Delinquent Classes of the Population of the United States, as Returned at the Tenth Census* (June 1, 1880) (Washington, D.C.: Government Printing Office, 1888), pp. vii–xli.

11. George Rosen, *Madness and Civilization: Chapters in the Historical Sociology of Mental Illlness* (London: Routledge & Kegan Paul, 1968), p. 278; Albert Deutsch, *The Mentally Ill in America: A History of Their Care and Treatment From Colonial Times* (New York: Doubleday, Doran, 1937, reprint New York: Columbia University Press, 1967), see ch. 8, p. 132.

12. Gerald N. Grob, *Mental Illness and American Society, 1875–1940* (Princeton, N.J.: Princeton Univ. Press, 1983), pp. 8, 10, 14–17.

13. "Dorothea L. Dix and Canadian Institutions," in Henry M. Hurd, ed., *The Institutional Care of the Insane in the United States and Canada* 4 vols. (Baltimore: Johns Hopkins University Press, 1916, reprint New York: Arno Press, 1973), vol. I: Appendix IX. Another influential advocate for the growth of mental institutions was public school movement leader, Horace Mann. See Jonathan Messerli, *Horace Mann: A Biography* (New York: Alfred A. Knopf, 1972), pp. 122–37.

14. Data compiled from the extensive survey conducted by Hurd, *The Institutional Care of the Insane.*

15. Hurd, *The Institutional Care of the Insane* IV, "Appendix to Journal of House of the Assembly on New Brunswick, 1936-37," pp. 98-99.

16. Hurd, *The Institutional Care of the Insane*, IV.

17. Names of board members were identified as wives and daughters in the Family Compact by Richard B. Splane, *Social Welfare in Ontario, 1791-1893: A Study of Public Welfare Administration* (Toronto: University of Toronto, 1965), p. 223, fn. 31; also see Upper Canada, *Statutes* (1851), ch. 34.

18. Susan Houston, "The 'Waifs and Strays' of a Late Victorian City: Juvenile Delinquency in Toronto," in *Childhood and Family in Canada* ed. Joy Parr (Toronto: McClelland & Stewart, 1982), pp. 129-142; Splane, *Social Welfare*, pp. 223-77.

19. For example: "An Act in Addition to an Act to Establish the Board of State Charities," in Massachusetts, *Acts and Resolves* (Boston, 1869), ch. 453; also "An Act Relating to the State Visiting Agency and Juvenile Offenders," in Massachusetts, *Acts and Resolves* (Boston, 1870), p. 262; New York passed similar legislation in 1892; Rhode Island in 1898; there were efforts to place children on probation or in families; see, Homer Folks, "The Care of Delinquent Children," *Proceedings of the National Conference of Charities and Correction*, (1891), pp. 136-44; Ontario legislation was passed in 1893, Ontario, *Statutes* (1893), ch. 45.

20. "An Act for the Prevention of Cruelty to and Better Protection of Children," Ontario, *Statutes* (1893), ch. 45; see Splane, *Social Welfare in Ontario*, pp. 268-75; and, Andrew Jones and Leonard Rutman, *In the Children's Aid: J. J. Kelso and Child Welfare in Ontario* (Toronto: University of Toronto, 1981).

21. J. D. Page [Chief Medical Officer of the Port of Quebec], "Immigration and the Canadian National Committee for Mental Hygiene," *Canadian Journal of Mental Hygiene* 1, 1 (Ap. 1919): 58-61; W. G. Smith, "Immigration and Defectives," *Canadian Journal of Mental Hygiene* 2, 1 (Ap. 1920).

22. On the child immigration movement see, Joy Parr, *Labouring Children: British Immigrant Apprentices to Canada, 1869*-1924 (London: Croom Helm, 1980); Gail H. Corbett, *Barnardo Children in Canada* (Petersborough, ON.: Woodland Publ., 1981); Rooke and Schnell, *Discarding the Asylum*, ch. 7; K. Bagnell, *The Little Immigrants* (Toronto: MacMillan, 1980).

23. N. C. Urquart and K. A. H. Buckley, eds., *Historical Statistics of Canada* (Toronto: MacMillan, 1965), p. 19.

24. Canada, Dominion Bureau of Statistics, *Census of Canada* vol. 1 (1921), pp. 542-3; vol. 2, pp. xii-xiii; also see Warren E. Kalbach, *The Impact of Immigration on Canada's Population* (Ottawa: Dominion Bureau of Statistics, 1970), pp. 71-74, 87-93.

25. W. G. Smith, "Immigration Past and Present," *Canadian Journal of Mental Hygiene* (hereafter CJMH) 1, 1 (Ap. 1919): 47; continued 1, 2 (July 1919): 130; also, "Oriental Immigration," *CJMH* 1, 3 (Ap. 1920): 73; C. K. Clarke, "Report of the

Medical Director," *CJMH* 2, 3 (Oct. 1920): 252–4; also see the *Fifth Annual Conference on Child Welfare, Proceedings and Papers, Ottawa 1925* (Ottawa: King's Printer, 1925), p. 59.

26. Robert H. Bremner, ed., *Children and Youth in America: A Documentary History* Vol. II: 1866–1932 (Cambridge: Harvard University, 1971), pp. 811–15, 817–31, Section II, School Health. Canada Commission of Conservation, *Report*, 1910, p. 132; also, Sutherland, *Children*, ch. 3, "Our Whole Aim is Prevention:' Public Health in the Schools," for a discussion. Early concerns in the United States and Canada for school inspections initially focused on sanitary school environments. Augustus Viele and W. H. B. Post, "Report on School-Buildings," *Third Annual Report of the Board of Health of the City of New York* (New York: N.Y.C. 1873), pp. 320–321 in Bremner, *Children and Youth*, Vol. II, pt. 7–8, pp. 895–6. The concern with sanitation extended to the collection of physical data, Taliaferro Clark, George L. Collins, and W. L. Treadway, "Rural School Sanitation," in U.S. Public Health Service, *Public Health Service Bulletin* No. 77 (Washington, D.C.: Government Printing Office, 1916), pp. 107–113; Ontario Board of Health, *Report* (1883), p. xvi; British Columbia Board of Health, Medical Inspection of Schools, *Reports* (1911); British Columbia, *Statutes* (1914), ch. 52.

27. James Kerr, *Newsholme's School Hygiene: The Laws of Health in Relation to School Life*, 14th ed. (London: George Allen & Unwin, Ltd., 1887, 1916); A. H. Hogarth, *Medical Inspection on Schools* (London: Henry Frowde, 1909).

28. Henry Maudsley, *The Physiology and Pathology of the Mind* (New York, 1867), p. 292, ch. on "Insanity of Early Life;" Charles West, *On Some Disorders of the Nervous System* (London, 1871); See Stephen Kern, "Freud and the Birth of Child Psychiatry," *Journal of the History of Behavioral Science* 6 (1970): 360–68, Kern argues that a medical specialty in child psychiatry had evolved in Europe.

29. Leo Kanner, *Child Psychiatry* (Springfield, Ill.: Charles C. Thomas, 1935); Leo Kanner, "History of Child Psychiatry," in *Comprehensive Textbook of Psychiatry* eds. A. M. Freedman and H. I. Kaplan (Baltimore: William & Wilkins, 1967).

30. Arthur Holmes, *The Conservation of the Child: A Manual of Clinical Psychology Presenting the Examination and Treatment of Backward Children* (Philadelphia: J. B. Lippincott & Co., 1912), see the "Historical Sketch," pp. 15–31, especially p. 18; Viviana Zelizer, *Pricing the Priceless Child: The Changing Social Value of Children* (New York: Basic Books, 1985).

31. Alfred Binet and Theodore Simon, *Enfants Anormoux* (Folin: Paris, 1907); George Sidney Brett, *A History of Psychology* Vol. III: Modern Psychology (London: George Allen & Unwin, New York: Macmillan Co., 1921), pp. 252–3; Mark Haller, *Eugenics: Hereditarian Attitudes in American Thought* (New Brunswick: Rutgers University Press, 1963), has a good discussion on this topic, see ch.7, pp. 95–110.

Chapter Two

1. William Henry Welch, "Opening Remarks by the President of the Section of Pathology and Bacteriology of Tuberculosis," *Papers and Addresses of William Henry Welch* 3 vols., Vol. I., ed. W. C. Burket (Baltimore and London: Johns Hopkins University Press, 1920).

2. William Osler, *Counsels and ideals* ed. C. N. B. Camac (New York, 1921), quoted in *The Medical Profession and Social Reform, 1855–1945* ed. Lloyd C. Taylor, Jr. (New York: St. Martin's Press, 1974), p. 5, fn. 21, p. 13.

3. Magali Sarfatti Larson, *The Rise of Professionalism: A Sociological Analysis* (Berkeley: University of Calif. Press, 1977), pp. 14–17.

4. Donald Fleming, *William H. Welch and the Rise of Modern Medicine* (Boston: Little, Brown & Co., 1954), p. 153.

5. Charles William Eliot, "Inaugural Address as President of Harvard, 1869," in *American Higher Education, A Documentary History* Vol. II, ed. Richard Hofstadter and Wilson Smith (Chicago: The University of Chicago Press, 1961), pp. 701–714; Henry James, *Charles W. Eliot, President of Harvard University 1869–1909*, Vol. II, (London: Constable and Co., 1930), see ch. 9.

6. Thomas Neville Bonner, *American Doctors and German Universities, A Chapter in International Intellectual Relations* (Lincoln: The University of Nebraska Press, 1963), "Frontpiece;" Daniel Coit Gilman, *The Launching of a University* (New York: Dodd & Mead Co., 1906); Richard Hofstadter and Walter P. Metzgar, *The Development of Academic Freedom in the United States* (New York: Columbia University Press, 1955), see ch. 8, "The German Influence," pp. 369–77.

7. James Morgan Hart, *German Universities: A Narrative of Personal Experiences* cited in Hofstadter and Smith, *American Higher Education*, pp. 569–583.

8. "The Governors of the Board and Faculty of the Sheffield Scientific School of Yale College, *Statement Presented to the State Board of Visitors At Their Annual Meeting, March 1967–8* (New Haven, Connecticut, 1968), p. 10–17, in Hofstadter and Smith, *American Higher Education*, p. 583. Also see Fernand Braudel, *On History* (Chicago: University of Chicago Press, 1980) in his discussion of "History and the Social Sciences: The Longue Duree," pp. 25–54, especially see p. 41.

9. A Stadtman, *The University of California, 1868–1968* (New York: McGraw-Hill Book Co., 1970), pp. 61–80; Harvey Cushing, *The Life of Sir William Osler* (London: Oxford University Press, 1926), p. 311–2; Daniel Coit Gilman, *The Launching of a University* (New York: Dodd, Mead & Co., 1906).

10. Stadtman, *The University of California*, p. 70.

11. James, *Charles W. Eliot*, pp. 4–5.

12. Charles W. Eliot to Daniel Coit Gilman, 17 January 1901, reproduced in James, *Charles W. Eliot*, pp. 131–2.

13. James, *Charles W. Eliot*, p. 8; Josiah Royce, *Scribner's Magazine* X (1891): 371–83.

14. The often reproduced painting by the well-known American portrait painter John Singer Sargent, "The Four Doctors," hangs in the William Henry Welch Medical Library at Johns Hopkins Medical School in Baltimore. Simon Flexner and James Thomas Flexner, *William Henry Welch and the Heroic Age of American Medicine* (New York: Viking Press, 1941), opposite p. 246.

15. Paul Starr, *The Social Transformation of American Medicine: The Rise of a Sovereign Profession and the Making of A Vast Industry* (New York: Basic Books, 1982).

16. Flexner and Flexner, *William H. Welch*, p. 349.

17. Flexner and Flexner, *Welch*, Appendix B. pp. 462–5.

18. Lloyd C. Taylor, Jr., *The Medical Profession and Social Reform, 1885–1945* (New York: St. Martin's Press, 1974), pp. 2–3; Also on Welch see, Fleming, *William H. Welch*. For good overviews see: James G. Burrow, *Organized Medicine in the Progressive Era: The Move Toward Monopoly* (Baltimore and London: The Johns Hopkins University Press, 1977); George Rosen, *Preventive Medicine in the United States 1900–1975: Trends and Interpretations* (New York: Science History Publications, 1975); A fictional work by James G. Mumford, *A Doctor's Table Talk* (Boston: Houghton-Mifflin, 1912) also describes this period.

19. Charles G. Roland, "William Osler, 1849–1919, Commemorative Issue," *Journal of the American Medical Association* 210 (December 22, 1969): 2213; Emile Holman, "Sir William Osler, Teacher and Bibliophile," *Journal of the American Medical Association* 210 (December 22, 1969); 2223; See Taylor, *The Medical Profession*, pp. 4–6; Cushing, *Sir William Osler*, vol. 1, part 2 on Baltimore; also, Fleming, *The Heroic Age*, chs. 7 to 12.

20. Frederick T. Gates, "Recollections of Frederick T. Gates on the Origins of the Institute," in George W. Corner, *A History of The Rockefeller Institute, 1901–1953: Origins and Growth* (New York: Rockefeller Institute Press, 1965), Appendix I, 576–84.

21. Abraham Flexner, *Medical Education in the United States and Canada*, Carnegie Foundation for the Advancement of Teaching Bulletin No. 4 (1910). This report reputedly "touched off a great movement of reform that in a decade or so made the departures of the Hopkins experiment standard all over the continent," Flexner and Flexner, *William H. Welch*, p. 308. For a good discussion see Ellen Condliffe Lagemann, *Private Power for the Public Good: A History of the Carnegie Foundation for the Advancement of Teaching* (Middletown, CT.: Wesleyan University Press, 1983), pp. 66–74; also Corner, *A History of the Rockefeller Institute*, pp. 149–51; Abraham Flexner, *Abraham Flexner: An Autobiography* (New York: Simon and Schuster, 1960). On Simon Flexner, Director of the Rockefeller Institute for Medical Research, see James Thomas Flexner, *An American Saga: The Story of Helen Thomas Flexner and Simon Flexner* (Boston and Toronto: Little, Brown & Co., 1984); and Lewellys F. Barker, *Time and the Physician: The Autobiography Lewellys F. Barker* (New York: G. P. Putnam's Sons, 1942).

22. John F. Fulton, *Harvey Cushing: A Biography* (Springfield, Ill.: Charles C. Thomas Publisher, 1946).

23. Cushing, *The Life of Sir William Osler*, p. 382, fn. 1; Barker, *Time and the Physician*.

24. Dorothy Ross, *G. Stanley Hall: The Psychologist As Prophet* (Chicago: University of Chicago Press, 1972), p. 381.

25. See Louis Hausman's "Introduction," in Eunice E. Winters, ed., *Collected Papers of Adolf Meyer* 4 vols. (Baltimore and London: The Johns Hopkins University Press, 1951–2), see especially Vols. I and II. Also see Clifford W. Beers, *A Mind That Found Itself*.

26. On Watson see David Cohen, *J. B. Watson The Founder of Behaviorism: A Biography* (London: Routledge & Kegan Paul, 1979); also John B. Watson, "Psychology as the Behaviorist Views It," *Psychological Review* 20 (1913): 158–77.

27. G. Stanley Hall, "The Contents of Children's Minds," *Princeton Review* 11 (May 1883): 249–72.

28. James M. Baldwin, "Psychology, Past and Present," *Psychological Review* 1 (July 1894): 363–91; Ross, *G. Stanley Hall* pp. 154–5, 180, 246–7.

29. G. Stanley Hall, *Life and Confessions of a Psychologist* (New York: Appleton-Century-Crofts, Inc., 1923). Also see E. L. Thorndike, *Biographical Memoir of G. Stanley Hall* (New York, 1923); Lorine Pruette's *G. Stanley Hall, A Biography of a Mind*, (New York, 1926); Edward Boring, *A History of Experimental Psychology* (New York: Appleton-Century-Crofts, 2nd ed., 1950, 1st ed., 1929), pp. 532–5.

30. Gerald Grob, *The State and the Mentally Ill: A History of Worchester State Hospital in Massachusetts, 1830–1920* (Chapel Hill: University of North Carolina Press, 1966); on Hall's influence in reforming psychiatry see New York *Evening Post* 6 (Feb. 1891); *New York Scientific American*, (Oct. 1891). Also see Adolf Meyer, "A Functional Approach to Dementia Praecox," in *Lectures and Addresses Delivered before the Department of Psychology and Pedagogy in Celebration of the Twentieth Anniversary of the Opening of Clark University*, September 1909 (Worchester, MA.: Clark University, 1910), pp. 156–7.

31. On Hall and Clark University see Ross, *G. Stanley Hall*, ch. 11; on the place of Clark University in American higher education see: Lawrence Russ Veysey, *The Emergence of the American University* (Chicago: University of Chicago Press, 1965); Merle Curti and Roderick Nash, *Philanthropy in the Shaping of American Higher Education* (New Brunswick, N.J.: Rutgers University Press, 1965); W. Carson Ryan, *Studies in Early Graduate Education: The Johns Hopkins, Clark University and the University of Chicago* (New York: Carnegie Foundation for the Advancement of Teaching, 1939); Hall, *Life and Confessions*, pp. 295–7.

32. Granville Stanley Hall, *Adolescence: Its Psychology and its Relation to Physiology, Anthropology, Sociology, Sex, Crime, Religion and Education* 2 vols. (New York: D. Apple-

ton, 1904), I, p. viii, x. Also see, Musgrove, *Youth and the Social Order*, pp. 56–7; and, John C. McCullers, "G. Stanley Hall's Conception of Mental Development," in *Rethinking Childhood* ed. Arlene Skolnick (Boston: Little, Brown & Co., 1976), pp. 68–77.

33. A review of the child study movement in the U.S. can be found in the *Pedagogical Seminary* 3 (1895): 189–212; 4 (1896): 111–25. The *Proceedings* of the National Education Association in 1895, pp. 893-906, also contain survey data of the early movement. G. Stanley Hall's most important work, *Adolescence*, a digest of his views on child study sold over 25,000 copies in the United States. Two years later the publisher came out with *Youth: Its Education, Regimen and Hygiene*, which was an abridgement directed at an audience of teachers and parents. Hall's other works include: *Morale: The Supreme Standard of Life and Conduct, Recreations of a Psychiatrist, Educational Problems* 2 vols.; *Aspects of Child Life and Education*. See Ross, *G. Stanley Hall*, p. 282 ; also, Wilber Harvey Dutton, "The Child Study Movement in American from its Origin (1880) to the Organization of the Progressive Education Association, (1920), Ph.D. Thesis, Stanford University, 1945." Robert E. Grinder and Charles E. Strickland, "G. Stanley Hall and the Social Significance of Adolescence," *Teachers College Record* 64 (February 1963): 390–9.

34. Theta H. Wolf, "Intuition and Experiment: Alfred Binet's First Efforts in Child Psychology," *Journal of the History of Behavioral Science* 2 (July 1966): 234–8; Ross, *G. Stanley Hall*, p. 284, fn. 24.

35. Ross, *G. Stanley Hall*, pp. 284, 352, 391–4; Nathan Hale, *Freud and the Americans: The Beginnings of Psychoanalysis in the United States* (London; Oxford Press, 1971).

36. See Luis M. Laosa, "Social Policies Toward Children of Diverse Ethnic, Racial and Language Groups in the United States," in *Child Development and Social Policy* Vol. I., eds. Harold W. Stevenson and Alberta E. Siegel (Chicago: University of Chicago, 1984), pp. 12–16 on Terman and Goddard with reference to the testing movement.

37. Ross, *G. Stanley Hall*, p. 352; John A. Popplestone and Marion White McPherson, "Pioneer Psychology Laboratories in Clinical Settings," in *Explorations in the History of Psychology in the United States* ed. Joseph Brŏzek (Lewisburg: Bucknell University Press, 1984), pp. 238–43.

38. See Haller, *Eugenics*, pp. 111–3; Popplestone and McPherson, "Pioneer Psychology Laboratories in Clinical Settings," pp. 238–43.

39. Lawrence A. Cremin, *The Transformation of the School: Progressivism in American Education 1876–1957* (New York: Vintage Books, 1964), p. 115, also p. 101 on Hall and pp. 110–1 on Thorndike. The 1932 *Dictionary of American Biography* vol. 8, ed. Malone Dumas (New York: Charles Scribner), pp. 127–9, cites Hall as second only to William T. Harris and John Dewey in his influence in education. His extended international impact is noted "especially recently in England." Wolf, "Intuition and Experiment," pp. 234–8.

40. See Paul Starr, *The Social Transformation of American Medicine: The Rise of a Sovereign Profession and the Making of A Vast Industry* (New York: Basic Books, 1982).

41. This is the title of Welch's biography, Flexner and Flexner, *The Heroic Age of American Medicine*. It reflects the perception of the age by the medical establishment and the philanthropies which supported medical research and higher education.

42. Ernest Gellner, *The Psychoanalytic Movement or the Coming of Unreason* (London: Granada, 1985), pp. 5, 163, 205.

Chapter Three

1. On the origins of the Charity Organization Movement see Frank Dexter Watson, *The Charity Organization Movement in the United States: A Study in American Philanthropy* (New York: MacMillan Co., 1922); Harold Coe Coffman, *American Foundations: A Study of Their Role in the Child Welfare Movement* (New York: Y.W.C.A., 1936); Edward Christian Lindemann, *Wealth and Culture* (New York: Harcourt Brace, 1936); Ernest Victor Hollis, *Philanthropic Foundations and Higher Education* (New York: Columbia University Press, 1938); more recently, Merle Curti and Roderick Nash, *Philanthropy and the Shaping of American Higher Education* (New Brunswick, N.J.: Rutgers University Press, 1965); on medical research, George Corner, *A History of the Rockefeller Institute*, 1901–1953 (New York: Rockefeller University Press, 1965); E. Richard Brown, *Rockefeller Men, Medicine and Capitalism in America* (Berkeley: University of California Press, 1960); general overviews include: Warren Weaver, *U.S. Philanthropic Foundations* (New York: Harper & Row, 1967); Waldemar A. Nielsen, *The Big Foundations* (New York: Columbia University Press, 1972); Ben Whitaker, *The Foundations: An Anatomy of Philanthropic Bodies* (London; Penguin, 1979); more recently, Ellen Condliffe Lagemann, *Private Power for the Public Good: A History of the Carnegie Foundation for the Advancement of Teaching* (Middletown, CT.: Wesleyan University Press, 1983); Robert F. Arnove, ed., *Philanthropy and Cultural Imperialism: The Foundations at Home and Abroad* (Bloomington, Indiana: Indiana University Press, 1982); and, Edward Berman, *The Influence of the Carnegie, Ford, and Rockefeller Foundations on American Foreign Policy: The Ideology of Philanthropy* (Albany, New York: State University of New York Press, 1983).

2. Mary O. Furner, *Advocacy and Objectivity: A Crisis in the Professionalization of American Social Science, 1865–1905* (Lexington, Kentucky: University of Kentucky Press, 1975; Thomas Haskell, *The Emergence of Professional Social Science* (Chicago: University of Chicago, 1977); Philip Abrams, *The Origins of British Sociology, 1834–1914* (Chicago: University of Chicago Press, 1968).

3. See Joseph M. Hawes, *Children in Urban Society: Juvenile Delinquency in Nineteenth Century America* (New York: Oxford University Press, 1971), pp. 27–60; Robert M. Mennel, *Thorns and Thistles: Juvenile Delinquents in the United States, 1825 to 1940* (Hanover, N.H.: University Press of New England, 1973); Barbara Brenzel, *Daughters of the State: A Social Portrait of the First Reform School for Girls in North America, 1856–1905* (Cambridge, MA.: MIT Press, 1983).

4. Watson, *The Charity Organization Movement*, makes this point.

5. Lindeman, *Wealth and Culture*, pp. 19–20 noted this in 1936.

6. F. Emerson Andrews, *Philanthropic Foundations* (New York: Russell Sage, 1956); *Philanthropic Giving* (New York: Russell Sage, 1950); also, *Legal Instruments of Foundations* (New York: Russell Sage, 1958).

7. Milton Katz, "Introduction," in *U.S. Philanthropic Foundations: Their History, Structure, Management, and Record*, ed. Warren Weaver (New York: Harper & Row, 1967), p. ix; Barbara Howe, "The Emergence of Scientific Philanthropy, 1900–1920, Origins, Issues, and Outcomes," pp. 52–54; also Sheila Slaughter and Edward T. Silva, "Looking Backward: How Foundations Formulated Ideology in the Progressive Period," pp. 55–85, both in *Philanthropy and Cultural Imperialism*, ed. Arnove; Lindeman, *Wealth and Culture*, pp. 19–20; Raymond B. Fosdick, *The Story of the Rockefeller Foundation* (New York: Harper, 1952), pp. 304–5.

8. The Rockefeller Foundation is one of the most prestigious of the foundations in the latter category. Foundation Library Center data, 1960, Government Tax Form 990-A, cited in Weaver, *U.S. Philanthropic Foundations*, p. 59.

9. The forty top philanthropies in the United States by the size of grant payments 1986–1987, range from 8.4 million (William Randolf Hearst Foundation), to over 200 million dollars (Ford Foundation). Only the top three donated over 100 million dollars in one year. Fewer than ten of the forty listed 1987 assets totaling more than one billion dollars. The smallest on the list dropped to 18.8 million in assets. The top ten represented two-thirds of the total assets for all forty listed. American Association of Fund-Raising Counsel, Trust for Philanthropy Statistics, *Giving U.S.A.* 33rd ed. (New York: AAFRC, 1988), cited in *The Chronicle of Higher Education* XXXIV, 42 (June 29, 1988): A1, A22.

10. Sigmund Diamond, *The Reputation of American Businessmen* (Cambridge, MA.: Harvard University Press, 1955), was interested in public perceptions of men who had accumulated great wealth during the nineteenth century; R. M. Galois and Alan Mabin, "Canada, the United States and the World-System," in *Heartland and Hinterland: A Geography of Canada*, ed. L. D. McCann (Scarborough, On.: Prentice-Hall, 1982), pp. 37–62, point out, from a world system perspective, the conditions which made the accumulation of great wealth possible. The deceleration of the world-economy between 1875 and 1895 occurred after the initial thrust of the industrial revolution. The economic growth of the United States began to challenge British dominance of world economic relations. Competition increased over the accumulation of markets, raw materials, outlets for profit and investment. These conditions fostered the growth of "large corporations with monopolistic powers such as Standard Oil of New Jersey in the United States and the Canadian Pacific Railway of Canada," p. 41.

11. Andrew Carnegie, "The Gospel of Wealth," in *The Gospel of Wealth and Other Timely Essays* (Garden City, N.Y., Doubleday, Doran, 1933); this essay first appeared in the *North American Review* (June 1889) with a supplement in December 1889; Howard J. Savage, *Fruit of an Impulse* (New York: Harcourt Brace, 1953); C.

Wright Mills, *The Power Elite* (London: Oxford University Press, 1956, reprint 1969), pp. 271–4.

12. "Charter of the Carnegie Institution of Washington," cited in Corner, *A History of the Rockefeller Institute,* p. 51.

13. Waldemar, A Nielsen, *The Big Foundations* (New York: Columbia University Press, 1971), p. 47, ch. 4.

14. Rockefeller Foundation, *Annual Reports*, Fosdick, *The Story*, "Introduction" p. ix–x; also see, Appendix III, p. 313–314 where areas of Rockefeller Foundation activities are listed for the 1913–1950 period, including: 28 European countries, 5 African, 33 in "The East," 5 in North America, 12 in South America, and 10 in the Caribbean, totaling 93.

15. Selections from Frederick Gates' manuscript autobiography were published in *American Heritage* 6, 3 (1955): 65–86; Gates manuscript, is also cited in Fosdick, *The Story of the Rockefeller Foundation*, p. 7; Simon Flexner and James Thomas Flexner, *William Henry Welch and the Heroic Age of Medicine* (New York: Viking, 1941), ch. 13, p. 269.

16. Gates' business acumen is witnessed by the fact that his first effort was to "thin out bad investments," where in one instance he added fifty million dollars to the fund of surplus wealth which he was to help disburse. Frederick Gates' manuscript autobiography, *American Heritage*, 6, 3 (1955): 65–86; see also Allan Nevins, *Study in Power: John D. Rockefeller, Industrialist and Philanthropist* (New York: Charles Scribner's Sons, 1953), p. 166; George Corner, *The History of the Rockefeller Institute*, p. 20.

17. Fosdick, *The Story of the Rockefeller Foundation*, p. 1.

18. Recollections of Raymond Fosdick, Alan Gregg, quoted in Fosdick, *The Story*, p. 1, p. 325, fn. 2.

19. Frederick T. Gates, "Recollections of Frederick T. Gates on the Origin of the Institute" Appendix I, pp. 575–584 in George Corner, *The History of the Rockefeller Institute.*

20. Gates, "Recollections" p. 576.

21. Donald Fleming, *William H. Welch and the Rise of Modern Medicine* (Boston: Little, Brown & Co., 1954), p. 106.

22. Fleming, *William H. Welch*, p. 109.

23. Also: L. Emmett Holt, the New York pediatrician and fellow parishioner of John D. Rockefeller Sr. at the Fifth Avenue Baptist Church; T. Mitchell Prudden, chair of pathology at College of Physicians and Surgeons since 1892; Hermann M. Biggs, of the Division of Bacteriology and Inspection of the New York City Department of Health; Theobald Smith, chair of comparative pathology at Harvard; and Christian A. Herter, professor of pathological chemistry at Bellevue

Hospital Medical Center, who was also professor of pharmacology at the College of Physicians and Surgeons in New York City.

24. Theobald Smith, had not studied in Europe; Corner, *A History of The Rockefeller Institute*, pp. 34–6, 62.

25. Corner, *A History*, pp. 31, 95.

26. Corner, *A History of the Rockefeller Institute*, pp. 44, 65.

27. Corner, *A History*, p. 95.

28. General Education Board, *The General Education Board: An Account of Its Activities 1902–1914* (New York: GEB, 1915); also see, James D. Anderson, "Education for Servitude: The Social Purposes of Schooling in the Black South, 1870–1930," Ph.D. Thesis University of Illinois, 1973.

29. The Sanitary Commission for the Eradication of Hookworm Disease in the Southern States had its precursors in William Osler's Laennec Society in the battle against tuberculosis. Welch's public health campaigns in Baltimore, and in even earlier work in fighting epidemics with clinical research in New York City.

30. Note that the academic department which had been headed by G. Stanley Hall at Johns Hopkins was unusual in that Hall was professor of psychology and pedagogy. When Hall left for Clark University, the department was taken over by James Baldwin and subsequently by John B. Watson, who insisted on a separate psychology department, a move supported by Adolf Meyer. This was accomplished in 1910; Joseph Brožek and Rand B. Evans, eds., *R. I. Watson's Selected Papers on the History of Psychology* (Hanover, New Hampshire: University of New Hampshire, 1977); George Sidney Brett, *A History of Psychology* Vol. III (London: George Allen & Unwin, 1921); Edwin G. Boring, *A History of Experimental Psychology* (New York: Appleton-Century-Crofts, 1950); Carl Murchison, ed., *A History of Psychology in Autobiography* (Worchester, MA.: Clark University Press, 1936); Richard J. Hernstein and Edwin G. Boring, *A Source Book in the History of Psychology* (Cambridge, MA.: Harvard University Press, 1965).

31. Fosdick, *The Rockefeller Foundation*, p. 141.

32. International Health Board, *Annual Report*; Fosdick, *The Story of the Rockefeller Foundation* cites sixty-two countries on six continents, "Areas of Rockefeller Foundation Activities (1913–1950)," Appendix III, pp. 313–314.

33. Nielsen, *The Big Foundations*, p. 50.

34. Nielsen, *The Big Foundations*, p. 48.

35. Jerome Greene, "Abstract of Address before the Commercial Club of Cincinnati," 18 March 1916, 900 Hist-1, 6, pp. 1518–1519, RAC, N. Tarrytown, N.Y.

36. Rockefeller Foundation, *Annual Reports* (New York: Rockefeller Foundation, 1917), pp. 302–303; (1913–1914), pp. 201–206; (1915), pp. 323–325; (1916), p. 356–358; (1917); also 900 Hist-1, 6, pp. 1531–1532, RAC, N. Tarrytown, N.Y.

37. Rockefeller Foundation, *Annual Report 1913–1914* (New York: Rockefeller Foundation, 1914), pp. 1, 11, 18, 21.

38. See Rockefeller Foundation, *Annual Report* (New York: Rockefeller Foundation, 1921), p. 21; also (1935), p. 69; (1940), p. 43; George Vincent, *President's Annual Review* (New York: Rockefeller Foundation, 1922), p. 8; also (1925), pp. 22, 39; 1926, pp. 39–40; Max Mason, *President's Annual Review* (New York: Rockefeller Foundation, 1933), p. xviii; Raymond B. Fosdick, *President's Annual Review* (New York: Rockefeller Foundation, 1936), pp. 9, 22; (1938), pp. 22–3. Fosdick, *The Story* pp. 123–34, see extended quote by Alan Gregg, p. 133.

39. Jerome Greene, "Statement to RF Board of Trustees, Oct. 27, 1915," cited in Rockefeller Foundation, "Minutes October 27, 1915," pp. 3108–09; J. D. Greene to J. Koren, 29 October 1915, RF 1.1, 200 A, 1913–1916, RFA; also see 900 Hist-1, 6, pp. 1589–90, RAC, N. Tarrytown, N.Y.

40. The Committee consisted of Starr J. Murphy, Harry Pratt Judson, Wickliffe Rose, John D. Rockefeller, Jr., and Jerome Greene. The Conference was held December 7, 1915, present: Murphy, Rose, Greene, Fosdick, with John Koren, Thomas Salmon and Abraham Flexner attending: see, *Report of the Conference*, 7 December 1915, Johns Hopkins School of Hygiene and Public Health, RF 1.1, 200 A, RFA, RAC, N. Tarrytown, N.Y.

41. J. D. Greene to C. W. Eliot, 11 November 1915, Johns Hopkins School of Public Health, RF 1.1, 200 A. RFA; also see 900 Hist-1, 6, pp. 1590–1591, RAC, N. Tarrytown, N.Y. This letter goes on to address the uplifting of cultural and moral values as an important role of philanthropy.

42. Fosdick, *The Story*, p. 300.

43. Rockefeller Foundation, *Annual Report*, (New York: Rockefeller Foundation, 1933), p. xviii; Raymond Fosdick, *The Rockefeller Foundation: A Review for 1936* (New York: Rockefeller Foundation, 1937), p. 8, "work in the medical sciences has chiefly to do with psychiatry, broadly interpreted."

44. *Historical Statistics of the United States*, Series H 398–411, p. 354; there have been four major congressional investigations of foundations in the United States lead by Frank P. Walsh, Montana, 1915; E. Eugene Cox, Georgia, (1952), B. Carroll Reece, Tennessee, (1954); and Wright Patman, Texas, (1962–1964); see Weaver, *U.S. Philanthropical Foundations*, p. 67; and Thomas C. Reeves, ed., *Foundations Under Fire* (Ithaca: Cornell University Press, 1970).

45. Edward Bellamy, *Looking Backward: 2000–1887* (New York: Modern Library, 1893, reprint 1917); Arthur Lipow, *Authoritarian Socialism in America: Edward Bellamy and The Nationalist Movement* (Berkeley: University of California Press, 1982); Robert Weibe, *The Search for Order: 1877–1920* (New York: Hill and Wang, 1967); also, George Bernard Shaw, ed., *Fabian Essays in Socialism* (Boston: Ball, 1911).

46. P. S. Foner, *History of the Labor Movement in the United States, Vol. II, The Industrial Workers of the World, 1905–1917* (New York: International Publishers, 1965); Patrick Renshaw, *The Wobblies: The Story of the Syndicalist Movement in the United States*

(Garden City, N.Y.: Anchor, 1968); on Canada see Seymour Martin Lipset, *Agrarian Socialism, The Cooperative Commonwealth Federation in Saskatchewan: A Study in Political Sociology* (Berkeley: University of California Press, 1950); and David J. Bercuson, *Fools and Wise Men: The Rise and Fall of the One Big Union* (Toronto: McGraw-Hill, 1978).

47. Sigmund Diamond, *The Reputation of American Businessmen* (Cambridge, MA.: Harvard University Press, 1955).

48. John D. Rockefeller, Sr. is quoted as saying: "A man should make all he can and give all her can," in Allan Nevins, *John D. Rockefeller* (New York: Charles Scribner's Sons, 1940), vol. II, p. 191; Ellen Condliffe Lagemann, *Private Power for the Public Good: A History of the Carnegie Foundation for the Advancement of Teaching* (Middletown, CT.: Wesleyan University Press, 1983), similarly notes that Andrew Carnegie gave away much of the fortune which threatened to make him the "richest man in the world," p. 3.

49. Diamond, *The Reputation*, p. 107.

50. Diamond, *The Reputation*, p. 107.

51. Diamond, *The Reputation*; also see Fernand Braudel, "History and the Social Sciences: The Longue Duree," in *On History* (Chicago: University of Chicago Press, 1980), pp. 25–47, p. 41, fn. 27; Raymond D. Fosdick, President of the Rockefeller Foundation, 1936–1948, expressly denies the interpretation of philanthropy as a "shield against public censure," p. 4, *The Story of the Rockefeller Foundation.*

52. Mary O. Furner, *Advocacy and Objective: A Crisis in the Professionalization of American Social Science, 1865–1905* (Lexington: Kentucky: University of Kentucky, 1975), pp. 33 and 38; Thomas Haskell, *Emergence of Professional Social Science* (Chicago: University of Chicago, 1977).

53. Richard Hofstader and Walter P. Metzger, *The Development of Academic Freedom in the United States* (New York: Columbia University Press, 1955), ch. IX pp. 413; and Furner, *Advocacy and Objectivity* illustrate this point.

Chapter Four

1. Lloyd C. Taylor, *The Medical Professional and Social Reform: 1885–1945* (New York: St. Martin's Press, 1974); George Rosen, *Preventive Medicine in the United States, 1900–1975: Trends and Interpretations* (New York: Science History Publications, 1975).

2. Robert Coles, "Introduction," in Clifford Whittingham Beers, *A Mind That Found Itself* (Pittsburgh: University of Pittsburgh, reprint 1981, original New York: Longmans Green, 1907), p. xvi.

3. Norman Dain, *Clifford W. Beers, Advocate for the Insane* (Pittsburgh: University of Pittsburgh Press, 1980), pp. 6–21.

4. CWB fragment from an original draft of *A Mind That Found Itself* [after Jan. 1905], 5 typed pages; *A Mind*, draft 1, Yale, pp. 266–68; 1st ed., p. 263; Beers Papers 2, AFMH Archives, CMC, NYC.

5. See Dain, *Clifford W. Beers*, ch. 6, pp. 61–86.

6. CWB "Notebook No. 1, Hartford, Jan. 1905," 6–10 January 1905, pp. 4–5, 18, Beers Papers 2, AFMH Archives, CMC, NYC; also see Dain, *Clifford W. Beers*, pp. 55–56.

7. Dain, *Clifford W. Beers*, p. 65.

8. CWB to Herbert Wescott Fisher, 20 June 1907, Beers Papers 2, AFMH Archives CMC, NYC.

9. Henry S. Noble to CWB, 15 March 1907; A. R. Diefendorf to CWB, 13 September 1905; Albert A. Thomas to CWB, 24 November 1905, Beers Papers 2, AFMH Archives, CMC, NYC.

10. Charles W. Page to CWB, 8 March 1906, and 14 March 1906; CWB to CWP, 18 September 1906, Beers Papers 2, AFMH Archives, CMC, NYC.

11. CWB to Herbert Wescott Fisher, 20 June 1907, Beers Papers 2, AFMH Archives, CMC, NYC.

12. CWB to William James, 9 June 1906; CWB to WJ, 27 January 1907; CWB to WJ, 17 April 1907; WJ to CWB, 12 March 1907, Beers Papers 2, AFMH Archives, CMC, NYC.

13. Dain, *Clifford W. Beers*, pp. 73–80, 120.

14. CWB, personal notes (typed, no heading), [probably June 1907], Beers Papers 2, AFMH Archives, CMC, NYC.

15. CWB to Anson P. Stokes, Falls Village, Conn., 9 September 1909, (handwritten and typesript copies), Beers Papers 2, AFMH Archives, CMC, NYC.

16. Stewart Paton to CWB, 9 January 1907; CWB to SP, 20 May 1907; SP to CWB, 20 May 1909. The Chapter to be included was an essay on "The Modern Hospital for the Insane," Beers Papers 2, AFMH Archives, CMC, NYC.

17. CWB, "Address Delivered at the 70th Birthday of Dr. Adolf Meyer," (typescript), pp. 174, 215, 228, Beers Papers 3, AFMH Archives, CMC, NYC.

18. CWB to Adolf Meyer, 24 September 1907, hand written copy of a letter transmitting a manuscript of *A Mind*; CWB, "Notebook," 22–25 September 1907; and 2, 6, 8, 9 October 1907, Beers Papers 2, CMC, NYC.

19. Grob, *The Inner World*, pp. 175–84.

20. Eunice Winters, "Adolf Meyer and Clifford Beers, 1907–1910," *Bulletin of the History of Medicine* 43 (Sept./Oct. 1969): 414–43.

21. See Dain's discussion in, *Clifford W. Beers*, pp. 80–83.

22. CWB to William James, 29 October 1907, Beers Papers 2, AFMH Archives, CMC, NYC.

23. CWB to WJ, 29 October 1907. Emphasis added.

24. CWB to Adolf Meyer, 27 October 1908, enclosed with a draft of a "Keynote Address" for the proposed National Association for Mental Hygiene. Beers Papers 2, AFMH Archives, CMC, NYC.

25. Adolf Meyer to CWB, 18 October 1908; CWB to AM, 19 October 1905, Beers Papers 2, AFMH Archives, CMC, NYC.

26. Beers, *A Mind* (1909); also drafts, *A Mind*, Beers Papers 2, AFMH Archives, CMC, NYC.

27. Penciled on his copy of the request he sent Meyer, CWB to Adolf Meyer, 26 October 2 1907; a return letter from Meyer is dated 27 October 1907, Beers Papers 2, AFMH Archives, CMC, NYC.

28. "A Visit with Dr. Meyer in Baltimore." Interview transcript with Paul O. Komora, (typescript), Salmon Papers 1, 3, AFMH Archives, Payne Whitney Clinic Library, CMC, NYC.

29. CWB to Adolf Meyer, 22 December 1908; AM to CWB, 16 January 1909, Beers Papers 2, AFMH Archives, CMC, NYC.

30. Adolf Meyer to CBW, 16 January 1909, Beers Papers 2, AFMH Archives, CMC, NYC.

31. Adolf Meyer to CWB, November 1908, Beers Papers 2, AFMH Archives, CMC, NYC.

32. CWB to Anson Phelps Stokes, 1 May 1908, Beers Papers 2, AFMH Archives, CMC, NYC; Everitt G. Hill, "Editorial: A Great Work Begun," *New Haven Evening Register*, May 7, 1908; "Mental Hygiene Society Founded," *The Morning Journal Courtier*, May 7, 1908; "Friends of the Insane Meet," *New Haven Evening Register*, 7 May 1908.

33. CWB to William James, 16 June 1908, cont. 18 June 1908, Beers Papers 2, AFMH Archives, CMC, NYC.

34. CWB to Adolf Meyer, 22 December 1908; AM to CWB, 16 January 1909, Beers Papers 2, AFMH Archives, CMC, NYC.

35. Minutes, "Meeting for the Founding of the National Committee For Mental Hygiene," 19 February 1909, Beers Papers 2, AFMH Archives, CMC, NYC.

36. Meyer wrote Beers, 2 March 1909: "No sooner do I mention the arrangement for the secretaryship preliminary of the Executive Committee, than I see you sitting on the fence flapping your wings. The part I have most at heart seems quite secondary." Beers Papers 2, AFMH Archives, CMC, NYC.

37. William James postcard to CWB, 22 September 1909; WJ to CWB, 22 May 1910, Beers Papers 2, AFMH Archives, CMC, NYC.

38. WJ to John D. Rockefeller, Sr., 31 January 1909, (copy), Beers Papers 2, AFMH Archives, CMC, NYC.

39. Adolf Meyer to CWB, 12 April 1909; AM to CWB, 13 April 1909, Papers 2, AFMH Archives, CMC, NYC.

40. Anson Phelps Stokes to CWB, 19 June 1909, Beers Papers 2, AFMH Archives, CMC, NYC.

41. George Blumer to Charles P. Emerson, April 1910; Adolf Meyer to Henry B. Favill, 8 May 1910; AM to CWB, 14 August 1910; Beers Papers 2, AFMH Archives, CMC, NYC.

42. Paul O. Komora Interview, "Visit with Dr. Meyer in Baltimore," Thomas Salmon Papers 1, 3, AFMH Archives, Payne Whitney Clinic Library, CMC, NYC.

43. Paul O. Komora Interview, "Visit with Dr. Meyer in Baltimore," p. 2, Thomas Salmon Papers 1, 3, AFMH Archives, Payne Whitney Clinic, CMC, NYC.

44. See Salmon's biography, Earl D. Bond, *Thomas W. Salmon: Psychiatrist* with Paul O. Komora (New York: W. W. Norton, 1950).

45. Paul O. Komora, Interview, "Visit with Dr. Duggan," (typescript), p. 1, Thomas Salmon Papers 1, 1, AFMH Archives, Payne Whitney Clinic Library, CMC, NYC; Raymond B. Fosdick, *The Story of the Rockefeller Foundation* (New York: Harper & Bro., 1952), pp. 26, 127–8.

46. NCMH, "How and by whom the work of the National Committee for Mental Hygiene has been financed, covering the organizing period, 1907–1911 and the period of its active work, 1912 to date 1918," 29 January, 1918, RG 1.1, 200, 33, 373; NCMH, "Bureau of Uniform Statistics," 1919, RG 1.1, 200, 33, 375, RFA, RAC, N. Tarrytown, N.Y.

47. Paul O. Komara notes, "Psychiatry in Medical Education," (typescript), Thomas Salmon Papers 1, 3; George H. Kirby, "The New York Psychiatric Institute and Hospital: A Sketch of Its Development from 1895–1929; " George H. Kirby, "Opening Address: Dedication of New York's New Psychiatric Institute and Hospital," 3 December 1929; with George H. Kirby to William Darrach, 20 May 1930, Thomas Salmon Papers 4, 11; New York State Hospital Commission, "Released for Morning and Evening Papers, Friday Dec. 31," 30 December 1926, Thomas Papers 4, 7, AFMH Archives, Payne Whitney Clinic Library, CMC, NYC.

48. NCMH, "Joint Meeting [of the Executive and Finance Committees]," 9 December 1911, Thomas Salmon Papers 1, 5, AFMH Archives, Payne Whitney Clinic Library, CMC, NYC.

49. NCMH, "First joint meeting of Executive and Finance Committees," 25 April 1911, Thomas Salmon Papers 1, 5, AFMH Archives, Payne Whitney Clinic Library, CMC, NYC.

50. TWS to Frederick Peterson (of the New York Psychiatrical Society regarding the Conference on Immigration) 14 November 1912, Thomas Salmon Papers 1, 6, AFMH Archives, Payne Whitney Clinic Library, CMC, NYC.

51. National Committee for Mental Hygiene and the Committee on Mental Hygiene of the New York State Charities Aid Association, "Mental Hygiene Conference and Exhibit, held at the College of the City of New York, 8–15 November 1912;" Jerome D. Greene, Memo, 15 November 1912; CWB to John D. Rockefeller, Sr., 7 November 1912, RG 1.1, 200, 32, 363, RFA, RAC, N. Tarrytown, N.Y.

52. NCMH, "Minutes Annual Meeting," 5 April 1913, pp. 82–143, AFMH Archives, CMC, NYC; Clarence Hincks and Helen MacMurchy, who became prominent in the Canadian mental hygiene movement, were among the Canadian delegates. Clarence Hincks, "International Conference on School Hygiene in Buffalo," *Toronto Star* (26 August 1913); John D. Griffin, "Mental Health—Canada: The Chronicle of a National Voluntary Movement, The Canadian Mental Health Association, 1918–1980," vol. 1 (May 1981), p. 13, Greenland-Griffin Archives, Toronto.

53. "Report of the Permanent International Committee," Meeting of the Permanent International Committee, Fourth International Congress on Social Hygiene, "Proceedings," (New York, 1913), pp. 113–63.

54. General Education Board, *The General Education Board: An Account of Its Activities, 1902–1914* (New York: G.E.B., 1915), pp. xiii–xiv.

55. Charles W. Eliot to CWB, 5 February 1914, Beers Papers 3, AFMH Archives, CMC, NYC.

56. August Hoch to Lewellys F. Barker (president of the NCMH), 30 December 1914, Thomas Salmon Papers 1, 6, AFMH Archives, Payne Whitney Clinic Library, CMC, NYC.

57. August Hoch to Lewellys F. Barker, 31 December 1914; Jerome D. Greene to AH, 4 January 1915; JDG to TWS, 4 January 1915; "Sumary of the negotiations with the Rockefeller Foundation," (typescript), 5 January 1915, Thomas Salmon Papers, 1, 6, AFMH Archives, Payne Whitney Clinic Library, CMC, NYC.

58. Steward Paton to CWB, 8 October 1923 discusses the origins of neuropsychiatric work in the army in 1917, Thomas Salmon Papers 3, 6; TWS to C. W. Gorgas, 12 May 1917, reports the management of mental cases in the Canadian Army, Thomas Salmon papers, 2, 3, AFMH Archives, Payne Whitney Clinic Library, CMC, NYC.

59. Stewart Paton to CWB, 8 October 1923, Thomas Salmon Papers 3, 6, AFMH Archives, Payne Whitney Clinic, CMC, NYC; Norman Fenton and Thomas Salmon, eds., "Neuropsychiatry," *U.S. Army in the World War* A.E.F. Section X (Washington, D.C.: U.S. Government Printing Office, 1950); Thomas W. Salmon, "Recommendations for the Treatment of Mental and Nervous Diseases in the United States Army," *Psychiatric Bulletin of New York State Hospitals* 2 (July 1917): 353–376; Thomas W. Salmon, "Psychiatric Lessons of the War," *Proceedings of the*

Canadian Public Health Association and Ontario Health Officers Association (May 6–8, 1919), also abstracted in the *New York Medical Journal* 110 (July 12, 1919): 84.

60. Thomas W. Salmon, "Memorandum Prepared at the Request of the Secretary of War," 18 July 1919, p. 1, Thomas W. Salmon Papers 3, 3, AFMH Archives, Payne Whitney Clinic Library, CMC, NYC; Fenton and Salmon, "Neuropsychiatry."

61. Thomas W. Salmon to Edwin Embree, 13 June 1919, Thomas Salmon Papers 2, 5, AFMH Archives, Payne Whitney Clinic Library, CMC, NYC.

Chapter Five

1. George A. Nader describes an urban system as: "territorial units of human organization which becomes specialized and therefore more interdependent, and in which the whole social system becomes more complex." *Cities of Canada, Vol. I: Theoretical, Historical and Planning Perspectives* (Toronto: MacMillan, 1975), p. 2; Gilbert A. Stelter and Alan F. J. Artibise, eds., *Shaping the Urban Landscape: Aspects of the Canadian City-Building Process* (Ottawa: Carleton University Press, 1982), L. D. McCann "Heartland and Hinterland: A Framework for Regional Analysis" in *Heartland and Hinterland: A Geography of Canada*, ed. L. D. McCann (Scarborough, ON.: Prentice Hall, 1982), pp. 2–34; also, in the same volume, R. M. Galois and Alan Mabin "Canada, the United States and World System: The Metropolitan Hinterland Paradox" pp. 37–62; see figure 2.3 which describes the patterns of economic core and periphery in North America in 1911, p. 53.

2. Irving Brecher and S. S. Reisman, *Canada-United States Economic Relations Royal Commission on Canada's Economic Prospects* (W. L. Gordon, chairman, July 1957), see pp. 18–24, and pp. 112–115 on the determinants of foreign investment in Canada in general, and 116–129 on the interdependence of the Canadian and U.S. economies; Nader, *Cities of Canada*, p. 210; Michael S. Cross and Gregory S. Kealey, eds., *The Consolidation of Capitalism, 1896–1929* (Toronto: McClelland and Stewart, 1983), see especially John C. Weaver, "Elitism and the Corporate Ideal: Businessmen and Boosters in Canadian Civil Reform, 1890–1920," pp. 143–168; Galois and Mabin, "Canada, the United States, and the World-System," see table 2.3 on direct foreign investments in Canada, p. 49.

3. Nader, *Cities of Canada*, p. 204.

4. Nader, pp. 204–205; on the wheat economy, pp. 206–207.

5. Dominion Bureau of Statistics, *Census of Canada*, Vol. II, (1921), p. xii–xiii; *Historical Statistics of the United States*, Series A 1–5, p. 8

6. Marshall Dees Harris, *Origins of the Land Tenure System in the United States* (Ames: Iowa, 1953), pp. 1–20; H. V. Nelles, *The Politics of Development, Forests, Mines, and Hydro-electric Power in Ontario, 1849–1941* (Toronto: MacMillan, 1975), pp. 30–41.

7. Kenneth McNaught, *The Pelican History of Canada* (Middlesex, England: Penguin, 1982), pp. 66.

8. Donald Creighton, *The Story of Canada* (Toronto: MacMillan, 1978), pp. 118–9; J. M. S. Careless, *Union of the Canadas: The Growth of Canadian Institutions, 1841–1857* (Toronto: MacMillan, 1967).

9. John Porter, *The Vertical Mosaic: An Analysis of Class and Power in Canada* (Toronto: University of Toronto, 1981), pp. 4–5; Peter Newman, *The Canadian Establishment* (Toronto: McClelland & Stewart, 1975); Pierre Fournier, *The Quebec Establishment: The Ruling Class and the State* (Montreal: Black Rose Books, 1975); Wallace Clements, *The Canadian Corporate Elite: An Analysis of Economic Power* (Toronto: McClelland & Stewart, 1975); Alfred A Hunter, *Class Tells: On Social Inequality in Canada* (Toronto: Butterworths, 1986).

10. S. Gilbert, "The Selection of Educational Aspirations." in R. A. Carlton, I. A. Colley and N. J. MacKinnon, eds., *Education, Change and Society* (Toronto: Gage, 1977), p. 284; I. Gillespie, "On the Redistribution of Income in Canada," in *Structured Inequality in Canada* eds. J. Harp, and J. R. Hofley (Scarborough: Prentice-Hall of Canada, 1980).

11. A. R. M. Lower, "The Origins of Democracy in Canada," *Canadian Historical Association Report* (1930), p. 70; C. P. MacPherson, *The Political Theory of Possessive Individualism* (New York: Oxford, 1979).

12. *Parliamentary Debates on the Subject of Confederation of the British North American Provinces*, Quebec, (1865), p. 59; S. F. Wise, "Upper Canada and the Conservative tradition," in Ontario Historical Society, *Profiles of a Province* (Toronto, 1967), pp. 20–33; Gad Horowitz, "Conservatism, Liberalism and Socialism in Canada: An Interpretation," *Canadian Journal of Economics and Political Science* 33 (1966): 143–171; W. L. Morton, *The Canadian Identity* (Toronto: University of Toronto Press, 1961, 1972), pp. 111–114; Richard Hofstadter, *Social Darwinism in American Thought* rev. ed. (New York: Braziller, 1955, 1969), p. 8; H. V. Nelles, *The Politics of Development: Forests, Minds and Hydro-electric Power in Ontario, 1849–1941* (Toronto: MacMillan, 1975), p. 41; Richard Hofstadter, *Anti-Intellectualism in American Life* (New York: Vintage, 1963); Peter Dobkins Hall, *The Organization of American Culture, 1700–1900: Private Institutions, Elites, and the Origins of American Nationality* (New York: New York University Press, 1982); T. H. Breen *Puritans and Adventurers: Change and Persistence in Early America* (New York: Oxford University Press, 1980).

13. D. G. Creighton, *The Road to Confederation* (Toronto, University of Toronto, 1964), see p. 142; W. L. Morton, *The Canadidan Identity* (Madison, University of Wisconsin, 1962, reprint 1972), pp. 111–140; Richard Hofstadter, *Social Darwinism in American Thought* (New York: Braziller, 1944, reprint 1969), pp. 8–9; C. Berger, *The Sense of Power: Studies in the Ideas of Canadian Imperialism, 1867–1914* (Toronto: University of Toronto, 1970), pp. 187–188; Seymour M. Lipset, "Canada and the U.S.: A Comparative View," *Canadian Review of Sociology and Anthropology* 1 (1964): 173–85; Seymour M. Lipset, "Historical Traditions and National Characteristics: A Comparative Analysis of Canada and the United States," *Canadian Journal of Sociology* 11, 2 (1986): 113–55.

14. Nelles, *The Politics of Development*, p. 47.

15. Nelles, *The Politics of Development*, p. 44.

16. M. C. Urquhart and K. A. H. Buckley, *Historical Statistics of Canada* (Toronto: Macmillan, 1965), p. 119.

17. Urquhart and Buckley, p. 119; also see, Nader, *Cities of Canada*, pp. 206–207; John Bradbury, "British Columbia: Metropolis and Hinterland in Microcosm," in *Heartland and Hinterland*, ed. L. D. McCann, pp. 339–370.

18. C. Dade, *Notes on the Cholera Seasons of 1932–4*, Pamphlet #1428, PAC Catalogue of Pamphlets, Vol. I, p. 18, cited in Richard Splane, *Social Welfare in Ontario: A Study of Public Welfare Administration* (Toronto: University of Toronto, 1965), p. 197 fn. 18; also see: T. J. Copp, *The Anatomy of Poverty: The Condition of the Working Class in Montreal, 1897–1929* (Toronto: McClelland & Stewart, 1974).

19. Neil Sutherland, *Children in English Canadian Society: Framing the Twentieth Century Consensus* (Toronto: University of Toronto, 1977); P. T. Rooke and R. L. Schnell, *Discarding the Asylum: From Child Rescue to the Welfare State in English-Canada, 1800–1950* (Lathan, MD: University Press of America, 1983); Susan Houston, "The Waifs and Strays of a Late Victorian City." in *Childhood and Family in Canadian History*, ed. Joy Parr (Toronto: McClelland & Stewart, 1982), pp. 129–142; Joseph Levitt, *Henri Bourassa and the Golden Calf* (Ottawa: University of Ottawa, 1972); for a look at the more recent phenomenon, see Philip Resnick, *The Land of Cain: Class and Nationalism in English Canada, 1945–1975* (Vancouver, New Star Books, 1977); on labor see, David J. Bercuson, *Foods and Wisemen: The Rise and Fall of the One Big Union* (Toronto: McGraw-Hill, 1978); James Struthers, *No Fault of Their Own: Unemployment and the Canadian Welfare State 1914–1941* (Toronto: University of Toronto, 1983); Desmond Morton with Terry Copp, *Working People: An Illustrated History of Canadian Labour* (Ottawa: Deneau, 1981); on the influence of religion, Richard Allen, *The Social Passion* (Toronto: University of Toronto, 1973); John C. Weaver, "Elitism and the Corporate Ideal: Businessmen and Boosters in Canadian Civic Reform, 1890–1920" in Cross and Kealey, *The Consolidation of Capitalism*, p. 143.

20. *Historical Statistics of the United States*, Series B148, p. 57.

21. Cited in Sutherland, *Children in English Canadian Society*, p. 68.

22. These figures soared in the first year of life, diminishing substantially in the one to four year old bracket and again in the five to fourteen year old range, *Historical Statistics of the United States*, Series B 181–192, p. 60; *Historical Statistics of the United States*, Series B107–115, p. 55; Series B 116–125, p. 56.

23. Emma Duke, "Infant Mortality: Results of a Field Study in Johnstown, Pennsylvania," U.S. Department of Labor, Children's Bureau Publication No. 9, (Washington, D.C.: Government Printing Office, 1915); Ontario Board of Health, *Reports* (1889), p. 16.

24. Grover Powers, "Developments in Pediatrics in the Past Quarter Century" *Yale Journal of Biology and Medicine* 12 (1939): 1–22, p. 9, cites that the majority of ad-

missions to children's wards prior to 1925 were due to diarrhea or vitamin D deficiencies; Robert Wodehouse, "Vital Statistics Pertaining to Infant Mortality" *Public Health Journal* II (August 1911): 363; Albert J. Mayer, "Life Expectancy in the City of Chicago, 1880–1950," *Human Biology* 21 (1955); 202–210; *Historical Statistics of the United States*, Series B 193-200, p. 63; Sutherland, *Children*, ch. 4, pp. 56–69.

25. New York Infant Asylum, *Twelfth Annual Report* (New York, 1884), pp. 44–45 in *Children and Youth in America* 3 vols., Vol. II, ed. Robert H. Bremner (Cambridge, MA.: Harvard University Press, 1971), p. 837.

26. John Spargo, *The Bitter Cry of the Children* (New York: The MacMillan Co., 1906); Ernest Poole, "Waifs of the Street," *McClure's Magazine* XXI (May 1903), described tuberculosis in tenements and attacked the notion that newsboys grew up to be wealthy capitalists.

27. Helen MacMurchy, "Report of the Committee on Mental Hygiene," *Canadian Medical Association Journal* (Sept. 1914): 75.

28. For a description of this movement, see Mark H. Haller, *Eugenics: Hereditarian Attitudes in American Thought* (New Brunswick: Rutgers University Press, 1963), pp. 71–3.

29. Jerome D. Greene, "Principles and Policies of Giving," 2 October 1913; R. B. Fosdick, "Plan for the Development of the Bureau of Social Hygiene," 23 October 1915; Rockefeller Foundation, "Minutes," 27 October 1915, pp. 3108–9; Hist. 900, 1, Vol. VI, pp. 1450, 1531, 1584–7, RAC, N. Tarrytown, N.Y.

30. Helen MacMurchy, "Report on Feebleminded," *Annual Report Ontario Hospital for Feebleminded and Epileptic* (1914).

31. Nova Scotia League for the Protection of the Feebleminded, "Minute Book," 4 June 1908, p. 1; Archives Nova Scotia Division of the CMHA, quoted in J. D. Griffin, "Mental Health Canada," ch. 1, vol. 2, Greenland-Griffin Archives, Toronto. This society expanded its charter and changed its name to the Nova Scotia Society for Mental Hygiene in 1920.

32. C. K. Clarke, *A History of the Toronto General Hospital* (Toronto: Wm. Briggs, 1913).

33. See *Public Health Journal* 4 (1914): 219.

34. Charlotte Heckler, *The Indomitable Lady Doctors* (Toronto: Clarke Irwin Co., 1974), pp. 140–224; E. A. Hardy and Honors A. Cochrane, eds., *Centennial Story: Board of Education for the City of Toronto, 1850–1950* (Toronto: Thomas Nelson, 1950), p. 129.

35. Ontario, Provincial Secretary's Department, Feebleminded in Ontario, *Reports*, (1908, 1920, 1913–15); Helen MacMurchy, "The Relation of Feeble-Mindedness to Other Social Problems," National Conference of Charities and Corrections, *Proceedings* XLIII (1916), pp. 229–5; Helen MacMurchy, *The Almosts: A Study of the Feeble-Minded* (Boston: Houghton-Mifflin, 1920).

36. C. K. Clarke, "The Story of the Toronto General Hospital Psychiatric Clinic," *Canadian Journal of Mental Hygiene* 1 (April 1919): This was the first Canadian court based psychopathic clinic and served as a forerunner to the Forensic Psychiatric Services and Family Court Clinic established in the 1950s.

37. Hincks, "Prospecting for Mental Health," p. 29.

38. John D. Griffin, "Mental Health—Canada: The Chronicle of a National Voluntary Movement, The Canadian Mental Health Association, 1918–1980," May 1981, vol. 1, p. 13, Greenland-Griffin Archives, Toronto; "Report of the Permanent International Committee," Meeting of the Permanent International Committee, Fourth International Congress on School Hygiene, "Proceedings," (New York, 1913), pp. 113–63. Hincks had attended the Fourth International Congress on School Hygiene in Buffalo, New York in 1913. He met Beers at that time and wrote about him in a column for the *Toronto Star*. Clarence Hincks, "International Conference on School Hygiene in Buffalo," *Toronto Star* (26 August 1913).

39. Clarence Hincks to CWB, 6 January 1918, Hincks Papers 4, 3; also Griffin, "The Canadian Mental Health Association," vol. 1, pp. 13, 17, Greenland-Griffin Archives, Toronto.

40. Clarence M. Hincks to CWB, 25 January 1918 and 5 December 1918, Hincks Papers 4, 3, Greenland-Griffin Archives, Toronto.

41. CMH to CWB, 12 February 1918, Hincks Papers 4, 3, Greenland-Griffin Archives, Toronto.

42. CWB to CMH, 23 November 1918, Clarence Hincks Papers 4, 3, Greenland-Griffin Archives, Toronto; NCMH, "How and By Whom the Work of the National Committee has Been Financed," RG 1.1, 200, 33, 373, RFA, RAC, N. Tarrytown, N.Y.

43. CMH to CWB, 12 February 1918, 16 February 1918; CWB to CMH 14 February 1918, "telegram," 21 February 1918, Hincks Papers 4, 3, Griffin-Greenland Archives, Toronto.

44. "List of the First Organizing Meeting, 26 February 1918;" CWB to D. A. Dunlap, 11 March 1918, Hincks Papers 4, 3, Greenland-Griffin Archives, Toronto; see *Toronto Globe* (27 February 1918).

45. CWB to C. K. Clarke, 14 March 1918, CWB to CMH, 20 March 1918, Hincks Papers, 4, 3, Greenland-Griffin Archives, Toronto.

46. Hincks, *A Recollection*, Recording; Griffin, "Mental Health—Canada," vol. 1, p. 25, Greenland-Griffin Archives, Toronto.

47. CMH to CWB, 18 November 1918, 22 November 1918, Hincks Papers 4, 3, Greenland-Griffin Archives, Toronto.

48. CMH to CWB, 8 May 1918, Hincks Papers 4, 3, Greenland Griffin Archives, Toronto.

49. CMH to CWB, 7 April 1922, 21 April 1922, 1 July 1922; C. K. Clarke to CWB, 4 December 1922, Beers Papers, 3, AFMH Archives, CMC, NYC.

50. John D. Griffin "The Amazing Careers of Hincks and Beers," *Canadian Journal of Psychiatry* 27, 8 (Dec. 1982): 668–71.

51. CMH to CWB, 24 June 1918; CWB to CMH, 26 June 1918, Hincks Papers 4, 3, Greenland-Griffin Archives, Toronto.

52. CWB to CMH, 12 April 1919, 21 November 1919; CMH to CWB, 29 February 1919, 6 November 1919, Hincks Papers 4, 3, Greenland-Griffin Archives, Toronto.

53. Canadian Medical Association, *Canadian National Committee for Mental Hygiene: Report of a Survey Made of the Organization* (Ottawa: Metropolitan Life Insurance Co., 1932), divides the early activities of the CNCMH into three phases: 1918–1923; 1924–1928; and 1928–1932.

54. For example, Clarke and Hincks arranged to keep the Manitoba survey confidential if reforms were carried out by government officials. Over two million dollars were, in fact, spent over the next three years on mental hygiene related public works. A report which was published in *Canadian Journal of Mental Hygiene*, 1, 1 (April 1919), applauded the government. The published report was in sharp contrast to the grim "Confidential Report," of the "Survey of Manitoba," (1918), especially in its description of the "Home for Incurables, October 8, 1918." J. M. Armstrong, the Provincial Secretary thanked Hincks and attributed the reforms in Manitoba to the CNCMH. See J. M. Armstrong to C. M. Hincks, 14 March 1919, Hincks Papers, Greenland-Griffin Archives, Toronto.

55. See "Mental Hygiene Survey of British Columbia," *Canadian Journal of Mental Hygiene* 2, 1 (April 1920); "Mental Hygiene Survey of the Province of Saskatchewan, *CJMH* 3, 4 (Jan. 1922); "Nova Scotia Survey," *CJMH* 3, 1 (April 1921); "Survey of the Province of Manitoba," *CJMH* 1, 1 (April 1919).

56. "Report of the Associate Medical Director, Montreal, P.Q." in the "Report of the Proceedings of the Second Annual Meeting of the Canadian National Committee for Mental Hygiene," Vancouver, B.C., 22 June 1920, pp. 7–9, CMHA Papers, MG 28 I 391, PAC, Ottawa.

57. Gordon Mundie, "The Out-patient Psychiatric Clinic." *The Canadian Journal of Mental Hygiene* 3, 2 (July 1921): 297–313.

58. Mundie, "The Out-patient Psychiatric Clinic."

59. Mundie, "The Out-patient Psychiatric Clinic."

60. "Minutes of the Combined Meeting of the Executive and Finance Committees," 17 February 1922, pp. 1–4, CMHA Papers, MG 28 I 391, PAC, Ottawa.

61. A. G. Morphy and William D. Tait, "Mental Hygiene Survey of Montreal Protestant Schools," *Canadian Journal of Mental Hygiene* 3, 1 (April 1921): 49–53; "Report of the Proceedings of the Second Meeting," p. 8.

62. Morphy and Tait, "Mental Hygiene Survey."

63. Morphy and Tait, "Mental Hygiene Survey;" William A. White, *The Mental Hygiene of Childhood* (Boston: Little, Brown & Co., 1919). See Gerald Grob, *The Inner World of American Psychiatry 1890–1940, Selected Correspondence* (New Brunswick, N.J.: Rutgers University Press, 1985), p. 106.

64. E. J. Pratt, "The Application of the Binet-Simon Tests (Stanford Revision) to a Toronto Public School," *Canadian Journal of Mental Hygiene* 3, 1 (April 1921): 95–116.

65. Pratt, "The Application," and, "Minutes of the First Meeting of the Sub-Committee on Educational and Industrial Psychology of the Canadian National Committee for Mental Hygiene," 3 December 1920, CMHA Papers, MG 28 I 391, PAC, Ottawa.

66. C. K. Clarke, "Study of 5,600 Cases Passing Through the Psychiatric Clinic of Toronto General Hospital," also, "A Study of 767 Cases of Illegitimacy," part of the "CNCMH Study of Toronto General," (typescript), Greenland-Griffin Archives, Toronto.

67. Clarke, "Study of 5,600 Cases."

68. Clarke, "Study of 5,600 Cases."

69. Clarke, "Study of 5,600 Cases," p. 1.

70. "February 1, 1921–April 22, 1921," in "CNCMH Study of Toronto General," Greenland-Griffin Archives, Toronto.

71. "February 1, 1921–April 22, 1921."

72. CNCMH reports and notations by Clarke, Hincks and the secretary, Marjorie Keyes, Greenland-Griffin Archives, Toronto.

73. Adolf Meyer to Gerry Morgan, 2 July 1930, Adolf Meyer Papers, I, reproduced in Grob, *The Inner World*, pp. 175–84.

74. "Cooperating Agencies of the Canadian Council on Child Welfare," *Fourth Conference on Child Welfare Proceedings*, p. 43.

Chapter Six

1. National Committee for Mental Hygiene and the Committee on Mental Hygiene of the New York State Charities Aid Association, "Mental Hygiene Conference and Exhibit," 8–15 Nov. 1912; see also Henry Goddard, *The Kallikak Family* (New York: MacMillan, 1912).

2. Theodore Roosevelt, "Conclusions of the White House Conference on Dependent Children, Special Message by the President of the United States," *Pro-*

ceedings of the Conference on the Care of Dependent Children Sixtieth Congress, 2nd ss., Senate Doc. No. 721, (Washington, D.C.: Government Printing Office, 1909), pp. 8–14.

3. Grace Abbott, "Part II: A Topical Abstract of State Laws Governing the Trial and Disposition of Juvenile Offenders," in *Juvenile Court Laws in the United States* ed. Hastings H. Hart (New York: Charities Publication, 1910), p. 122.

4. "An act to regulate the treatment and control of dependent, neglected and delinquent children," 1899, see ch. 23. *Revised Statutes of the State of Illinois 1899* (Chicago, 1899), p. 131; John Koren, "A Summary of Juvenile Court Laws in the United States," in Hart, *Juvenile Court Laws*. Note, Massachusetts and New York had earlier legislation which designated separate court sessions for children in 1872 and 1892 respectively, but they did not enact statutes specifying unique courts until 1906 and 1909.

5. Dominion of Canada, *Statutes* (1980), ch. 40; Neil Sutherland "Towards 'Intelligent and Progressive Legislation for the Prevention of Crime:' Preparing the Way for the Juvenile Delinquent Act, 1886–1908," in *Children in English Canadian Society*, ch. 8, p. 122.

6. Emma O. Lundberg and Mary E. Milburn, "Stories Illustrating the Problems Dealt with by the Board of Children's Guardians," *Child Dependency in the District of Columbia* U.S. Department of Labor, Children's Bureau Publication No. 140 (Washington, D.C.: Government Printing Office, 1924), p. 86.

7. Illinois, *Revised Statutes*, ch. 23, sec. 169, and ch. 122, sec. 144; see, Breckenridge and Abbott, *The Delinquent Child and the Home*, p. 11.

8. "Testimony of Judge Merritt W. Pickney," given before the Cook County Civil Service Commission, Nov. 22 and 23, 1911," reproduced in Breckenridge and Abbott, *Delinquent Child*, Appendix II, p. 203.

9. See Anthony M. Platt, *The Child Savers: The Invention of Delinquency* (Chicago: University of Chicago, 1969), pp. 92–100 on the role of both Jane Addams and Julia Lathrop.

10. Ethel S. Dummer, "Life in Relation to Time," on *Orthopsychiatry, 1923–1948, Retrospect and Prospect* eds. Lawson G. Lowrey, and Victoria Sloane (Menasha, Wis.: George Banta for the American Orthopsychiatric Assoc., 1948), pp. 3–13.

11. "Testimony of Judge Merritt W. Pinckey," see p. 234.

12. Lightner Witmer, "Clinical Psychology," *The Psychological Clinic* 1, 1 (March 18, 1907): 1–9.

13. Arthur Holmes, *The Conservation of the Child: A Manual of Clinical Psychology Presenting The Examination and Treatment of Backward Children* (Philadelphia: J. B. Lippincott Co., 1912), pp. 28–9. *The Psychological Clinic* was explained as "A Journal of Orthogenics For the Study and Treatment of Retardation and Deviation," edited by Witmer. It contained occasional articles on insanity, i.e., vol. 2, 4 (June 15, 1908), had an article by Adolf Meyer, p. 89, and a review of Beers', *A Mind That Found Itself*, by Clara Harrison Town, p. 116–7.

14. William Healy and Augusta F. Bronner, "The Child Guidance Clinic, Birth and Growth of an Idea," in Lowrey and Sloane, *Orthopsychiatry*, pp. 14–49.

15. William Healy, *The Individual Delinquent: A Text-Book of Diagnosis and Prognosis for All Concerned In Understanding Offenders* (Boston: Little, Brown & Co., 1915); Augusta Bronner, *The Psychology of Special Abilities and Disabilities* (Boston: Little, Brown & Co., 1917, reprint 1926).

16. See W. Norton Grubb and Marvin Lazerson, *Broken Promises: How Americans Fail Their Children* (New York: Basic Books, 1982), p. 114.

17. Thomas W. Salmon, "Bureau of Social Hygiene, Institute of Criminology: Study of the Psychopathology of Crime," proposal submitted to the Rockefeller Foundation, [probably 1915]; also "Memorandum Regarding A Director for Studies in the Psychopathology of Crime." Thomas Salmon Papers 4, 2, AFMH Archives, Payne Whitney Clinic Library, CMC, NYC.

18. Glueck's statement on the Sing Sing Study in the "Mental Hygiene Section," of the National Conference of Social Work, *Proceedings of the 44th Annual Session*, Pittsburgh, PA., June 16 to 17, 1917, pp. 3191–454; Salmon, "Memorandum Regarding the Director."

19. Thomas W. Salmon, "Appeal to the Rockefeller Foundation," 19 November 1918, Thomas Salmon Papers 3, 4, AFMH Archives, Payne Whitney Clinic Library, CMC, NYC.

20. Thomas W. Salmon, "Mental Hygiene: A Report on Work Carried on by the National Committee for Mental Hygiene with Appropriations Made by the Rockefeller Foundation, Jan. 1, 1915 to Dec. 31, 1916," Thomas Salmon Papers 2, 3, AFMH Archives, Payne Whitney Clinic Library, CMC, NYC; Clifford Beers, "Report to the Rockefeller Foundation," February 1918, see pp. 1–2, RG 1.1, 200, 33, 373, RFA, RAC, N. Tarrytown, N.Y.

21. Bernard Glueck, "Thomas W. Salmon and The Child Guidance Movement," *The Journal of Juvenile Research* XIII, 2 (April 1929): 80.

22. Beers, "Report to the Rockefeller Foundation," February 1918.

23. Thomas W. Salmon to Walter B. James, 9 April 1919 with TWS to George E. Vincent, 9 April 1919, RG 1.1, 200, NCMH 1919; RF Hist 900–1, vol. 6, pp. 1424–6, RFA, RAC, N. Tarrytown, N.Y.

24. Thomas W. Salmon to Walter B. James, 9 May 1919, RG 1.1, 200, NCMH 1919, RFA, RAC, N. Tarrytown, N.Y.

25. The Memorial produced annual reports from 1919 to 1930, the last is a synopsis of its activities and finances; see LSRM, *Annual Report* (New York: Rockefeller Foundation, 1930).

26. LSRM, *Annual Report 1930*, pp. 10–11.

27. LSRM, *Annual Report 1930*, p. 17.

28. Arthur H. Ruggles to Edward S. Harkness, 7 June 1924, Thomas Salmon Papers 4, 5, AFMH Archives, Payne Whitney Clinic Library, CMC, NYC.

29. "Report of the Conference on the Prevention of Juvenile Delinquency Held at Lakewood, N.J., March 11–14, 1921," Thomas Salmon Papers 4, 2, AFMH Archives, Payne Whitney Clinic Library, CMC, NYC.

30. Bernard Glueck, "Thomas W. Salmon and the Child Guidance movement," *Journal of Juvenile Research* 13, 2 (April 1929), p. 8; also, Paul O. Komora, "Child Guidance Clinics: One of the Promising Developments in the Field of Mental Hygiene," newsclipping dated Jan. 7, 1927, (typed notations), probably from P. Komora, "Child Guidance," [about 1927] Thomas Salmon Papers 4, 8, AFMH Archives, Payne Whitney Clinic Library, CMC, NYC.

31. William Healy, "Oral History Interviews conducted by John C. Burnam, Jan. 1960," (transcript), pp. 94–95, 195; note that the Judge Baker Foundation received funds from the NCMH and RF in the 1920s and 1930s. Thomas W. Salmon, "Some New Problems for Psychiatric Research in Delinquency," read at the Eleventh Annual Meeting of the American Institute of Criminal Law and Criminology, Boston, Mass., 3 September 1919, p. 10, reprinted *Mental Hygiene* IV, 1 (Jan. 1920): 29–42; also reprint No. 73 NCMH, draft copy in Thomas Salmon Papers 3, 4, AFMH Archives, Payne Whitney Clinic Library, CMC, NYC.

32. Salmon, "Some New Problems," p. 10.

33. Salmon, "Some New Problems," p. 11.

34. "Conclusions and Recommendations," *Report of the Conference, Part III,* p. 4, Thomas Salmon Papers 4, 2, AFMH Archives, Payne Whitney Clinic Library, CMC, NYC.

35. "Conclusions and Recommendations."

36. "Conclusions and Recommendations," pp. 4, 6.

37. "Conclusions and Recommendations," p. 6.

Chapter Seven

1. Arthur H. Ruggles to Edward S. Harkness, 7 June 1924, Thomas Salmon Papers 4, 5, AFMH Archives, Payne Whitney Clinic Library, CMC, NYC.

2. "Preliminary Report to the Commonwealth Fund from the New York School of Social Work on the Operation of Division I of the Delinquency Program During the Period Dec. 1, 1921 to June 30, 1927," pp. 1–3, CF 65, RAC, N. Tarrytown, N.Y.

3. "Annual Report to the Commonwealth Fund on the Operation of the Bureau of Children's Guidance by the New York School of Social Work as Section I

of the Program for the Study of Methods for the Prevention of Delinquency Covering the Year 1924–1925," pp. 4–6; Porter R. Lee, "Annual Report of the New York School of Social Work to the Commonwealth Fund on the Operation of the Bureau of Children's Guidance as Section I of the Program for the Study of Methods for the Prevention of Delinquency Covering the Year Ending September 30, 1926," pp. 4–5, Tables I and IV, CF 65, RAC, N. Tarrytown, N.Y.

4. Bernard Glueck, "Annual Report of the Bureau of Children's Guidance," 22 December, pp. 2–34; "Memorandum from Dr. Glueck covering the work of the Bureau of Children's Guidance as of October 1, 1923," CF 65, RAC, N. Tarrytown, N.Y.

5. "Preliminary Report to the Commonwealth Fund from the New York School of Social Work on the Operation of Division I of the Delinquency Program During the period Dec. 1, 1921 to June 30, 1927." CF 65, RAC, N. Tarrytown, N.Y.

6. Lois Meredith French, *Psychiatric Social Work* (New York: Commonwealth Fund, 1940), p. 40; Roy Lubove, *The Professional Altruist: The Emergence of Social Work as a Career 1880–1930* (New York: Atheneum, 1969), pp. 98–99.

7. B. C. Smith to C. M. Hincks, 7 January 1932, CF 67, RAC, N. Tarrytown, N.Y.

8. Barry C. Smith, "Report of the General Director, November 1921, Child Welfare, Program for the Prevention of Delinquency," p. 35, LSRM 3, 111, 1113, RAC, N. Tarrytown, N.Y.; on juvenile courts see, Katharine F. Lenroot and Emma O. Lundberg, "Juvenile Courts at Work: A Study of the Organization and Methods of Ten Courts," in U.S. Department of Labor, Children's Bureau Publication No. 142 (Washington, D.C.: Government Printing, 1924), p. 97.

9. Benjamin W. Fraizer, "Teacher Training," In United States Department of the Interior, Office of Education, *Biennial Survey of Education 1926–1928* Bulletin No. 16 (Washinton, D.C.: Government Printing, 1930), p. 344.

10. Smith, "Report of the General Director," p. 32.

11. Members included Thomas Salmon, as chair, Judge Charles W. Hoffman of Cincinnati, J. Prentice Murphy of Philadelphia and Emma Lundberg, a researcher with the federal Children's Bureau. Commonwealth Fund, "Minutes of Joint Committee on the Methods of Preventing Delinquency," 26 April 1922, CF 376. Also see Katharine F. Lenroot and Emma O. Lundberg, *Juvenile Courts At Work: A Study of the Organization and Methods of Ten Courts* U.S. Department of Labor, Children's Bureau Publication No. 141 (Washington, D.C.: Government Printing, 1923).

12. "List of Publications Published by the NCMH," November 1927, LSRM 3, 35, 368; "The Mental Hygiene Program of the Commonwealth Fund and Some Evidences of Its Value," pp. 13–4, [1928], CF 66, RAC, N. Tarrytown, N.Y.

13. Arthur H. Ruggles to Edward S. Harkness, 7 June 1924, Thomas Salmon Papers, 4, 5 AFMH Archives, Payne Whitney Clinic Library, CMC, NYC.

14. Commonwealth Fund, "Minutes of the Joint Committee on Methods of Preventing Delinquency," 22 February 1922, CF 376, RAC, N. Tarrytown, N.Y.

15. "The Mental Hygiene Program of the Commonwealth Fund and Some Evidences of Its Value," pp. 2–5.

16. George S. Stevenson and Geddes Smith, *Child Guidance Clinics: A Quarter Century of Development* (New York: Commonwealth Fund, 1934), pp. 23–26.

17. E. G. Steger, et al, "The Psychiatric-Child Guidance Clinic: A Study by the Department of Health of the Community Council, St. Louis Missouri," n.d. received by the Commonwealth 8 January [presumably 1925], CF 66, RAC, N. Tarrytown, N.Y.

18. V. V. Anderson and Thomas W. Salmon, "Address on the Work of the St. Louis Clinic" presented to the American Association for the Study of the Feebleminded, in St. Louis, cited in Commonwealth Fund, "Minutes," 24 May 1922, CF 376, RAC, N. Tarrytown, N.Y.

19. Commonwealth Fund, "Minutes," 22 March 1922, 24 May 1922, p. 77, CF 376, RAC, N. Tarrytown, N.Y.

20. E. G. Steger, "To the Consultant Staff of the Psychiatric-Child Guidance Clinic," p. 2, CF 66, RAC, N. Tarrytown, N.Y.

21. Steger, "To the Consultant Staff."

22. Steger, "To the Consultant Staff."

23. Barry C. Smith, "Conference with Dr. Stevenson and Miss Bassett," 12 March 1929, CF 66, RAC, N. Tarrytown, N.Y.

24. "Report of the Division on Community Clinics of the National Committee for Mental Hygiene July 1, 1927 to October 1, 1927," p. 5, CF 66, RAC, N. Tarrytown, N.Y.

25. Mildred Scoville to Barry C. Smith, "Memorandum, Re.: Interview with George Stevenson," 13 June 1932, CF 67; RAC, N. Tarrytown, N.Y.; also see Stevenson and Geddes, *Child Guidance*, p. 26.

26. William Nelson, "Report of the Psychiatric Clinic," 18 August 1925, pp. 1–4, CF 66, RAC, N. Tarrytown, N.Y.

27. Nelson, "Report," p. 4.

28. Nelson, "Report."

29. The study group had a median age of forty-three years. Five percent of the subjects were determined to be schizophrenic, fully five times the expected or normal incidence rate of schizophrenia. Lee N. Robins, *Deviant Children Grown Up: A Psychiatric and Sociological Study of Psychopathic Personality* (Baltimore: Williams & Wilkins, 1966), pp. 239–44.

30. Robbins, *Deviant Children*; also see Lee N. Robbins, "Antecedents of Character Disorder," in Merrill Roff and David F. Ricks, eds., *Life History Research in Psychopathology* (Minneapolis: University of Minnesota Press), pp. 226–239.

31. See August B. Hollingshead and Frederick C. Redlich, *Social Class and Mental Illness* (New York: John Wiley & Son, 1965), where significant differences are found between class position and diagnosis and treatment of mental illness. However, schizophrenia tended to have the same incidence across class lines, pp. 226–7. On class and life cycle differences, see pp. 360–7.

32. George S. Stevenson, "Child Guidance and the National Committee," in *Orthopsychiatry 1923–1948: Retrospect and Prospect* eds. Lawson G. Lowrey and Victoria Sloane (Menasha, Wis.: George Banta Publ. for the Am. Orthopsychiatric Assoc., 1948), pp. 66–7.

33. Anderson, "Report of the Division," p. 14.

34. Anderson, "Report of the Division," p. 16.

35. Anderson, "Report of the Division," p. 18.

36. "Dallas Child Guidance Clinic," CF 66, RAC, N. Tarrytown, N.Y.

37. "Dallas Child Guidance Clinic."

38. Barry C. Smith to Harold I. Gosline, 6 August 1925, attached: "Report of Study of Dallas Child Guidance Clinic Made at the Request of Its Board of Directors," 27–30 July 1925, initialed by Ralph P. Truitt and Lawson G. Lowrey, CF 66, RAC. N. Tarrytown, N.Y.

39. "Report of the Division of Community Clinics of the National Committee for Mental Hygiene July 1, 1927 to October 1, 1927," p. 5, CF 66, N. Tarrytown, N.Y.

40. Abraham Flexner, *Medical Education in the United States and Canada*, Carnegie Foundation for the Advancement of Teaching, Bulletin No. 4 (New York: Carnegie Foundation for the Advancement of Teaching, 1910).

41. Stevenson and Smith, *Child Guidance Clinics*, pp. 33–38.

42. "Instructions for Using the Rating Scale," and attached, "Case Reports, Longfellow School Survey, Minneapolis, Minnesota, 1924," CF 66, RAC, N. Tarrytown, N.Y.

43. "Instructions for Using the Rating Scale."

44. "Case Reports, Longfellow School Survey, Minneapolis, Minnesota, 1924," CF 66, RAC, N. Tarrytown, N.Y.

45. "Case Reports, Longfellow School Survey."

46. Smiley D. Blanton and M. G. Blanton, *Child Guidance* (New York: Century, 1927); Also typescript of Salmon's introduction dated 12, 15 December 1926, Thomas Salmon Papers 4, 7, AFMH Archives, Payne Whitney Clinic Library, CMC, NYC.

47. Blanton and Blanton, *Child Guidance*, pp. 3–9, 288–294.

48. Max Seham wrote a parent training manual, *The Tired Child*, which was the result of his studies of fatigue. He advised that sleeping schedules be adjusted in order to assure the formation of good sleep habits.

49. Blanton and Blanton, *Child Guidance*, pp. 212–24.

50. Blanton and Blanton, *Child Guidance*, pp. 221–2.

51. "Case Reports, Longfellow School Survey."

52. "Report of the Division on Community Clinics of the National Committee for Mental Hygiene, July 1, 1927 to October 1, 1927," pp. 5–7, CF 66; George S. Stevenson, "Visit to Minneapolis - May 10, 1927," "Vist to St. Paul - May 10, 1927," attached to Barry C. Smith to George S. Stevenson, 1 June 1927, CF 66; Memorandum to B. C. Smith from M. Scoville, 13 June 1932, p. 3, CF 67, RAC, N. Tarrytown, N.Y.

53. Stevenson, "Visit to Minneapolis," and "Visit to St. Paul."

54. Stiffler felt Blanton was "discourteous," "Visit to St. Paul."

55. Stevenson, "Visit to Minneapolis," and "Visit to St. Paul."

56. Stevenson and Smith, *Child Guidance*, p. 43.

57. Stevenson and Smith, *Child Guidance*, p. 44.

58. "Foundations Showing an Interest in the Mental Hygiene Field," May 1935, CF 67, RAC, N. Tarrytown, N.Y.

59. Letitia D. Fairchild, "Child Guidance in America," London County Council of Education Committee, Special Services Sub-Committee, for information of members only, S.O. 450, enclosure 209A, 7 May 1928." Fairchild was the Divisional Medical Officer. A copy of her report was sent to the Commonwealth Fund which promoted child guidance demonstrations in Britain as well as the United States, CF 66, RAC, N. Tarrytown, N.Y., pp. 1–6.

60. *Laws of Pennsylvania*, (1902), No. 185 and 297; *Laws of Pennsylvania*, (1903), No. 205 (Preamble); See also, Thomas J. Homer, *Juvenile Court Laws in the United States* (New York: Charities Publication Committee, 1910).

61. This was sometimes worded as "assisting the applicant into making an independent decision not to continue." Almena Dawley, "Treatment Possibilities in the Application Interview." *The News-Letter of the American Association of Psychiatric Social Workers* (Sept. 1932): 8–9.

62. Stevenson and Smith, *Child Guidance*, p. 46.

63. Stevenson and Smith, *Child Guidance*.

64. "Report of the Division on Community Clinics of the National Committee for Mental Hygiene, July 1, 1927 to October 1, 1927," p. 10, CF 66, RAC, N. Tarrytown, N.Y.

65. Margo Horn, "The Moral Message of Child Guidance, 1925–1945," *Journal of Social History* (Sept. 1984): 25–36.

66. Horn, "The Moral Message of Child Guidance, 1925–1945," pp. 25–36.

67. Stevenson and Smith, *Child Guidance,* p. 39.

68. Stevenson and Smith, *Child Guidance,* pp. 39–40.

69. "Report of the Division on Community Clinics of the National Committee for Mental Hygiene July 1, 1927 to October 1, 1927," p. 7; "Memorandum," Barry Smith to M. Scoville, 20 February 1929, p. 2; "Conference with Dr. Stevenson and Miss Bassett," 12 March 1929; CF 66, RAC, N. Tarrytown, N.Y.

70. M. C. Scoville, "Psychiatric Activities in the Los Angeles Area," 11–18 May 1936, pp. 1–7, CF 67, RAC, N. Tarrytown, N.Y.

71. Scoville, "Psychiatric Activities," p. 5.

72. Scoville, "Psychiatric Activities," pp. 6–7.

73. Norman Fenton, *Mental Hygiene in School Practice* (Stanford: Stanford University Press, 1949); similar texts for teachers include: P. M. Symonds, *Mental Hygiene and the School Child* (New York: MacMillan, 1934); H. N. Rivilin, *Educating for Adjustment* (New York: Appleton-Century, 1936); L. A. Averill, *Mental Hygiene for the Classroom Teacher* (New York: Pitman, 1939).

74. Fenton, *Mental Hygiene.*

75. Fenton, *Mental Hygiene,* Appendix I, pp. 403–411; Appendix II, pp. 412–3 provides four classification systems: his own, that of the Worchester State Hospital Child Guidance Clinic, Lawson Lowrey's and Sprague's Universal Classification of Psychiatric problems. The manuals cited were published by Stanford University and the textbook *Mental Hygiene in School Practice* was also produced in mimeograph form for distribution to teachers.

76. Fenton, *Mental Hygiene in School Practice,* pp. 16–17.

77. Fenton, *Mental Hygiene,* p. 17.

78. Fenton, *Mental Hygiene,* p. 24.

79. Fenton, *Mental Hygiene,* pp. 335, 341.

80. Lewis Terman, *The Teacher's Health* (Boston: Houghton Mifflin, 1913).

81. L. G. Lowrey, "Psychiatry for Children," *American Journal of Psychiatry* 101 (Nov. 1944): 375–88.

82. Lowrey, "Psychiatry for Children," pp. 375–388; M. A. Clarke, "Directory of Psychiatric Clinics in the United States–1936," *Mental Hygiene* 20 (January 1936): 66–129; Leo Kanner, *Child Psychiatry* (Springfield, Ill.: Charles C. Thomas, 1935).

83. Ray Lyman Wilber, "A Survey and Challenge," *White House Conference on Child Health and Protection, 1930: Addresses and Abstract of Committee Reports* (New York: Century Co., 1931), p. v.; Section IV, p. 305.

84. Section IV, Committee B, William J. Ellis, chairman, "Physically and Mentally Handicapped," *White House Conference on Child Health and Protection, 1930: Addresses and Abstracts of Committee Reports* (New York: Century, 1931), p. 305; includes a "Bill of Rights for the Handicapped Child," see p. 291.

85. David M. Levy, *New Fields of Psychiatry* (New York: W. W. Norton & Co., 1947), p. 41.

Chapter Eight

1. RF presidents include: George Vincent (1917–1929, Max Mason (1929–1936) and Raymond B. Fosdick (1936–1948). Directors of the Division on Medical Sciences include: Richard Pierce (1919–1930) and Alan Gregg (1930–1954). See Raymond B. Fosdick, *The Story of the Rockefeller Foundation* (New York: Harpers & Bro., 1952); Rockefeller Foundation, *Annual Report* (New York: RF, 1933), p. xviii; Raymond B. Fosdick, *The Rockefeller Foundation: A Review for 1937* (New York: RF, 1937), pp. 22–5, 26–7.

2. "Application to the Laura Spelman Rockefeller Memorial for an Appropriation of $12,000 a year for a Mobile Mental Hygiene Clinic in Monmouth County, New Jersey," 12 July 1921, LSRM 3, 34, 558, RAC, N. Tarrytown, N.Y.

3. President Theodore Roosevelt's Country Life Commission (1907) is a witness to the official concern expressed over the backwardness of the rural areas, similarly rural sociology was a burgeoning applied science. See Paul H. Landis, *Rural Life in Process* (New York: McGraw-Hill, 1940); Thomas James, "Applied Social Science and Planned Change in Education: The Case of Rural Sociology and School Consolidation," paper presented at the History of Education Society Annual Meetings, Stanford University, October 17, 1986.

4. Geraldine (Mrs. Lewis S.) Thompson quote in, "Conference Laura Spelman Rockefeller Memorial in Connection with the Monmouth County Organization for Social Service," 11 February 1926, LSRM 3, 34, 364, RAC, N. Tarrytown, N.Y.

5. Katherine B. Davis, (typed report), 1 August 1921 attached to "Monmouth County Organization for Social Service, Inc., An Application from Mrs. Lewis S. Thompson." Also see K. B. Davis, "A Supplemental Report on the Request of Mrs. Lewis S. Thompson," 14 September 1921. K. B. Davis to William S. Richardson (Bureau of Social Hygiene), 14 September 1921, mentions a trip to Monmouth County and suggestions from Salmon concerning personnel. Raymond B. Fosdick to W. S. Richardson, 19 September 1921, LSRM 3, 34, 358, RAC, N. Tarrytown, N.Y.

6. V. V. Anderson to Beardsley Ruml, 3 October 1923; Geraldine (Mrs. Lewis S.) Thompson to B. Ruml, 27 October 1923, LSRM 3, 34, 358, RAC, N. Tarrytown, N.Y.

7. Barry C. Smith to T. W. Salmon, 30 September 1921, Thomas Salmon Papers, 4, 2, Payne Whitney Clinic Library, CMC, NYC.

8. V. V. Anderson, "Clinic Conducted by the Division on the Prevention of Delinquency by the National Committee for Mental Hygiene," pp. 9–10, LSRM 3, 34, 364, RAC, N. Tarrytown, N.Y.

9. Anderson, "Clinic Conducted by the Division on the Prevention of Delinquency by the National Committee for Mental Hygiene," p. 13, LSRM 3, 34, 364, RAC, N. Tarrytown, N.Y.

10. Anderson, "Clinic Conducted By the Division on the Prevention of Delinquency."

11. V. V. Anderson to Beardsley Ruml, 3 October 1923, attached schedule for the meeting; Geraldine (Mrs. Lewis S.) Thompson to B. Ruml, 27 October 1923, LSRM 3, 34, 358, RAC, N. Tarrytown, N.Y.

12. Geraldine Thompson to Lawrence K. Frank, 25 February 1924, (copy), LSRM 3, 34, 359, RAC, N. Tarrytown, N.Y.

13. Barry C. Smith to John L. Montgomery (executive secretary of the Monmouth Co. Organization), 29 December 1923, LSRM 3, 34, 359, RAC, N. Tarrytown, N.Y.

14. L. K. Frank, "Monmouth County Organization for Social Service Memorandum," 12 January 1924; L. K. Frank, "Memorandum: Monmouth County Clinic," 22 January 1924; John L. Montgomery to Barry Smith, 7 January 1924, 16 January 1924, 19 January 1924, LSRM 3, 34, 359, RAC, N. Tarrytown, N.Y.

15. V. V. Anderson to John L. Montgomery, 22 January 1924; George Stevenson to John L. Montgomery, 15 January 1924, LSRM 3, 34, 359, RAC, N. Tarrytown, N.Y.

16. L. K. Frank to Kenneth Chorley, "Memorandum," 7 April 1925, LSRM 3, 36, 360 RAC, N. Tarrytown, N.Y.; Roy Lubove, *The Professional Altruist: The Emergence of Social Work as a Career, 1880–1930* (New York: Atheneum, 1969), pp. 106–7, 1915 address by Abraham Flexner National Conference on Charities and Correction.

17. J. D. Ketchum, "Report II on Social Psychology," in E. A. Bott, "Research Planning in the Canadian Psychological Association," *Canadian Journal of Psychology* 2 (1948): 14–15.

18. Edwin G. Boring, *A History of Experimental Psychology* (New York: Appleton-Century-Crofts, 1929, 1950); Richard J. Hernstein and Edwin G. Boring, *A Source Book in the History of Psychology* (Cambridge, MA.: Harvard University Press, 1965); Rand B. Evans, "The Origins of American Academic Psychology," in *Explorations in the History of Psychology in the United States* ed. Josef Brožek (Lewisburg: Bucknell University Press, 1984), pp. 17–60.

19. C. R. Myers, "Notes on the History of Psychology in Canada," *The Canadian Psychologist* 6, 1 (January 1965): 5.

20. Myers, "Notes on the History of Psychology in Canada," pp. 4–19.

21. C. R. Myers, "Edward Alexander Bott (1887–1974)," *The Canadian Psychologist* 15, 3 (July 1974): 292; Karl S. Bernhardt, "Professor E. A. Bott," *Canada's Mental Health* (June 1957).

22. Canadian Medical Association, *Report of a Survey of the Organization [Canadian National Committee for Mental Hygiene]* (Ottawa: Metropolitan Life Insurance Co., 1932), pp. 14–30.

23. "Minutes of the First Meeting of the Sub-Committee on Educational and Industrial Psychology of the Canadian National Committee for Mental Hygiene," 3 December 1920, CMHA Papers, MG 28 I 391 84/63, PAC, Ottawa.

24. "Minutes of the First Executive Meeting (2nd Year) of the Canadian National Committee for Mental Hygiene, held in the office of Dr. C. F. Martin," 17 October 1919, p. 38, CMHA Papers, MG 28 I 391 84/63, PAC, Ottawa.

25. E. A. Bott, "Juvenile Employment in Relation to Public Schools and Industries in Toronto," outlined in "Minutes of the First Meeting of the Sub-Committee on Educational and Industrial Psychology of the Canadian National Committee for Mental Hygiene," 3 December 1920, CMHA Papers, MG 28 I 391, 84/63, PAC, Ottawa.

26. "Minutes of the Sub-Committee on Educational and Industrial Psychology CNCMH," 3 December 1920, CMHA Papers, MG 28 I 391, 84/63, PAC, Ottawa.

27. "Minutes of the Sub-Committee," 3 December 1920.

28. C. M. Hincks to Edwin Embree, 25 February 1924, RG 1.1, 1, 427 1, RFA, RAC, N. Tarrytown, N.Y.

29. A series of correspondence between Hincks and Embree in the 1930s records personal events and Edwin Embree's continuing support for CNCMH as president of the Rosenwald Fund. Clarence Hincks Papers, 2, 9, Greenland Griffin Archives, Toronto; Edwin Embree to Alan Gregg, 15 September 1939, A. G. to E. E., 15 September 1939; A. G. to C. M. Hincks, 22 September 1939, RFA RG 1.1, 427, 1, 6, RAC, N. Tarrytown, N.Y.

30. C. M. Hincks to E. Embree, 25 February 1924.

31. The early eugenic societies for the care of the feebleminded argued for special classes. These societies also formed the basis for the CNCMH. "Minutes of the Rockefeller Foundation," 27 February 1924, pp. 24033–24034, RG 1.1 427, 1, 1, RFA, RAC, N. Tarrytown, N.Y.

32. E. Embree to C. M. Hincks, 3 March 1924, RG 1.1 427, 1, 1, RFA, RAC, N. Tarrytown, N.Y.

33. C. M. Hincks to E. Embree, 3 March 1924.

34. C. M. Hincks to E. Embree, 5 March 1924; E. E. to C. M. H., 5 March 1924, RG 1.1, 427, 1, 1, RFA, RAC, N. Tarrytown, N.Y.

35. C. M. Hincks to E. Embree, 28 April 1924, RG 1.1, 427, 1, 1, RFA, RAC, N. Tarrytown, N.Y.

36. "Minutes of the Rockefeller Foundation," pp. 1920–24, pp. 24114–16, RG 1.1 427, 1–11, RFA, RAC, N. Tarrytown, N.Y.

37. C. M. Hincks to E. Embree, 30 May 1924; C. M. H. to E. E., 5 June 24; E. E. to C. M. H., 10 June 1924, RG 1.1, 427, I, RFA, RAC, N. Tarrytown, N.Y.

38. "Report of the Special Meeting held in Montreal on Saturday, June 7th to consider the administration of the Rockefeller Foundation appropriation of $75,000 to the Canadian National Committee for Mental Hygiene." CMHA Papers, MG 28 I 391 84/63, PAC, Ottawa.

39. "Report of the Special Meeting."

40. C. M. Hincks to Norma S. Thompson, 26 June 1925, N. S. T. to C. M. H. 1 July 1925, RG 1.1, 427, 1, 1, RFA, RAC, N. Tarrytown, N.Y.

41. "Medical Director's Report," 19 June 1925, CMHA papers, MG 28 I 391 84/63, PAC, Ottawa.

42. "Medical Director's Report," 19 June 1925.

43. "Medical Director's Report," 19 June 1925.

44. "Medical Director's Report," 19 June 1925.

45. "Report of the Annual Meeting of the Board of Directors and of the Executive and Finance Committees of the Canadian National Committee for Mental Hygiene," 14 November 1924, CMHA Papers, MG 28 I 391 84/63, PAC, Ottawa.

46. C. M. Hincks to E. Embree, 17 March 1924, RG 1.1, 427, 1, 1, RFA RAC, Tarrytown, N.Y.; Karl S. Bernhardt, "Dr. William E. Blatz," *The Canadian Psychologist* 6, 1 (Jan. 1965): 1–3. John B. Watson and Beardsley Ruml were also students of Angell. See Carl Murchison, ed., *A History of Psychology in Autobiography* (Worcester, MA.: Clark University Press, 1936), pp. 1–38 on Angell, pp. 69–82 on Carr.

47. Hincks to Embree, 17 March 1924.

48. J. G. Fitzgerald to R. H. Crowley, (chief inspector of schools, Toronto Board of Education), 6 May 1926, RG 1.1, 427, 1, 2, RFA, RAC, N. Tarrytown, N.Y.

49. Canadian Medical Association, *Report of a Survey.*

50. Canadian Medical Association, *Report of a Survey*, J. G. Fitzgerald to R. H. Crowley, 6 March 1926.

51. C. M. Hincks, "Report of Medical Director to Board of Directors and Supporters of the CNCMH," 19 October 1925, CMHA papers, MG 28 I 391 84/63, PAC, Ottawa.

52. Toronto Research Division, "Report Upon a Five Year Experiment in Mental Hygiene Research in Regal Road School, Toronto," 31 March 1930, RG 1.1, 427, 1, 7, RFA, RAC, N. Tarrytown, N.Y.

53. Toronto Research Division, "Report."

54. Toronto Research Division, "Report."

55. Hincks, "Report," p. 2; Viviana A. Zelizer in *Pricing the Priceless Child: The Changing Social Values of Children* (New York: Basic, 1985) gives us some hints about why companies like Metropolitan were eager to support research such as described here. Zelizer argues that children's insurance was sold on a "child saving rhetoric, stressing the priceless emotional value of children above their cash value," pp. 117–37, 125. A perusal of papers read before the American Life Convention between 1906 and 1952 and the Medical Section Papers from 1910 show an early and increasing interest in public education as a means of selling insurance and as a means of reducing the outlay of insurance companies by preventable accidents and illness. By 1919 the conservation of health and insurance were well linked. See R. Carlyle Buley, *The American Life Conventon 1906–1952: A Study in the History of Life Insurance* 2 vols. (New York: Appleton-Croft, 1953), see appendices, vol. 2, pp. 1188–1279.

56. Mary J. Wright, "The History of Developmental Psychology in Canada, Note 4: The Saga of William Emet Blatz," part 1, (typescript), Greenland-Griffin Archives, Toronto.

57. Mary J. Wright, "The Saga of William Emet Blatz," part 1.

58. For example, Murphy Gardner (Columbia Univ.) wrote to L. K. Frank, 23 January 1935, regarding a GEB sponsored conference on child psychology held in New York City, 19–20 January 1935: "Of course folks like Bill Blatz are going to go ahead with their ideas without regard for disturbing questions of this sort, but, most of us I like to think are still educable." GEB 930 1, 3, 370, 3866, RAC, N. Tarrytown, N.Y.

59. William E. Blatz and Helen Bott, *The Management of Young Children* (New York: Morrow, 1930); William E. Blatz and Helen Bott, *Parents and the Pre-School Child* (New York: Morrow, 1929); Blatz's other instructional works included *Nursery Education: Theory and Practice* with Dorothy Millichamp and Margaret Fletcher, and *We Go to Nursery School* with Marjorie Poppleton, both (New York: Morrow, 1935).

60. Mary J. Wright, "The Saga of William Emet Blatz," part 1, p. 9

61. William E. Blatz, et al., *The Five Sisters* (Toronto: University of Toronto, 1937, 1938).

62. Albert R. Gilgen, *American Psychology Since World War II. A Profile of the Autobiography* Vol. III, ed. Carl Murchison (Worchester, MA.: Clark University

63. See James R. Angell, "James Rowland Angell," in *A History of Psychology in Autobiography* Vol. III, ed. Carl Murchison (Worchester, MA.: Clark University Press, 1936), pp. 28–29.

64. William E. Blatz, *Understanding the Young Child* (Toronto: Clarke, Irwin & Co. 1944), see the "Introduction."

65. See William E. Blatz, *Human Security* (Toronto: University of Toronto, 1966).

66. B. F. Skinner, *Beyond Freedom and Dignity* (New York: Knopf, 1971).

67. William E. Blatz, *Human Security.*

68. Mary D. Salter, *An Evaluation of Adjustment Based Upon the Concept of Security* University of Toronto Studies in Child Development Series, No. 9 (Toronto: University of Toronto, 1940); for a list of publications and tests on human security see Blatz, *Human Security*, pp. 129–131.

69. Mary D. Salter Ainsworth, "The Significance of Service in England," in Agnes N. O'Connell and Nancy Felipe Russo, eds., *Models of Achievement Reflection on Eminent Women in Psychology* (New York: Columbia University Press, 1983), pp. 201–19.

70. William E. Blatz, *Hostages to Peace: Parents and Children of Democracy* (New York: Morrow, 1940).

71. William E. Blatz, *Understanding the Young Child* (Toronto: Clarke, Irwin, 1944), pp. v–vii.

72. Mary J. Wright, "The History of Developmental Psychology in Canada, Note 5: The Saga of William Emet Blatz, Part II, 1938–1950," (typescript), Greenland-Griffin Archives, Toronto.

73. William E. Blatz, *Understanding the Child* (Bickley Kent, U.K.: University of London, 1944; New York; William Morrow, 1944, with 8 reprints between 1945 and 1965).

74. Mary J. Wright a senior staff member of the Institute and Garrison Lane makes this argument in "The Saga of William Emet Blatz," part 2, p. 5; also interview with John D. Griffin, July 20, 1986, Toronto.

75. Wright, "The Saga."

76. Anna Freud, a refuge from occupied Europe, was also actively disseminating her ideas on child psychiatry during this period.

77. Central Advisory Council for Education, *Children and Their Primary Schools* 2 vols., "The Plowden Report" (London: Her Majesty's Stationary House, 1967).

78. Lillian Weber, *The English Infant School and Informal Education* (Englewood Cliffs, N.J.: Prentice-Hall, 1971); also Wright, "The Saga," part 2, p. 5.

79. Featherstone published these articles in *The New Republic* (August 19, September 2, and September 9, 1967). Joseph Featherstone, *An Introduction: Informal Schools in Britain Today* Anglo-American Primary School Project (New York: Citation Press, 1971). Marvin Lazerson, ed., *American Education in the Twentieth Century* (New York: Teachers College Press, 1987), "Introduction" p. 44 and the selection from Joseph Featherstone, pp. 177–182, notes this influence in the context of American educational reform in the 1960s.

80. See the three excerpts from Lillian Weber in Charles Silberman, *The Open Classroom Reader* (New York: Random House, 1973), pp. 22–6, 148–66, 467–80; also Featherstone, pp. 133–8.

81. E. M. Stapleford, *History of the Day Nursery Branch* (Toronto, Ontario: Ministry of Community and Social Services, 1976), p. 2.

82. Mary J. Wright, "The Saga," part 2, p. 6.

83. Dorothy Millichamp and Mary L. Northway, *Conversations at Caledon: Some Reminiscences of the Blatz Era* (Toronto: Brora Centre, 1977).

84. Ontario, Department of Education, *Living and Learning: The Report of the Provincial Commission on the Aims and Objectives of Education in Ontario* (1968), pp. 76–77, known as the Dennis-Hall Report. See also Charles Silberman, *Crisis in the Classroom: The Remaking of American Education* (New York: Random House, 1970), p. 115 where he quotes the Ontario report.

85. Douglas Meyers, *The Failure of Educational Reformism in Canada* (Toronto: McClelland & Stewart, 1973).

86. Alan Gregg, "Canadian National Committee for Mental Hygiene," p. 2, RF 1.1, 427, 1, 6, RFA, RAC, N. Tarrytown, N.Y.

87. Gregg, "Canadian National Committee."

Chapter Nine

1. Dorothy Ross, *G. Stanley Hall: The Psychologist As Prophet* (Chicago: University of Chicago Press, 1972), pp. 148–79, 179; also see G. Stanley Hall, *Life and Confessions of a Psychologist* (New York: D. Appleton, 1923).

2. See Louise J. Kaplan, *Adolescence: The Farewell to Childhood* (New York: Simon and Schuster, 1984).

3. Laura Spelman Rockefeller Memorial, *Annual Report* (New York: Rockefeller Foundation, 1930), p. 10.

4. LSRM, *Annual Report* (New York: Rockefeller Foundation, 1930), p. 9.

5. "The Present Situation in Child Research," GEB 930 1, 3, 369, 3849, RAC, N. Tarrytown, N.Y.

6. "Minutes of the Meeting of Committee on Child Growth and Development," 22 December 1936, GEB 930 1, 3, 369, 3849; "Minutes of the Meeting of Committee on Child Growth and Development," 15 March 1937; "Minutes of the Meeting of Committee on Growth and Development," 3 June 1937, GEB 930 1, 3, 369, 3850, RAC, N. Tarrytown, N.Y.

7. George D. Stoddard and Dorothy E. Bradbury, *Pioneering in Child Welfare: A History of the Iowa Child Welfare Research Station 1917–1933* (Iowa City: University of Iowa Press, 1933); Ginalie Swaim, "Cora Bussey Hillis: Woman of Vision," *The Palimpsest* 60, 6 (1979): 162–177; Cora Bussey Hillis, "How the Iowa Child Welfare Research Station Came into Being," unpublished manuscript, August 1919, Cora Bussey Hillis Papers, Iowa State Historical Department, Division of the State Historical Society of Iowa, Iowa City, cited in Henry L. Minton, "The Iowa Child Welfare Research Station and the 1940 Debate on Intelligence: Carrying on the Legacy of a Concerned Mother," *Journal of the History of Behavioral Sciences* 20 (April 1984): 160–175.

8. Carl E. Seashore, "Carl Emil Seashore," in Carl Murchison, ed., *History of Psychology in Autobiography* (Worchester, MA.: Clark University Press, 1930), pp. 225–97; Carl E. Seashore, *Pioneering in Psychology* (Iowa City: University of Iowa, 1942).

9. George D. Stoddard, "The Second Decade: A Review of the Activities of the Iowa Child Welfare Research Station, 1928–38," *Aims and Progress of Research* 58, New Series, 366 (Feb. 1, 1939):1.

10. State of Iowa, "Chapter 282, Iowa Child Welfare Research Station: An Act to establish and maintain the Iowa Child Welfare Research Station and making an appropriation therefor." *Acts & Joint Resolutions passed at the Regular Session of the Thirty-Seventh General Assembly of the State of Iowa.*

11. Undated news clipping, "Entire Families May Enter Lists For Blue Ribbons," LSRM 3, 43, 450, RAC, N. Tarrytown, N.Y.

12. George B. Mangold, *Problems of Child Welfare* (New York: MacMillan, 1914, 2nd ed. 1924), p. 123.

13. "An Act for the promotion of the Welfare and Hygiene of Maternity and Infancy, 1921," *U.S. Statutes at Large* XLII, part 1 (April 1921–March 1923), pp. 224–6; see U.S. Department of Labor, Children's Bureau, "The Promotion of the Welfare and Hygiene of Maternity and Infancy: The Administration of the Act of Congress of November 23, 1921," Bureau Publication No. 146 (Washington: Government Printing, 1925); also, Robert Bremner, ed., *Children and Youth in America, Vol. II* (Cambridge, MA.: Harvard Univ. Press, 1971), pp. 1003–1025.

14. May Pardee Youtz, "Iowa State Program of Parent Education," in *Child Study Conference on Parent Education* Bronxville, New York, October 1925, pp. 93–98, LSRM 5, 27, 284, RAC, N. Tarrytown, N.Y.

15. Bird T. Baldwin to Mr. Richardson, 8 December 1920, LSRM 3, 40, 416, RAC, N. Tarrytown, N.Y.

16. "Child Study and Parent Training," LSRM 3, 30, 315, RAC, N. Tarrytown, N.Y.

17. "Memorandum Concerning Child Study Program," September 1925, LSRM 3, 30, 351, RAC, N. Tarrytown, N.Y.

18. See George D. Stoddard, "The Second Decade: A Review of Activities of the Iowa Child Welfare Research Station," *Aims and Progress of Research* 58, New Series 366 (Feb. 1, 1939): 2–9, 14.

19. Stoddard, "The Second Decade," p. 2.

20. Nutrition studies were conducted by Amy L. Daniels.

21. Stoddard, "The Second Decade," pp. 11–12.

22. Bird T. Baldwin, Heredity and Environment-Or Capacity and Training? *Journal of Educational Psychology* 19 (1928): 405–9; Bird T. Baldwin and Lorle I. Stecher, "Mental Growth Curve of Normal and Superior Children," *University of Iowa Studies in Child Welfare* 2, 1 (1922); Bird T. Baldwin, Eva A. Fillmore and Lora Hadley, *Farm Children: An Investigation of Rural Life in Selected Areas of Iowa* (New York: Appleton, 1930); this was published two years after Baldwin's death.

23. Stoddard, "The Second Decade," p. 6; Harold M. Skeels, "Iowa Studies of the Mental Growth of Children in Relation to the Differentials of the Environment: A Summary," in *The Thirty—Ninth Yearbook of the National Society for the Study of Education - Intelligence its Nature and Nurture*, Vol. II, ed. Guy M. Whipple (Bloomington, Ill.: Public School Publishing, 1940), pp. 281–308.

24. Beth L. Wellman, "The Effect of Preschool Attendance upon the IQ," *Journal of Experimental Education* 1 (1932/3): 48–69; Beth L. Wellman, "Some New Basis for Interpretation of the IQ," *Journal of Genetic Psychology* 41 (1932): 116–126; Beth L. Wellman, "Physical Growth and Motor Development and Their Relation to Mental Development in Children," in *Handbook of Child Psychology* ed. Carl Murchison (Worchester, MA.: Clark University Press, 1931), pp. 242–77; Beth L. Wellman, "Iowa Studies on the Effects of Schooling," in Whipple, *The Thirty-Ninth Yearbook*, pp. 281–308.

25. Michael M. Sokal, "James McKeen Cattell and American Psychology in the 1920s," in *Explorations in the History of Psychology in the United States*, ed. Josef Brožek (Lewisburg: Bucknell University Press, 1984), pp. 298, 300–1; Robert Castel, Francoise Castel and Anne Lovell, *The Psychiatric Society* (New York: Columbia University Press, 1982), pp. 289, 294.

26. Hamilton Cravens, *The Triumph of Evolution: American Scientists and the Hereditarian - Environment Controversy 1900–1941* (Philadelphia: University of Pennsylvania Press, 1978).

27. Haller, *Eugenics*, pp. 125–9.

28. N. J. Blcok and G. Dworkin, *The IQ Controversy* (New York: Pantheon Books, 1974), see "The Lippman-Terman Debate," pp. 4–44; Cravens, *The Triumph of Evolution.*

29. See for example: H. H. Goddard, *The Kallikak Family: A Study of the Heredity of Feeblemindedness* (New York: MacMillan, 1912), and *Feeblemindedness: Its Causes and Consequences* (New York: Macmillan, 1919): L. M. Terman, *The Measurement of Intelligence* (Boston: Houghton Mifflin, 1916); and *The Intelligence of School Children* (Boston: Houghton Mifflin, 1919); Robert M. Yerkes, "How May We Discover the Children Who Need Special Care?" *Mental Hygiene* 1 (1917); 252–9; and Man Power and Military Effectiveness: The Case for Human Engineering," *Journal of Consulting Psychology* 5 (1941): 205–9.

30. Minton, "The Iowa Child Welfare Research Station," pp. 160–3.

31. Minton, "The Iowa Child Welfare Research Station," pp. 168–72.

32. Guy Montrose Whipple, ed., *The Twenty-First Yearbook of the National Society for the Study of Education-Intelligence Tests and Their Use* (Bloomington, Ill.: Public School Publishing, 1922).

33. See Gould, *The Mismeasure of Man*, ch. 6, pp. 234–320.

34. Flier, Assembly Bill 161, "Save the Children," n.d., LSRM 3, 43, 452, RAC, N. Tarrytown, N.Y.

35. "Mrs. Rogers Sends Message by Radio: Address on Child Welfare Bill Broadcasted From Hale's Before Its Defeat," *Mercury Herald* 10 May 1923, LSRM 3, 43, 453, RAC, N. Tarrytown, N.Y.

36. Lawrence K. Frank to Faculty and Officers, U. C. Berkeley, 6–12 March 1925, LSRM 3, 43, 452, RAC, N. Tarrytown, N.Y.

37. L. B. D. to Beardsley Ruml, "Your Memorandum of March 11th to the Memorial's Trustee Committee of Review on Child Study and Parent Education," 15 March 1927, LSRM 3, 31, 329, RAC, N. Tarrytown, N.Y.

38. L. B. D. to Ruml, "Your Memorandum."

39. Edmund E. Day to Beardsley Ruml, "Child Study and Parent Education," 17 March 1927, LSRM 3, 31, 329, RAC, N. Tarrytown, N.Y.

40. "Interview with President Sproul, U.C. with Mr. L. K. Frank," 21 November 1932, GEB 930, 1, 3, 374, 3907, RAC, N. Tarrytown, N.Y.

41. L. K. Frank to Ethel Richardson, 15 April 1927, LSRM 3, 43, 452, RAC, N. Tarrytown, N.Y.

42. Stoltz secured an LSRM grant of $22,500 from 1926 to 1929 for parent education. "Extract from a letter on the Conference of Modern Parenthood, Los Angeles," January 1927; Beardsley Ruml to W. J. Cooper [Superintendent of the California State Department of Education] 19 November 1928; "Sponsor's Report," 4 October 1928, LSRM 3, 27, 281, RAC, N. Tarrytown, N.Y.

43. L. K. Frank, "Visit to U.C. Institute of Child Welfare, 4–9 Feb. 1934," GEB 930, 1, 3, 374, 3908, RAC, N. Tarrytown, N.Y.

44. Rockefeller Foundation, Grant No. 77, For Research in Adolescence.

45. Robert Sproul to GEB, 3 May 1934, "Summary of Principal Activities in the Growth Study of Adolescents at the End of Two Years of Data Collection," 1 January 1934, GEB 930, 1, 3, 374, 3908, RAC, N. Tarrytown, N.Y.

46. R. Sproul to GEB, [Note that funds were distributed from the Spelman Fund as the successor to the LSRM] L. K. Frank to H. Stoltz, 21 May 1934; LKF, "Interviews, Visit to the U. C. Study of Adolescents," 4–9 Feb. 1934, GEB 930, 1, 3, 374, 3908, RAC, N. Tarrytown, N.Y.

47. L. F. K. to A. Gregg, Memo "Subject: California Guidance Study," 28 May 1935, GEB 930, 1, 3, 374, 3909, RAC, N. Tarrytown, N.Y.

48. Alan Gregg Diary, 25 June 1935; 27 June 1935, GEB 930, 1, 3, 374, 3909, RAC, N. Tarrytown, N.Y.

49. R. J. Havighurst to Professor E. Tolman, 9 September 1940, GEB 930, 1, 3, 375, 3912, RAC, N. Tarrytown, N.Y.

50. R. J. Havighurst, "The Programs of Adolescent Study at the Univ. of Calif. and in the Oakland Public Schools, in Relation to Educational Problems," 22 May 1935, GEB 930, 1, 3, 374, 3909, RAC, N. Tarrytown, N.Y.

51. Harold Jones to R. J. Havighurst, "Report: Adolescent Growth Study," 4 April 1939, GEB 930, 1, 3, 374, 3914, RAC, N. Tarrytown, N.Y.

52. Jones to Havighurst, "Report."

53. R. J. Havighurst, "Summary of Visit to Institute of Child Welfare," 29 April 1937 to 12 May 1937, GEB 930, 1, 3, 374, 3910, RAC, N. Tarrytown, N.Y.

54. Herbert Stoltz, *Yearbook on Adolescence* (New York: MacMillan, 1950).

55. "Abstract of the Chapters," draft of the *Yearbook*.

56. R. J. Havighurst, "Memo Concerning the Guidance Study at the Univ. of California," 19 January 1938; W. W. Brierley to R. Sproul, 16 December 1938, GEB 930, 1, 3, 374, 3911, RAC, N. Tarrytown, N.Y.

57. R. J. Havighurst, "Publication of Results of Research at the California Institute of Child Welfare," 22 December 1938, GEB 930, 1, 3, 374, 3911, RAC, N. Tarrytown, N.Y.

58. Havighurst, "Publication of Results."

59. Jean W. MacFarlane, "Statement of Objectives, Points of View," 26 Oct. 1938, GEB 930, 1, 3, 374. 3911, RAC, N. Tarrytown, N.Y.

60. Stoltz, *Yearbook*, was subsidized with a publication grant of five thousand dollars, cited under "grants in Aid to I 48049," F. M. Rhind, "Interview with Harold Jones Re: Publication Yearbook," 4 May 1943 and outline of "Yearbook on Adolescence," GEB 930, 1, 3, 374, 3911, RAC, N. Tarrytown, N.Y.

61. F. M. Rhind, "Request from Dr. Tyler for continued support of the Univ. of Chicago's Center of Documentation and Collaboration for the Study of Human Development and Behavior," 5 January 1943; R. Hutchins to F. M. Rhind, 8 April 1943; W. W. Brierley to R. Hutchins, 11 Dec. 1943; FMR, "Interview Univ. of Chicago Child Development Center Collaborators, D. A. Prescott, R. J. Havighurst," 17 Nov. 1943, 23 July 1943, 16 Aug. 1943; R. J. Havighurst to F. M. Rhind, 11 Oct. 1943, GEB 930, 1, 3, 375, 3920, RAC, N. Tarrytown, N.Y.; See Alice B. Smuts, "The National Research Council on Child Development and the Founding of the Society for Research in Child Development, 1925–1933," in *History and Research in Child Development*, eds. A. B. Smuts and J. W. Hagen, *Monographs of the S.R.C.D.*, Serial No. 211, Vol. 50, Nos. 4–5 (1985), pp. 108–125.

62. "Inter-University Collaboration to Further Research in Human Development and Behavior and to Extend the Use of Research Findings in the Education of Professional Persons," 15 March 1944, GEB 930, 1, 3, 375, 3920, RAC, N. Tarrytown, N.Y.

63. "The University of Chicago Announcement of the Continuation of the Collaboration Center on Human Development and Education," 6 October 1943, p. 2. Collaborators included: J. E. Anderson of the University of Minnesota, H. H. Anderson of the University of Illinois, William Greulich of Western Reserve University, Kai Jensen of the University of Wisconsin, Arthur Jersild of Teacher's College Columbia University, Harold Jones of U.C. Berkeley, Mark A. May of Yale University, Willard Olsen of the University of Michigan, Sidney Pressey of Ohio State University, L. W. Sontag of Antioch College, Alfred Washburn of the University of Colorado, Robert Sears of the University of Iowa, and Harvey Murray of Harvard University. "Document D," 15 March 1944, GEB 930, 1, 3, 375, 3920, RAC, N. Tarrytown, N.Y.

64. R. Sproul to R. J. Havighurst, 17 March 1937; R. J. H. to R. S. 25 March 1937, GEB 930, 1, 3, 375, 3914; R. J. Havighurst, "Summary of Visit," 29 April 1937 to 12 May 1937; R. J. H. to J. MacFarlane, 4 April 1938; J. M. to R. J. H., 6 April 1938; R. J. H. to J. M., 18 Ap. 1838, GEB 930, 1, 3, 375, 3910; R. J. Havighurst, "Interview - Visit U.S. Institute of Child Welfare," 28 June 1938 to 5 July 1938, GEB 930, 1, 3, 375, 3911, RAC, N. Tarrytown, N.Y.

65. Flora M. Rhind, "Interview Erik Homburger," 17 September 1947, GEB 930, 1, 3, 375, 3914, RAC, N. Tarrytown, N.Y.

66. Erik H. Erikson, *Childhood and Society* (New York: W. W. Norton, 1950, 2nd ed. 1963, 3rd ed. 1985).

67. R. J. Havighurst, Interview, "Erik Homburger Erikson Guidance Study U.C.," 20 Dec. 1940, GEB 930, 1, 3, 375, 3912; J. MacFarlane to A. Gregg, 18 Nov. 1941, A. Gregg to J. MacFarlane, 21 Nov. 1941, GEB 930, 1, 3, 375, 3914, RAC, N. Tarrytown, N.Y.

68. Erikson also had problems at Yale with Arnold Gesell, whose work in child study had begun in 1911, funded in part by Rockefeller philanthropy from 1920 to 1944. A. Gesell, "Memo," 21 Oct. 1938; A. Gregg, "Note," and "Correspondence between Gesell and Homburger," 19, 18, 16, 20, 29 Oct. 1937; A. Gregg, "Diary" 3 Jan. 1938; J. R. Angell to A. Gregg, 31 Oct. 1938, GEB 930, 1, 3, 376, 3925, RAC, N. Tarrytown, N.Y.

69. Glen H. Elder, Jr., *Children of the Great Depression: Social Change in Life Experience* (Chicago: University of Chicago, 1974).

Chapter Ten

1. Warren I. Susman, *Culture as History: The Transformation of American Society in the Twentieth Century* (New York: Pantheon, 1984), p. 284.

2. Paul Boyer, *Urban Masses and the Moral Order in America 1880–1920* (Cambridge, MA.: Harvard University Press, 1978), pp. 167–8.

3. *Annual Reports of the Chiefs of the Children's Bureau to the Secretary of Labor* (Washington, D.C.: Government Printing Office, 1915); George Rosen, *Madness in Society: Chapters in the Historical Sociology of Mental Illness* (London: Routledge & Kegan Paul), p. 296.

4. *Proceedings of the National Conference of Social Work* 44th Annual Session, Pittsburgh, PA, June 16–17, 1917, pp. 391–454; *Proceedings* 45th Annual Session, Kansas City, MO., May 15–20, 1918, pp. 513–28; *Proceedings* 46th Annual Session, Atlantic City, N.J., June 1–8, 1919, pp. 335–413; *Proceedings* 47th Annual Session, New Orleans, LA., Ap. 14–21, 1920. Canada Department of National Health and Welfare, *Community Mental Health in Canada* (Ottawa, Mar. 1954), pp. 1–6, documents poor facilities, and the need for trained personnel.

5. *White House Conference 1930: Addresses and Abstracts of Committee Reports* (New York: Century Co., 1931).

6. White House Conference 1930, p. 275; Michael B. Katz, *In the Shadow of the Poorhouse: A Social History of Welfare in America* (New York: Basic Books, 1986), p. 144; Sheila M. Rothman, *A Woman's Proper Place: A History of Changing Ideals and Practices, 1870s to the Present* (New York: Basic Books, 1978), p. 126.

7. U.S. Department of Labor, Children's Bureau, *Conference on Children in a Democracy - Papers and Discussions at the Initial Session, April 26, 1939* (Washington, D.C.: U.S. Government Printing Office, 1939).

8. U.S. Department of Labor, *Proceedings 1940*, p. 3.

9. Francis Perkins, "Opening Statement by the Chairman," General Session, 18 Jan. 1940, pp. 1–5; W. R. Ogg, p. 21 both in *Proceedings*, 1940; see Katz, *Shadow of the Poorhouse*, pp. 124–9.

10. "General Report Adopted by the Conference, January 19, 1940," in *Proceedings* after p. 126, pp. 1–81, see p. 10.

11. Perkins, "Opening," *Proceedings*, pp. 4–5.

12. U.S. Department of Labor, Children's Bureau, *Proceedings of the White House Conference on Children in a Democracy, Washington, D.C. Jan. 18–20, 1940* Bureau Publ. No. 266, (Washington, D.C.: U.S. Government Printing Office, 1940), pp. 4–5.

13. K. D. Fisher, pp. 12–13; G. Mitchell, pp. 13–17, *Proceedings.*

14. "The mechanism of democratic government requires a citizen body that is strong, intelligent, secure and happy, and that for the annoying internal aggression of poverty, suffering, disease, and insecurity there must be effort to the same degree that there is against external aggression." Address by Charlotte Whitton in *Proceedings*, pp. 27–8.

15. See "General Report," pp. 32–74.

16. Edward A. Richards, ed., *Proceedings of the Mid-century White House Conference on Children and Youth: Report of Conference Sessions* Washington, D.C., December 3–7, 1950, (Raleigh, N.C.: Health Publications Institute, 1951), pp. 150–65, see "Contents."

17. Nina Ridenour, *Mental Health in the United States: A Fifty Year History* (Cambridge: MA.: Harvard University Press for the Commonwealth Fund, 1961), pp. 122–5, 66–70.

18. *Report on the Activities of the National Committee for Mental Hygiene (Canada) for the Year 1944*, 1 December 1944, CMHA Papers, PAC, MG 28, I, 391, 84/63, Ottawa.

19. *Report of the General Director to Meeting of Board of Directors, National Committee for Mental Hygiene (Canada). Held in the Head Office, Royal Bank of Canada, Montreal, June 13, 1945*, p. 2, CMHA Papers, PAC, MG 28, I, 391, 84/63, Ottawa.

20. Not to be confused with the American Foundation for Mental Hygiene founded by Beers in the 1920s; Dain, *Beers*, pp. 236, 247.

21. Ridenour, *Mental Health*, p. 106.

22. Mary J. Ward, *The Snake Pit* (N.Y.: Random House, 1946); Albert Deutsch, *The Shame of the Cities* (N.Y.: Harcourt Brace, 1948); U.S. Senate Commit-

tee on Education and Labor, *Hearings on S1160, National Neuro-Psychiatric Institute Act*, 79th Cong., 2d sess., (1946), p. 107.

23. Albert Deutsch, *The Mentally Ill in America: A History of Their Care and Treatment from Colonial Times* (Garden City, N.Y.: Doubleday Doran & Co. for the American Foundation for Mental Hygiene, 1937, revised and enlarged Columbia University Press, 1949). Deutsch's book became the "standard comprehensive work on the subject." See Dain, *Clifford W. Beers*, pp. 279–81.

24. *Report on the Activities of the NCMH (Canada) for the Year 1944*, pp. 4–5.

25. See Ridenour, *Mental Health*, pp. 106–19, 102–3, and 88–90.

26. U.S. Senate Committee on Education & Labor, *Hearings on S. 1160, National Neuro-Psychiatric Act*, 79th Cong., 2d sess., 1946, p. 107; Robert Felix, *Mental Illness, Progress and Prospects* (New York: Columbia University Press, 1967).

27. Rockefeller Foundation, *Minutes*, 22 June 1951, pp. 51375–77 RG 1.1, 200, 32, 358, RFA, RAC, N. Tarrytown, N.Y.: Ridenous, *Mental Health*, pp. 78–9, 127–31.

28. Rockefeller Foundation, *Minutes*, pp. 51375–7.

29. Arthur H. Bunker to Alan Gregg, 12 March 1951; AG Diary, "Feb. 16, 1951—New York," Re.: interview Owen Root and Arthur Bunker of the NMHA, RG 1.1, 200, 32, 358, RFA, RAC, N. Tarrytown, N.Y.

30. Charles Dollard (President of the Carnegie Corp.) to A. Gregg, 29 Mar. 1951, 22 May 1951; R.S.M. interview Charles Dollard, 14 May 1951; A. G. Diary on Oren Root and A. L. Van Ameringen, National Association of Mental Health, 15 May 1951; Robert M. Lister to Oren Root, 13 May 1951; F. M. Rhind to Oren Root, 22 June 1951; National Association for Mental Health, "Summary of Contributions and Pledges Received Jan. 1, 1951 through Dec. 31, 1951," 10 Jan. 1952, RG 1.1, 200, 32, 365, RFA, RAC, N. Tarrytown, N.Y.

31. A. Gregg, "Main Points Amalgamation of National Committee for Mental Hygieine," (memo) 4 June 1951, RG 1.1, 200, 32, 365, RFA, RAC, N. Tarrytown, N.Y.

32. Cited in Robert Castel, Francoise Castel and Anne Lovell, *The Psychiatric Society*, trans., Arthur Goldhammer (New York: Columbia University Press, 1982), pp. 59–60; also see, Eli A. Rubinstein and George V. Coelho, "Mental Health and the Behavioral Sciences," *American Psychologist* 25 (1970): 517–523.

33. Eli A. Rubinstein and George V. Coelho, "NIMH Role in the Behavioral Sciences," in E. A. Rubinstein and G. V. Coelho, eds., *Behavioral Sciences and Mental Health: An Anthology of Program Reports*, U.S. Public Health Service Publication 2064, (1970), pp. 1–11.

34. P.L. 182, passed 84th Cong., 1st sess., 28 July 1955.

35. Joint Commission on Mental Illness and Health, *Action for Mental Health, Final Report* (N.Y.: Basic Books, 1961); John F. Kennedy, "Message from the Presi-

dent of the U.S. Relative to Mental Illness and Mental Retardation," 88th Cong., House of Rep., 5 Feb. 1963, No. 58, p. 4; Felix, *Mental Illness* p. 82.

36. See Castel, Castel and Lovell, *The Psychiatric Society* for a discussion of the psychiatrization of difference, pp. 202–13.

37. C. Hincks, "Memo Presented to the Board of Directors," *Minutes of the Meeting of the Board of Directors, NCMH Held in Montreal, Nov. 8, 1945*, CMHA Papers, PAC, MG 28, I, 391, 84/63, Ottawa; John D. Griffin, "Mental Health—Canada: The Chronicle of a National Voluntary Movement. The Canadian Mental Health Association, 1918-1980," (May 1981), p. 230, J. D. Griffin Papers, Greenland-Griffin Archives, Toronto.

38. "Minutes of the Meeting of the Board of Directors of the NCMH (Canada) Held in Montreal September 30, 1948," CMHA papers, PAC, MG 28, I, 391, 84/63, Ottawa; Griffin, "Mental health," p. 230.

39. J. F. Boys, "The Birth of a Community Mental Health Clinic," MSW Thesis, Univ. of Toronto, 1953; M. A. Briault, "History of the Toronto Mental Health Clinic, 1946-1954," MSW Thesis, Univ. of Toronto, 1954; Griffin, "Mental Health," pp. 223–4.

40. "Minutes of the Board of Directors," 30 Sept. 1948, p. 3, CMHA Papers, MG 28, I, 391, 84/93, PAC, Ottawa: National Committee on School Health Research, (NCSHR), *A Health Survey of Canadian Schools 1945–1946: A Survey of Existing Conditions in the Elementary and Secondary Schools of Canada*, Report No. 1, (Toronto: NCSHR, 31 Mar. 1947); NCSHR, "A Health Survey of Canadian Schools, 1945–1946, Report No. 1, *Canadian Education* 2, 2 (Jan./Feb./Mar. 1947): 77–92; NCSHR, "Second Report," *Canadian Education* 3, 2 (Mar. 1948): 1–79.

41. "Minutes, Meeting of the Board of Directors," 3 October 1949, CMHA Papers, MG 28, I, 391, 84/63, PAC, Ottawa; J. D. Griffin and J. R. Seeley, "Education for Mental Health: An Experiment," *Canadian Education* 7 3 (1952); J. R. Seeley et al., *Crestwood Heights* (Toronto: University of Toronto Press, 1956).

42. Griffin, "Mental Health," p. 236.

43. "Minutes of the Board of Directors," 17 December 1946, CMHA Papers, MG 28, I, 391, PAC, Ottawa.

44. Board of Directors, "Proposed Activity of the NCMH (Canada) During 1949–1950, Exploration of the Possibilities of Seeking the Partnership of the Canadian Public Through the Organization of Provincial Divisions and Local Branches," Sept. 1949, CMHA Papers, MG 28, I, 391, 84/63, PAC, Ottawa.

45. This arrangement is not without its problems, David Randall and Paul Grocott, "Advocacy and the Delivery of Community Health Services: Do They Mix? A Saskatchewan Perspective," *Canadian Mental Health* 34, 1 (March 1986): 9–10.

46. Christian Smith, untitled report to the Board of Directors Re: visit to Saskatchewan in *Annual Report for the Year 1949 of the National Committee for Mental Hygiene*, CMHA Papers, MG 28, I, 391, 84/63, PAC, Ottawa; Murray Cherneskey, "A Touch of Laycock: A Study of S. R. Laycock: Educator and Apostle of Mental Health," M.Ed. Thesis, Univ. of Saskatchewan, 1978; Billie E. H. Housego, "Some Reflections on the Life and Times of S. R. Laycock," (typescript), Univ. British Columbia, p. 161.

47. John Bowlby, *Maternal Care and Mental Health* (New York: Columbia University Press, 1951), a summary was published as *Child Care and the Growth of Love* ed. Margery Fry (New York: Penguin, 1953).

48. Dain, *Beers*, pp. 244–53; Ridenour, *Mental Health*, pp. 66–70.

49. Fosdick, *The Story*, pp. 130–1.

50. Chester I. Barnard to Joseph H. Willis, "Inter-office Correspondence," 2 Dec. 1946; J. H. W. to A. Gregg; R. B. Fosdick, "Memo," 27 Dec. 1946; J. H. W. to A. G., "Cantril's Letter of November 21st and article," 2 Jan. 1947; J. H. W. to A. G., 25 June 1948; C. I. Barnard to A. G. 5 Aug. 1948; C. I. B. to A. G., "Memo," 5 Aug. 1948, RG 3, 906, 2, 18, RFA, RAC, N. Tarrytown, N.Y.

51. Robert S. Morison to C. I. Barnard, "Memo," 30 Sept. 1948, p. 2, RG 3, 906, 2, 18, RFA, RAC, N. Tarrytown, N.Y. Robert S. Morrison, a biologist, became director of the Divisions of Medical Science and Natural Science of the RF in 1952 upon the retirement of Alan Gregg and Warren Weaver.

52. C. I. Barnard to A. Gregg, 5 Aug. 1948, RG 3, 906, 2, 18, RFA, RAC, N. Tarrytown, N.Y.

53. Deutsch, *The Mentally Ill in America*, p. 191; Norman Dain, *Mental Illness and American Society 1875–1940* (Princeton: Princeton University Press, 1983), pp. 266–87.

54. See Dain, *Mental Illness*.

55. B. C. Smith to M. C. Scoville, "Memorandum," 24 Oct. 1944, CF 74, RAC, N. Tarrytown, N.Y.

56. M. C. Scoville to B. C. Smith, "Memorandum," 22 May 1944, CF 74, RAC, N. Tarrytown, N.Y.

57. "Conference on Psychiatric Needs in Post-war Situation and Plans to Meet Them," 24 Nov. 1944, (typescript), pencil; "personal for B. C. S. for Bd. Report"; G. S. Stevenson to M. Scoville, 20 Oct. 1944, CF 74, RAC, N. Tarrytown, N.Y.

58. "Appendix I - Skeleton Report on the Hershey Conference, Presented to the Directors at a Meeting on 14 June 1945," CF 74, RAC, N. Tarrytown, N.Y.

59. M.C. Scoville, "Group for the Advancement of Psychiatry Interview with Brig. Gen. William C. Menninger, Dr. Henry Brosin and Dr. Thomas A.C. Rennie," 29 June 1946, CF 74, RAC, N. Tarrytown, N.Y.

60. Scoville, "GAP Interview," p. 5, the "Circular Letter No. 1," downplays the exclusiveness of the membership described as "informal" and comprised of "well established" APA members, p. 1.

61. Wm. C. Menninger to M. C. Scoville, 20 Ap. 1948, CF 74, RAC, N. Tarrytown, N.Y.

62. M. C. Scoville, "GAP Interview with Menninger, Brosin and Rennie," 29 May 1946; "Circular Letter No. 1, Group for the Advancement of Psychiatry," by Wm. C. Menninger, is more conciliatory toward the APA than Scoville's interview indicates: "there is no desire to capture offices or promote rivalries, or to set up a new organization," p. 1, CF 74, RAC, N. Tarrytown, N.Y.

63. "Circular Letter No. 1," pp. 3–7; "GAP Meeting 4–6 Nov." [1946] (typescript), pp. 1–6, CF 74, RAC, N. Tarrytown, N.Y.

64. Mennninger to Scoville, 20 April 1948, p. 10.

65. Felix, *Mental Illness, Progress and Prospects*.

66. Felix, *Mental Illness, Progress and Prospects*, pp. 10–11.

67. Felix, *Mental Illness, Progress and Prospects*, p. 8.

68. "Agenda Steering Committee Meeting—Asbury Park," 7 Ap. 1949; The Committee for the Preservation of Medical Standards in Psychiatry, "Letter No. 2," APA, CF 74, RAC, N. Tarrytown, N.Y.

69. Karl Bowman to Wm. C. Menninger, n.d., in "Agenda," 7 Ap. 1949.

70. John Whitehorn to Wm. C. Menninger, n.d., "Agenda," 7 Ap. 1949.

71. Winfred Overholser to Wm. C. Menninger, n.d., in "Agenda," 7 Ap. 1949.

72. "Aims and Objectives of GAP," Circular Letter No. 127, GAP; "Agenda," pp. 4, 6, CF 74, RAC, N. Tarrytown, N.Y.

73. "Agenda."

74. Isabel Dickson, (Executive Secretary, CPA] "The Canadian Psychiatric Association 1951–1958," *Canadian Journal of Psychiatry* 25, (Feb. 1980): 86–97, original 1958, reprint 1980, ed. O. A. Roberts.

75. "Report on the Activities of The NCMH (Canada) for the Year 1944," 1 Dec. 1944, MG 28, I, 391, 84/63, PAC, Ottawa.

76. C. A. Roberts, "Major Changes in the Administration of Psychiatric Services in Canada." *Canadian Psychiatric Association Journal*, 11, 3 (June 1966): 229.

77. "Report of the General Director to Meeting of Board of Directors, NCMH (Canada)," Montreal, 13 June 1945.

78. Dickson, "Canadian Psychiatric Association," p. 86. This is important because the forerunner to the APA in the United States predated the American Medical Association. The medical profession only began to overtake the superintendents of asylums in prestige in the late nineteenth century. American psychiatrists as medical scientists had to live down their background as administrators. Psychiatry and medicine came to have an ambivalent, competitive and jealous relationship with formal medical organizations. This was less the case in Canada partly because medicine never achieved the high status it did in the United States.

79. "Agenda Steering Committee—Asbury Park," 7 April 1949, CF 74, RAC, N. Tarrytown, N.Y.

80. The CPA was incorporated June 1, 1951. K. G. Gray, J. D. Griffin and Q. C. Griffin were instrumental in drafting the constitution and legal papers for incorporation, see Dickson.

81. Dickson, "The Canadian Psychiatric Association," p. 93.

82. CPA, "Minutes of the 4th Annual Meeting, August 30, 1954;" see Dickson, "The Canadian Psychiatric Association," p. 96.

83. Jean L. Lapointe, "Child Psychiatry Across Canada: An Outline of Current Facilities and Resources," *Canadian Psychiatric Association Journal* 6, 5 (October 1961): 241-6.

84. McConville, "The Future," p. 209-11.

85. J. S. Pratten, "Presidential Address: Discipline and Disciplines," *Canadian Psychiatric Association Journal* 22, 8 (Dec. 1977): 405-415.

86. *Promotion of Mental Health in the Primary and Secondary Schools: An Evaluation of 4 Projects*, GAP Report No. 18 (Jan. 1951); *The Contribution of Child Psychiatry to Pediatric Training and Practice*, GAP Report No. 21, (Jan. 1952); *Integration and Conflict in Family Behavior*, GAP Report No. 27, (Aug. 1954); *Illustrative Strategies for Research on Psychopathology of Mental Health*, GAP Report No. S-2, (July 1956); *The Diagnositc Process in Child Psychiatry*, GAP Report No. 38, (Aug. 1957); *Basic Considerations on Mental Retardation: The Family Crisis—The Therapeutic Role of the Physician*, GAP Report No. 56, (Dec. 1963); *Sex and the College Student*, GAP Report No. 61, (Nov. 1965).

87. *The Diagnostic Process in Child Psychiatry*, GAP Report No. 38.

88. GAP, Committee on Child Psychiatry, *Psychopathological Disorders in Childhood: Theoretical Considerations and a Proposed Classification* VI, GAP Report No. 62, (New York: GAP, 1966).

89. American Psychiatric Association, *DSM-III-R, Diagnostic and Statistical Manual of Mental Disorders* 3rd ed. rev. (Washington, D.C.: APA, 1984), p. 35; World Health Organization, *ICD-9, International Classification of Diseases* 9th ed. (Geneva:

WHO, 1978). Note, the Canadian Psychiatric Association officially recognizes the APA's DSM-III-R.

90. NIMH, *Statistical Note, No. 115* (April 1975); Castel, Castel and Lovell, *The Psychiatric Society*, see ch. 4.

91. B. M. Rosen, M. Kramer, S. G. Willner and R. W. Redick, "Utilization of Psychiatric Facilities By Children: Current Status," *Public Health Service Bulletin* No. 1868 (1968).

92. NIMH, *Statistical Note,* No. 130 (April 1976).

93. There is reason to believe that there are substantial differences in age (child/adolescent), sex, rural-urban residence, income and psychiatric incidence and prevalence rates of mental disorders. In the U.S., for the institutionalized age group under fifteen, there were seven times the number of boys as girls. Castel, Castel and Lovell, *The Psychiatric Society*, pp. 107–8; NIMH, *Statistical Note*, No. 91 (Sept. 1973); and, No. 112, (Mar. 1975); In the fifteen to nineteen age group females dominate outpatient and general hospital facilities. Urban statistics are higher than rural. See Hamish Nichol, "Incidence of Psychiatric Treatment of Adolescents," *Canadian Journal Psychiatry* 24, 6 (Oct. 1979): 521–530, survey of B. C. in 1966; also, B. M. Rosen, M. Kraimer, R. W. Redick and S. G. Willner, *Utilization of Psychiatric Facilities by Children: Current Status, Trends and Implications* PHS Publ. 1868 (Washington, D.C.: U.S. Dept. of Health, Educ. and Welfare, 1968); B. M. Rosen, A. K. Bahn, S. Shellow and E. M. Bower, "Adolescent Patients Served in Out Patient Psychiatric Clinics," *American Journal of Public health* 55 (1965): 1563–77.

94. Castel, Castel and Lovell, *The Psychiatric*, pp. 108–9.

95. Naomi I. Rae-Grant, "Roadblocks and Stopgaps: A Review of Factors Obstructing the Development of Comprehensive Child Mental Health Services," *Canadian Psychiatric Association Journal* 21, 6 (Oct. 1976): 433.

96. Nichol, "Incidence," p. 529; Rae-Grant, "Roadblocks," pp. 433–40.

97. Only two to three percent of adolescent patients receive what amounts to expensive and long-term psychotherapy, see Nichol, "Incidence," p. 529.

98. Jacques Donzelot, *The Policing of Families* fwd. G. Deleuze, trans. R. Hurley (New York: Pantheon, 1979); Allan V. Horwitz, *The Social Control of Mental Illness* (New York: John Wiley & Sons, 1976); also August B. Hollingshead and Frederick C. Redlich, *Social Class and Mental Illness: A Community Study* (New York: John Wiley & Sons, 1958, 1965).

99. See DSM-III-R, p. 19.

Chapter Eleven

1. Oscar E. Ewing, "The Mid-Century White House Conference on Opportunity and A Responsibility for Americans," in Edward A. Richards, gen. ed., *Proceedings of the Mid-Cenltury White House Conference on Children and Youth: Report of Con-*

ference Sessions, Washington, D.C. December 3-7, 1950 (Raleigh, N.C.: Health Publications, 1951), pp. 42-3.

2. Alexander S. Rogawski, "Mental Health Programs in Welfare Systems: Child and Adolescent Psychiatry, Sociocultural and Community Psychiatry" in *American Handbook of Psychiatry*, vol. II, ed. Gerald Caplan (New York: Basic Books, 1974), pp. 749-72; *The Consultant in a Family Service Agency*, GAP Report No. 34, (1956); *The Welfare System and Mental Health*, GAP Report No. 85, (1973); *Roles of the Psychiatrist in Welfare Agencies*, GAP Report No. 86 (1974).

3. See Dennis Guest, *The Emergence of Social Security in Canada* (Vancouver: University of British Columbia Press, 1982).

4. Guest, *The Emergence*, pp. 83-103; The Canadian Welfare Council, *The Rowell-Sirois Report and the Social Services in Summary* (Ottawa: Canadian Welfare Council, 1940).

5. Guest, *The Emergence*, pp. 49-61; Margaret K. Strong, *Public Welfare Administration in Canada* (New York: Patterson Smith, 1969, reprint University of Chicago, 1930).

6. Guest, *The Emergence*, p. 52, fn. 12; on British Columbia see William Rasmussen, "An Evaluation of the Mother's Allowances Programme in British Columbia," MSW Thesis, University of British Columbia, 1950.

7. Guest, *The Emergence*, pp. 73-7, 79.

8. Canada, *Report of the Royal Commission on Dominion-Provincial Relations, Book I, Canada 1867-1939* (Ottawa: Queen's Printer, 1940)); *Book II, Recommendations* (Ottawa: Queen's Printer, 1940); Canada, *Royal Commission on Health Services*, Vol. I (Ottawa: Queen's Printer, 1964).

9. Tamara Hareven, "An Ambiguous Alliance: Some Aspects of American Influence on Canadian Social Welfare," *Social History/histoire sociale* 3 (April 1969): 82-98.

10. Guest, *The Emergence*, p. 56.

11. Charlotte Whitton (editorial), "Family Allowance," *Social Welfare* 11, 7 (1929): 147.

12. Roy Lubove, *The Struggle for Social Security* (Cambridge: MA.: Harvard University Press, 1968), p. 103.

13. Peter Bryce, "Mothers' Allowances," *Social Welfare* 1, 6 (1919): 131-2.

14. Thomas Haskell, *The Emergence of Professional Social Science* (Chicago: University of Chicago Press, 1977); Roy Lubove, *The Professional Altruist: The Emergence of Social Work as A Career, 1880-1930* (New York: Atheneum, 1969); James L. Lieby, *A History of Social Welfare and Social Work in the United States* (New York: Columbia University Press, 1978).

15. Paul Starr, *The Social Transformation of American Medicine: The Rise of A Sovereign Profession and the Making of A Vast Industry* (New York: Basic Books, 1982), pp. 232–290; Viviana A. Zelizer, *Pricing the Priceless Child: The Changing Social Value of Children* (New York: Basic Books, 1985); R. Carlyle Buley, *The American Life Convention, 1906–1952: A Study in the History of Life Insurance*, Vol. II (New York: Appleton-Century-Crofts, 1953).

16. See Guest, *The Emergence.*

17. Daniel S. Hirshfield, *The Lost Reform: The Campaign for Compulsory Health Insurance in the United States From 1932 to 1943* (Cambridge, MA.: Harvard University Press, 1970).

18. Bertram S. Brown and James D. Isbister, "U.S. Government Organization for Human Services - Implications for Mental Health Planning," in *American Handbook of Psychiatry*, p. 573.

19. Advisory Commission on Intergovernmental Relations, *Block Grants: A Comparative Analysis* (Washington, D.C.: Government Printing Office, 1979); T. W. Schultz, "Human Capital Approaches in Organizing and Paying for Education," in *Financing Education: Overcoming Inefficiency and Inequaity* eds. W. W. McMahon and T. G. Geske (Urbana: University of Illinois Press, 1982).

20. C. Philip Kearney, "Value Polarities and Complimentarities in American Education Policy Making: Efficiency and Choice," paper presented at the American Educational Research Association Annual Meeting, April 1988, New Orleans; C. Philip Kearney, "Michigan's Experiences with the Federal Education Block Grant," *Economics of Education Review* 4 (1985): 181–7.

21. See W. Norton Grubb and Marvin Lazerson, *Broken Promises: How Americans Fail Their Children* (New York: Basic Books, 1982).

22. Alexis de Tocqueville, *Democracy in America* ed. Richard D. Heffner (New York: New American Library, 1956), pp. 189–92.

23. De Toqueville was no champion of individualism: "Individualism, at first, only saps the virtues of public life; but, in the long run, it attacks and destroys all others, and is at length absorbed in downright selfishness," p. 193. While de Tocqueville saw individualism as originating in democracies and fostered by equality of condition, the modern new use of the concept was to mediate between equality of condition and equality of opportunity.

24. John Hutcheson, *Dominance and Dependency in Liberalism and National Policies in the North America Triangle* (Toronto: McClelland & Stewart, 1978), pp. 99–124.

25. Larson, *The Rise of Professionalism*, p. 154.

26. W. L. Morton, *Canadian Identity* 2nd ed. (Madison: University of Wisconsin: 1961, 1972), p. 99; also see Jacques Monet, "Maintaining A Constitution Worthy of Such a country: Reflections on Values in Canadian Society," *The Nash Lecture, The Fifth, 1982* (Regina: Champion College, University of Regina, 1982).

27. Morton, *The Canadian Identity*, pp. 105-6.

28. Monet, "Maintaining," p. 11; see Canada, Department of Justice, *A Consolidation of The Constitution Act 1867 to 1982* (Ottawa: Minister of Supply and Services, 1983), see "Canadian Charter of Rights and Freedoms," pp. 61-76.

29. John Porter, "Canadian Character in the Twentieth Century," in *The Measure of Canadian Society: Education, Equality and Opportunity* (Ottawa: Gage, 1979), p. 92.

30. Porter, "Canadian Character," p. 90.

31. C. Wright Mills, *The Power Elite*, (New York: Free Press, 1956); G. William Domhoff, *Who Rules America?* (Englewood Cliffs, N.J.: Prentice-Hall, 1967); Mary Anna Culleton Colwell, "The Foundation Connection: Links among Foundations and Recipient Organizations," in *Philanthropy and Cultural Imperialism: The Foundations at Home and Abroad* ed. Robert Arnove (Bloomington: University of Indiana Press, 1980, 1982), pp. 412-52.

32. Seymour Martin Lipset, "Revolution and Counter Revolution: The United States and Canada," in Thomas R. Ford, ed., *The Revolutionary Theme in Contemporary America* (New York: Basic Books, 1970), pp. 21-64; "Historical Traditions and National Characteristics: A Comparative Analysis of Canada and the United States," *Canadian Journal of Sociology* 11, 2 (1986): 113-55.

33. Porter, "Canadian Character," p. 99; Lipset, "Revolution," and "Historical;" also see: S. D. Clark, *The Developing Canadian Community* (Toronto: University of Toronto Press, 1960); Dennis Wrong, *American and Canadian Viewpoints* (Washington, D.C.: American Council on Education, 1955).

34. Kathleen McConnachie, "The Mental Hygiene and Eugenics Movements in the Inter-War Years," paper presented at the History of Education Society, Vancouver, B.C., October 1983.

35. Nielsen, *The Big Foundations*, p. 397.

36. John Porter, "Canadian Character," makes the point that Canada gained almost as many immigrants (7.1 million) as it lost to emigration (6.1 million) between 1851 and 1951. Considering that the total population of Canada was 2.5 million in 1881, at any one time a large percentage of the population was strongly tied to its origins or in transition. This accounts in part for the importance of ethnic differences and the greater acceptance and retention of ethnic cultural variations in Canada as compared with the U.S. which was able to inundate immigrant groups into a majority culture. It also gives some insight into the absence of a stereotypic Canadian identity.

37. S. F. Wise and Robert Craig Brown, *Canada Views the United States: Nineteenth Century Political Attitudes* (Seattle: University of Washington Press, 1967).

38. Jacob Viner, *Canada and Its Giant Neighbor* Alan B. Plaunt Memorial Lectures, Carleton University, Ottawa, 30 January and 1 February, 1958 (Ottawa: Carleton University Press, 1958); Morton, *Canadian Identity*, p. 107.

39. Hugh MacLennan, "A Society in Revolt," in *Voices of Canada: An Introduction to Canadian Culture* ed. Judith Webster (Burlington, VA.: Association for Canadian Studies in the United States, 1977); Steven J. Arnold and Douglas J. Tigert, "Canadians and Americans: A Comparative Analysis," *International Journal of Comparative Sociology* 15 (March-June 1974): 68–83; Robert Presthus, ed., *Cross National Perspectives: United States and Canada* (Leiden: E.J. Brill, 1977); S. D. Clarke, in H. F. Angus, ed., *Canada and Her Great Neighbor: Sociological Surveys of Opinion and Attitudes Concerning the United States* (New York: Ryerson, 1938); see also Porter, "The Measure;" Lipset, "Revolution," and "Historical Traditions."

40. See the classic, Kingsley Davis and W. E. Moore, "Principles of Stratification," *American Sociological Review* X (1945). For a critique see Dennis H. Wrong, "The Functional Theory of Stratification: Some Neglected Considerations," *American Sociological Review* XXIX, 6 (Dec. 1959).

41. Warren Weaver, "Concluding Remarks to Part II: The Consensus," in *U.S. Philanthropic Foundations: Their History, Structure, Management and Record* (New York: Harper & Row, 1967), p. 441.

42. Charles E. Lindblom and David K. Cohen, *Useable Knowledge: Social Sciences and Social Problem Solving* (New Haven: Yale Univ. Press, 1979).

43. "Report of the Committee on Medical Education," n.d. [Jan. 1947] CF 71, RAC, N. Tarrytown, N.Y.

44. Sheila Slaughter and Edward T. Silva, "Looking Backward: How Foundations Formulated Ideology in the Progressive Period," in *Philanthropy and Cultural Imperialism*, pp. 55–86.

45. See, E. Richard Brown, "Rockefeller Medicine in China: Professionalism and Imperialism," pp. 123–46; Edward H. Berman, "Educational Colonialism in Africa: The Role of American Foundations, 1910–1945," pp. 179–202; and, Berman, "The Foundations' Role in American Foreign Policy: The Case of Africa, post 1945," pp. 203–32, in Philanthropy and Cultural Imperialism.

46. Mary Anna Culleton Colwell, "The Foundation Connection: Links Among Foundations and Recipient Organizations," in *Philanthropy and Cultural Imperialism*, pp. 413–52.

47. Edward H. Berman, *The Influence of the Carnegie, Ford, and Rockefeller Foundations on American Foreign Policy: The Ideology of Philanthropy* (Albany: State University of New York Press, 1983); Waldemar A. Nielsen makes a similar point, *The Big Foundations* (New York: Columbia University Press, 1972), p. 394.

48. Gilgen, *American Psychology Since World War II*, p. 26.

49. Jeanne L. Brand, "The National Mental Health Act of 1946: A Retrospect," *Bulletin of the History of Medicine* 39 (May-June): 231–244; Commission on Hospital Care, *Hospital Care in the United States*, (New York: Commonwealth Fund, 1947): Dan Fishback, "What's Inside the Black Box: A Case Study of Allocative Politics in the Hill-Burton Program," *International Journal of Health Services* 9 (1979):

313–339; see also Starr's discussion in *The Social Transformation of American Medicine*, pp. 344–346, 348–350.

50. Joseph H. Hinsey, "The Role of Private Foundations: The Development of Modern Medicine," in *U.S. Philanthropic Foundations: Their History, Structure, Management and Record*, ed. Warren Weaver (New York: Harper & Row, 1967), p. 261.

51. Hinsey, "The Role of Private Foundations: The Development of Modern Medicine," pp. 260–275; Nielsen, *The Big Foundations*, pp. 78–98; Carnegie Corp. funding was for a survey of mental health services in education, Griffin, *Mental Health* Book II, p. 236; Isabel Laird and H. Whitney, *Mental Health in Education—An Evaluation of Special Mental Health Training of Selected Teachers* (1954), Greenland-Griffin Archives, Toronto.

52. See Starr, *The Social Transformation of American Medicine*; Nielson, *The Big Foundations*, pp. 256–62; E. Richard Brown, *Rockefeller Medicine Men: Medicine and Capitalism in America* (Berkeley: University of California Press, 1960).

53. George Stevenson, who had been head of the Division on Community Clinics of the NCMH, took over the general directorship after Clarence Hinck's resignation in 1939. Stevenson began to prod official channels to fund programs in community mental health: "Project Designed to Develop Community Functions of a Mental Hospital," 1939; Stevenson's acceptance of the position as general director was announced in April: NCMH to News Editor, (memo), "The National Committee for Mental Hygiene Announces Staff Changes," 6 April 1939, CF 67, RAC, N. Tarrytown, N.Y.

54. The original statement was from William Welch. The Cinderella notation comes from an editorial "Cinderella's Cinderella," in the *Canadian Psychiatric Association Journal* 10, 5 (October 1965): 323.

55. Chester I. Barnard to Alan Gregg, 5 August 1948, RG 3, 906, 2, 18, RFA, RAC, N. Tarrytown, N.Y.

56. Four million dollars had been spent before the formalized policy emphasis in the Medical Division in 1932; Fosdick, *The Story*, p. 129.

57. "Tentative Divisional Reports on the Postwar Program of The Rockefeller Foundation," June 1944, p. 16, (mimeograph), cited in Raymond B. Fosdick, *The Story of The Rockefeller Foundation* (New York: Harper & Row, 1952), pp. 127, fn. 4.

58. Discussion on the program in psychiatry began in 1928, "Report of the Special Committee on the Division of Medical Education of the Rockefeller Foundation presented to the Board of Trustees meeting, 9 November 1928;" "A Brief Summary of the Conferences of Trustees and Officers," Princeton, November 1930; citations on the value of psychiatric research come from David L. Edsall, "Memorandum Regarding Possible Psychiatric Developments," 3 Oct. 1930. (Edsall was Dean of Harvard Medical School and a RF Trustee), see Fosdick, *The Story*, pp. 128–130; "Agenda for Special Meeting, Westchester Country Club," 11 April 1933; Flora M. Rhind to C. I. Barnard, 21 June 1948, RG 3, 906, 2, 18, RFA, RAC, N. Tarrytown, N.Y.

59. Training fellowships and the development of departments of psychiatry, neurology and related fields took precedence in the ten years of effort to develop psychiatry. The Universities of Chicago and Yale were "given" departments of psychiatry; McGill's Institute for Neurology and Neuro-surgery was supported. Teaching was rounded out and extended by grants to the Institute of Psychoanalysis at Chicago, as well as to Tulane, Duke, McGill, Washington University, Harvard, Johns Hopkins, University of Colorado, University of Michigan and the Institute of Pennsylvania Hospital. A variety of studies were supported at institutes and universities in the United States, Canada and Europe, which included research on brain chemistry, epilepsy, optics, neuro-anatomy, cytology, biochemistry, child psychology, physiology and neuro-histology. "The Emphasis on Psychiatry," excerpts from Trustees' Confidential Report, October 1943, pp. 12–16, RG 3, 906, 2, 18, RFA, RAC, N. Tarrytown, N.Y.

60. Coser, "Foundations," p. 337.

61. Harry R. Brickman, "Organization of a Community Mental Health Program in a Metropolis," in *American Handbook of Psychiatry*, p. 663.

62. Margaret Atwood, *Second Words: Selected Critical Prose* (Boston: Beacon, 1984), p. 392.

Chapter Twelve

1. Michel Foucault, "Truth and Power," in *Power/Knowledge: Selected Interviews and Other Writings 1972–1977* ed. Colin Gordon (New York: Pantheon, 1980), pp. 109–133.

2. Norbert Elias, *Power and Civility*, The Civilizing Process: Volume II, trans. Edmund Jephcott (New York: Pantheon, 1939, 1982), p. 118.

3. Norbert Elias, *The History of Manners*, The Civilizing Process: Volume I, trans. Edmund Jephcott (New York: Pantheon, 1939, 1978), p. 182.

4. Elias, *The History of Manners*, pp. 182–3.

5. Jurgen Habermas, *Legitimation Crisis* (Boston: Beacon, 1976).

6. Marc Bloch, *The Royal Touch: Sacred, Monarchy and Scrofula in England and France* (London: Routledge and Kegan Paul, 1973).

7. "Report on the Program in Adolescent Growth and Development," pp. 8–9, GEB 930, 1, 3, 369, 3850, RAC, N. Tarrytown, N.Y.

8. The Thomas Theorm as quoted by Robert Merton: "If men define situations as real, they are real in their consequences." For a discussion see, Robert K. Merton, "The Self-fulfilling Prophecy," in Lewis A. Coser, *The Pleasures of Society* (New York; New American Library, 1980), pp. 29–47; Thomas, *The Unadjusted Girl* see pp. 41–69 on the "definition of the situation," also, W. I. Thomas and D. S.

Thomas, *The Child In America* (New York: Alfred A. Knopf, 1928, New York: Johnson Reprint, 1970).

9. Lawrence K. Frank, "Social Problems," *American Journal of Sociology* 30, 4 (Jan. 1925): 462–473.

10. Frank, "Social," p. 467.

11. Humanitarian mores are defined as the urge to make the world better and to remedy the misfortunes of others. Organizational mores are the basic structures upon which the social order rests such as national identity, religious and family organization. Problems according to Waller emanate from organizational mores, Willard Waller, "Social Problems and the Mores," *American Sociological Review* 1, 6 (Dec. 1936): 922–33.

12. Waller, "Social," p. 932.

Index